Human

Human Geography

Society, Space, and Social Science

edited by

Derek Gregory

Ron Martin

and

Graham Smith

1994 c

University of Minnesota Press
Minneapolis

Editorial matter, selection, and Chapter 1 © Derek Gregory, Ron Martin, and Graham Smith 1994

Individual chapters © Tim Bayliss-Smith and Susan Owens; Morag Bell; Derek Gregory; Ron Martin; Linda McDowell; Chris Philo; Graham Smith; Susan J. Smith; Nigel Thrift 1994

First published 1994 by
THE MACMILLAN PRESS LTD

Published simultaneously in the United States 1994
by the University of Minnesota Press
2037 University Avenue S.E., Minneapolis, MN 55455–3092

Printed in China

Library of Congress Cataloging-in-Publication Data

A catalog record for this book is
available from the Library of Congress.

ISBN 0–8166–2618–9 (hc)
ISBN 0–8166–2619–7 (pb)

Contents

List of Figures and Tables

Figures

Tables

Preface

This book on human geography and its relationship to the other social sciences is designed primarily with undergraduates in mind. During the mid-1980s the three editors were given the responsibility of introducing first-year geography undergraduates at Cambridge to human geography. What we wanted to convey to students embarking upon their geography careers was not only a sense that geography had much to contribute to the other social sciences but that recent advances, particularly in critical theory, were pivotal to making sense of our geographical world. Armed with such theoretical insights, we attempted to convey the utility of such approaches to understanding the geographical restructuring of our economies, polities and societies. Given the rapidly changing nature of human geography, we also felt it important to expand the project to include leading geographers working in various sub-disciplines of the subject. This book is the product of this endeavour, and of our attempts to show how central the cross-fertilisation of ideas and concepts within the social sciences are to the continuing process of rethinking human geography and of the importance of a geographical imagination to good social science.

The major acknowledgement that editors of a volume such as this need to make is to the contributors. All of them responded with enthusiasm to the project and produced their chapters within the deadline. We are also grateful for their forbearance in awaiting the volume's final editing. The same goes for our publisher Steven Kennedy, whose encouragement, interest and support we appreciate more than he is probably aware.

Cambridge

DEREK GREGORY
RON MARTIN
GRAHAM SMITH

List of Contributors

Tim Bayliss-Smith is Lecturer in Geography at the University of Cambridge and a Fellow of St John's College. His research interests focus on population and environment in the human tropics, with a particular focus on Melanesia. He is author of *The Ecology of Agricultural Systems* and coauthor of *Islands, Islanders and the World*.

Morag Bell is Reader in Geography at the University of Loughborough with research interests in cultural and environmental relations in Britain and southern Africa in the colonial and postcolonial eras.

Derek Gregory is Professor of Geography at the University of British Columbia and was formerly Lecturer in Geography at the University of Cambridge and Fellow of Sidney Sussex College. His research interests focus primarily on the relationships between social theory and human geography. Major publications include *Ideology, Science and Human Geography, Social Relations and Spatial Structures, Horizons and Human Geography* and *Geographical Imaginations*.

Ron Martin is Lecturer in Geography at the University of Cambridge and Fellow of St Catharine's College, where he lectures in economic and political geography. His main publications include *Regional Wage Inflation and Unemployment, Geography as Spatial Science, the Geography of De-Industrialisation, Regional Development in the 1990s,* and *Money, Power and Space*. His main research interests cover the geography of labour markets, uneven regional development, state intervention and the space economy, the geography of money, and the global economy.

Linda McDowell is Lecturer in Geography at the University of Cambridge and Fellow of Newnham College. Her interests straddle social/cultural and economic geography, and she is currently working on a study of sexuality and subjectivity. She is coeditor and coauthor of several books including, *Landlords and Property, The Transformation of Britain,* and *Defining Women*.

Susan Owens is Lecturer in Geography at the University of Cambridge and a Fellow of Newnham College. Her interests are in the field of environmental policy in Britain and Europe and her research is concerned with energy and environmental issues, land-use planning, pollution and environmental taxes. She is also interested in the political development of environmentalism. She has written many articles and reports on these issues, and is the author or editor of a number of books, including *Energy Planning and Urban Form* and *Environment, Resources and Conservation*.

Chris Philo is Lecturer in Geography at St David's University College, Lampeter, Wales. His research interests include the historical geography of 'madness', 'outsiders' and institutions designed to treat and control such perceived social threats. He has coauthored *Approaching Human Geography: An Introduction to Contemporary Theoretical Debates* and coedited *Selling Places: The City as Cultural Capital, Past and Present*.

Graham Smith is Lecturer in Geography at the University of Cambridge and Fellow of Sidney Sussex College. His research interests focus on nationalism, ethnic relations and citizenship in the post-Soviet republics and in Eastern–Central Europe, and the geopolitics of the post-Cold-War era. His publications include *Planned Development in the Socialist World*, *The Nationalities Question in the Soviet Union*, and *The Baltic States: The National Self-Determination of Estonia, Latvia and Lithuania*.

Susan J. Smith is Professor of Geography at the University of Edinburgh. Her current research focuses on racism and migration in Britain and Canada, housing opportunities for people with health problems, and the prevention of child accidents in a community setting. She is author of *The Politics of 'Race' and Residence*, coauthor of *Housing and Social Policy*, and coeditor of *Housing for Health*.

Nigel Thrift is Professor of Geography at the University of Bristol. His main interests are in the international financial system (especially the City of London), the countries of the Pacific Basin and social theory. He is currently working on the economic significance of social networks in the City of London and on the growth of landscapes of light and power.

1

Introduction: Human Geography, Social Change and Social Science

DEREK GREGORY, RON MARTIN AND GRAHAM SMITH

> One thing all social theories have in common .. is that they all
> in time, become obsolete as historical events unfold along lines
> no theory could have possibly anticipated. . . . Then comes the
> problem of reconstruction, after the patchwork attempts of the
> theoretical diehards fail.
>
> Stephen Rousseas, *Capitalism and Catastrophe*

> One side of the preferred attitude is to accept at least the possi-
> bility that we stand on the brink of a new social epoch, the dis-
> tinctiveness of which may require us to introduce categories and
> discourses which severely puncture the modernist ambience of
> conventional Marxism and pluralism. . . . On the other hand . . .
> it is not the decisive replacement of outworn criteria by fresh
> insight which will mark social theory in the coming period, but
> rather the relatively inconclusive jostling of theoretical traditions,
> the scrambling of ground-rules for comparison and assessment,
> and the oscillation between post-modernist disruption and mod-
> ernist retrenchment.
>
> Gregor McLennan, *Marxism, Pluralism and Beyond*

Changing Concepts in a Changing World

These passages capture a mood that over the past few years has
spread with increasing momentum through the social and political
sciences. The dual contention this mood expresses, that modern

1

society stands poised on some critical 'hinge of history', on the threshold of a new reality, the onset of which requires a commensurate remoulding of our theoretical and conceptual schemas, of our ways of viewing and comprehending the world, has become the focus of wide-ranging discussion and debate. Of course, against this position it can be argued that every generation lives through social, economic and political change, and thus that contrary to what is claimed the present era is not exceptional in this respect; or that because the end of the twentieth century is drawing near there is the irresistible but erroneous urge to believe that we have entered a particularly uncertain but formative age, another *fin-de-siècle*. Such cautionary objections, however, seem to have few supporters. Rather the belief that we are passing through a major transition in the historical trajectory of global socio-economic and geopolitical development is now pervasive. The dramatic upheaval, restructuring and destabilisation of world capitalism; the increased globalisation of production, finance, and even culture; the collapse of state socialism in Eastern and Central Europe; the resurgence of ethnic and sociopolitical localisms and regionalisms; the search for new national and international systems of socioeconomic regulation; the growing emphasis on environmentalism: these and other major developments of our times are interpreted by many to mark the waning of the old order and the crystallisation of a new. As McLennan argues, to accept the *possibility* that we stand on the brink of a new social epoch at least compels us to reexamine our accepted orthodoxies and theories. For there is in fact an undeniable feeling of disorientation and disruption in contemporary social science, a growing impatience to be moving on beyond the theoretical, methodological and epistemological paradigms of the postwar period. Far from remaining immune from such issues, human geography has become inextricably caught up in this intellectual maelstrom, and in many respects has moved to the forefront in the conceptual reappraisal and exploration that has ensued.

In one sense, of course, the current disruption and reappraisal in human geography is nothing new, for the subject has been undergoing a more or less continuous process of vigorous development and 'rethinking' for the past three decades. Nevertheless, without necessarily subscribing to any episodic model of disciplinary evolution, whether Kuhnian 'paradigm shifts' or Lakatosian 'research programmes', it is possible to argue that this is the third time that a particularly important phase of change has punctuated this continuity. We now look back on the 1960s as a decade when the 'new geography' successfully supplanted the old 'areal differentiation' tradition as the vanguard approach. For a while this new geography, based on a union of quantitative techniques, liberal neoclassical (marginalist) economics and the *esprit geometrique* bequeathed by earlier 'location theorists', appeared to offer a rational and logical approach to the study of the spatial organisation of modern society, indeed to provide the foundations of a theoretically rigorous and empirically exact 'spatial science' (see Harvey, 1969; Billinge, Gregory and Martin, 1984). During the 1970s, however, mounting criticism of the limited empirical reach and positivistic underpinnings of this school of 'locational analysis' stimulated the search for alternative procedures and perspectives (for example, Harvey, 1973; King, 1976; Gregory, 1978).

Of particular significance in the emergence of 'radical' post-positive human geography during the course of that decade was what might be called the 'Marxist turn'. Human geography was not exceptional in this respect; indeed a similar (re)discovery of Marxism had already begun within several areas of the social sciences and humanities, from political economy (for example, Harry Braverman) through social theory (Louis Althusser), social history (E. P. Thompson) and literary criticism (Raymond Williams), and eventually to the still wider terrain of cultural studies (for example T. J. Clarke and Stuart Hall). As far as human geography was concerned the dominant form of Marxism that was imported derived in practice more from specific strands of Marxian political economy (the labour process, and the 'laws of motion' of capitalism as a mode of production) than from Althusser's much more ambitious scheme. Nevertheless the result, especially as articulated and stimulated by the writings of David Harvey, was that the research agenda in human geography shifted away from a preoccupation with the statistical laws of spatial distribution to the historical and material processes of uneven urban and regional development inherent in the 'laws of motion' and 'crisis tendencies' of capitalism. To be sure, like its predecessors Marxist geography embraced a number of variants, including non-structuralist and even 'humanistic' forms, was by no means universally adopted throughout the discipline, and coexisted with several other approaches, including an attenuated but still evolving literature in the location-theoretic tradition. But there can be no doubt that by the early 1980s the 'Marxist turn' had influenced the empirical and theoretical orientation of much of human geography, and had exposed the subject to important dialogues between Marxism and other discourses, such as critical social theory. Yet no sooner had this reorientation seemingly taken place than the most recent wave of debate and reappraisal began.

This latest wave of rethinking has already proved to be particularly significant, not just because Marxism as a perspective has come under critical scrutiny and rejection, but because the whole project of radical postpositive human geography is being reassessed. The initial impression one has in reading through the literature in and about human geography that has appeared during the past few years is that of increasing disarray, exploration and debate. Everything seems to be 'up for grabs'. There is a distinct lack of consensus – except amongst the members of the same subschool – about the proper research procedures, the most promising theoretical approaches, what bodies of social, political, economic and cultural theory to draw upon, the language and textual strategies to be employed, and even about the very nature of our subject matter. There are claims and counterclaims, a veritable plethora of critiques and fresh insights all clamouring for our allegiance. This sense of turmoil and redirection is evident right across human geography as a whole, whether in the proliferation of 'new models' (Peet and Thrift, 1989), the search for 'new horizons' (Gregory and Walford, 1989) or the prosecution of new proposals for 'remodelling', 'remaking', 'approaching' or 'changing' human geography (Macmillan, 1989; Kobayashi and Mackenzie, 1989; Cloke, Philo and Sadler, 1991; Johnston, 1993). Similarly, and also a sign of the inchoate nature of this upheaval, numerous epithets have been invoked to describe these recent movements in human geography: post-Marxist, poststructuralist, critical-realist, structurationist, feminist and, perhaps most contentious but also most elusive of all, postmodernist.

The responses to this break-up of postpositive human geography are as diverse as the debates and alternative approaches themselves. Quite early on some feared what they saw as an emergent fragmentation of the subject, a branching 'towards anarchy' (Johnston, 1983), involving numerous specialised formulations each concerned with only a limited range of phenomena and using a separate 'non-geographical' language of its own (Stoddart, 1987). There are others, however, who see in this growing multiplicity of approaches and methods 'tantalizing opportunities for a renewed human geography' (Ley, 1989), or the foundations for a postmodern reconstruction of human geography which realigns it with the 'mainstream of social theory' (Dear, 1988). Whatever view is taken, one thing is clear, namely that (to apply McLennan's apt phrase) the modernist ambience of the subject has been severely punctured, and that we have entered an era of epistemological relativism and methodological pluralism. The question of whether some coherence can or should be imposed upon this intellectual fragmentation is itself a central issue of contention.

But the present turmoil is by no means confined to geography. Across the whole field of the social sciences and the humanities there is a heightened sense of intellectual experimentation and self-appraisal, a blurring of boundaries and genres, and a determined attempt to reach out beyond the centralisms and parochialisms of the Western academy. Discipline after discipline has been drawn into these endlessly multiplying conversations – so much so that most 'disciplines' these days are, by their very nature, multidisciplinary – and if one takes the wider view that this implies it becomes possible to identify some signals in the noise.

One pervasive theme is what might be called the 'lowering of the capitals': a rigorous questioning of the privileges so often ascribed to (among others) Philosophy, Science, Theory and History. These terms, and the sets of assumptions that they have been understood to carry with them, have been tacitly capitalised in most academic work, and until very recently their authority and assumptions have usually been taken for granted. However these normalising conventions are now busily being interrupted. The social sciences as a whole have been extraordinarily deferential to the claims of philosophers and their ability to adjudicate between competing discourses and practices: much more so, probably, than the physical sciences. Human geography has been no exception, in its appeals to logical positivism to underwrite spatial science and then to phenomenology and realism (among others) to undermine it. But many philosophers now have a much more modest sense of purpose. While the end of 'Philosophy with a capital P', as Rorty once put it does not automatically mean the end of philosophy *tout court*, it does mean that its imperial claims have been qualified. Its task is now seen to involve dialogue with other disciplines rather than instruction of them, to produce complication as much as simplification, and to issue admissions of doubt as often as declarations of certainty (Baynes, Bohman and McCarthy, 1987). In much the same way it is increasingly unusual to find science placed on a pedestal or set up as a target. In the past the social sciences either based themselves on or distanced themselves from the received model of the natural sciences. Hence, for example, the schism between the geometrical abstractions of spatial science – the empty geometries of Christaller and Losch – and the spirited evocations of place within humanistic geography. But the stereotype of 'science' on which such responses turned has since been shattered by a wonderfully rich history, sociology, ethnography and even poetics of science which together have advanced a scrupulously careful consideration of science as a fully *social* practice. Like other spheres of social life it is shot through with grids of power and scored by hermeneutic circles which enter into its most basic procedures and protocols (Latour, 1987; Rouse, 1987).

This evidently opens a considerable space for investigations of what geographers *do* (and have done) rather than what they *claim* to be doing. Theory, too, has been reappraised; while the critique of empiricism remains as important as ever, the imperialism of what Mills once called 'Grand Theory', indifferent to content, context or positionality, has been called into ever sharper question. Theoretical work has become much more attentive to the transgressive rather than the stipulative possibilities it makes available, to its capacity to enlarge our critical imaginations rather than police our empirical enquiries, and it is not surprising that a number of writers have redescribed theory through metaphors of travel and displacement. These metaphors are not without their problems and privileges, but the new sensibility they have helped to install has been accompanied by a deepening suspicion of self-sufficient metanarratives that imply an unproblematic access to some singular truth from which 'vantage-point history' is to be simultaneously judged and made. This radical doubt heralds not the 'end of history' that some conservative commentators seek to celebrate so much as the end of a history that inscribed 'the West' so unproblematically at its centre (Young, 1990). In both registers, human geography has much to offer as well as much to learn.

A second theme was identified by Clifford Geertz (1983) when he wrote so eloquently about what he called 'the blurring of the genres'. What he had in mind was the exploration of a series of metaphors – of social life as a game, a drama and a text – which, he argued, had recast the critical imagination and brought about a 'reconfiguration' of social thought. Since then, whatever the merits (or otherwise) of those particular images, the most significant ecumenical gesture has probably been the still more general dismantling of the barriers between the social sciences and the humanities. This is, in part, the result of exploring those other, 'little-p' philosophies that directly address the relations between philosophy and literature and in some cases conceive of philosophy as a 'form of writing'; in part, too, the result of acknowledging the textuality of much of what happens in science; of treating 'theory' as a guerilla discourse that cannot be kept within the boundaries of normally scientific disciplines; and of worrying away at the conceptions of human subjectivity and human agency put to work in most of the stories the West tells itself about itself.

But it is also directly connected to the explosion of interest in cultural studies. Geertz himself suggested that the blurring of the genres was most visibly indexed by the ways in which the social sciences were drawing more and more 'from the contrivances of cultural performance than those of physical manipulation', and in many ways the resurgence of cultural geography speaks to exactly the same point (and indeed often to the same audience). But Geertz's phrasing threatened to reinstate the old opposition between culture and science, whereas cultural studies have moved to address the intricate entanglements of culture, science and technology that enter so forcefully into the constitution of the late-twentieth century world and the convulsive transformations of capitalist modernity (Penley and Ross, 1991). These developments may have a particular salience for human geography, not only because those entanglements – what Harraway (1991a) termed 'the integrated circuit' – have their own, highly uneven, geographies, but also because human geography, by virtue of its involvements in cartography, remote sensing, spatial science and geographical information systems, and its sometimes tense association with physical geography, probably still provides one of the most technically sophisticated arenas within contemporary social sciences and humanities. This plainly imposes an obligation to reflect carefully on the cultural politics of the technologies in which it is implicated. But the blurring of the genres also affects more mundane – though hardly less complicated – practices, and there is no doubt that the 'cultural turn' has had a profound impact on reading and writing within the academy: on the interrogation of texts and images, on the use of language and voice(s), on the strategies of representation that enter so deeply into *what* we say (Clifford and Marcus, 1986; Spivak, 1988). This is confined neither to cultural geography nor to cultural studies more generally, but increasingly informs all our inquiries.

These two themes braid into a third: the spatialisation of critical enquiry. It would be wrong to interpret this as a purely disciplinary affair. Like history, the discourse of geography is much wider than any formal discipline, and some of the most consequential discussions of spatiality and social life have been conducted without reference to our intramural debates. If metaphors of place and space, landscape and location, have now become commonplace, however, one of the most significant contributions of human geography may well be to insist on the materiality of those terms. In his remarkable account of *La production de l'espace*, first published almost twenty years ago, the philosopher Henri Lefebvre suggested that one of the least remarked consequences of the contemporary production of abstract space was a process of constant 'metaphorisation' through which living bodies were 'transported out of themselves, transferred and emptied out as it were, via the eyes' (Lefebvre, 1991, p. 98). He saw it as a task of the first importance not to celebrate such a process of decorporealisation – as so many postmodern writers have since urged – but instead to call attention to its consequences and to assert a stubborn, even subversive materiality. The politics of vision, of the gaze, of landscape as a way of seeing, of the 'scopic regimes' of modernity, have played a particularly prominent part in critical responses to the geographies of postmodernity sketched by Harvey (1989) and Soja (1989). Those critiques ought not to be undervalued, but the joint attentiveness of these two authors to both the metaphorical and the material implications of spatiality, of socially produced space, may turn out to be one of their most enduring contributions.

In fact Neil Smith (1990) suggested that such a project (though probably not exactly the *same* project) might make it possible to fashion what he calls 'spatial difference that is not the same time fragmentation'. This declaration of faith intersects with a fourth theme: the situatedness of knowledge. Invocations of 'difference', of processes of 'othering' and of intersection of different and sometimes competing subject-positions, are now almost standard. This does not mean, however, that these are simply ritual performances and empty gestures. To be sure, the politics of location that they imply is sometimes laid at the door of postmodernism alone, where its critics fear the admission of relativism and even nihilism. But this is hardly what Smith has in mind, and many writers now argue that a sensitivity to difference does not so much erase objectivity as transform its terms: it does not denote a search for some Archimedean point

(margin note: 3rd theme)

(margin note: 4th theme)

from which to make unassailable claims to truth, but is instead an open recognition of the (inescapable) partiality of one's point of view and positionality, and a scrupulous interrogation of the consequences (Harraway, 1991b). Put like that, it is not difficult to see why feminism and postcolonialism have had such a deservedly disconcerting impact on the Western academy, and indeed on public culture more generally, and why so many commentators should try to dismiss both of them as signs of a censorious 'political correctness'. For they do indeed strike at the very heart of traditional Western conceptions of intellectual inquiry and they challenge some of the most basic assumptions, concepts and practices that have governed (literally so) the place of academy in social life. Here too geography has been neither immune nor silenced, as the development of feminism within geography, and latterly of geography within feminism, testifies. Geography's complicity in colonialism, in various forms and for various purposes, invites an equally unsettling consideration of the postcolonial critique that is animating so many other disciplines, but it also allows, through a process of what Spivak (1988) would call 'unlearning', quite *other* geographies to contribute to that critique and enlarge our horizons of meaning and responsibility.

These four themes are not exhaustive, and they certainly do not constitute a new orthodoxy. Each of them can be interpreted and challenged in different ways. But they run through much of the present conversation, inside and outside human geography. They also inform and, we hope, will be informed by the contributions to this book. Our aim is thus not to attempt to construct any general framework or set of principles, nor to offer yet one more methodological or theoretical manifesto to add to the multiplicity that already exists. It is rather to take stock of some of the key arguments and alternatives that have already been advanced. The need for some sort of considered assessment, both in general terms and within the different subdisciplines of the subject, of the challenges and responses raised by the current reorientation(s) is needed for at least two reasons. In the first place, although there is unquestionably a certain excitement to be derived from the abandonment of established viewpoints and the exploration of new ones, such enthusiasm should always be tempered with caution. We should be as suspicious of sheer novelty as we ought to be of rigid orthodoxy, not out of any distrust of conceptual innovation but simply to ensure that new ideas do not pass unexamined into new dogmas. For there are signs that a number of new dogmas have already begun to emerge, in the sense that the claims that have been made for some new arguments appear to be exaggerated beyond what is actually justified by the evidence. The now-obligatory references to 'post-Fordism' and 'postmodernity' are two important cases in point.

Secondly, the novelty of new approaches, even when set against the alleged weaknesses or irrelevance of existing schemas, is not of itself sufficient to proclaim an advance in problem specification or understanding. It is vital to remember that new ideas can be quite as problematic as the orthodoxies they seek to overthrow, and that existing perspectives may still contain valid heuristic and substantive strengths. This issue is amply illustrated by the 'postmodern turn' in human geography. The postmodern turn, with its trenchant critique of rationalist and foundationalist epistemology, and its emphasis on the relativism of our knowledge claims, has certainly opened up valuable space for creative and innovative enquiry within human geography. It has sensitised geographers to the importance of micro and marginal phenomena largely ignored by our (high) modernist theories and perspectives, and has valorised differences, pluralities and heterogeneities suppressed by the generalising and universalising models that have dominated human geography over the past three decades (see Soja, 1989). But in prioritising the mapping of fragments and differences, a postmodern human geography runs the risk of ignoring the more systemic features and relations of social, political and economic structure: the geographical imagination may well be broadened in one direction, but is simultaneously eclipsed in another.

Just as individuals need cognitive maps of their cities to negotiate their spatial environment, so we need maps of society to intelligently analyse, discuss and intervene in social processes. Synoptic or macroconceptualisations are vital to the elucidation of contemporary society: its organisation, its constitutive social relations, practices, discourses and institutions; its integrated and interdependent features; and its structures of power and modes of oppression and domination. Social theory, of which human geography is such an integral part, analyses how these elements fit together to constitute specific societies, and how societies work or fail to function (Best and Kellner, 1991). Large-scale macromodels and cognitive mappings, the 'big pictures' that modern theory strives to construct, continue to have a central role to play in enabling us to see how, for example, the economy, the polity, culture, and social institutions and practices

interact to produce a social system. As we move through the passage from one historical phase of global socio-economic development to another, both modern and postmodern theories are needed
to grasp the continuities with the past and the novel features of a
rapidly changing present. Neither perspective is adequate on its own.
How these two approaches to theory and explanation are articulated
will, we believe, be a major factor in shaping the course and content of human geography over the rest of the present decade.

Plan of the Book

The central task of the following chapters is to flesh out in a more
focused and systematic way what an enriched imagination of the
relationship between geography and the rest of the social sciences
can offer. The plan of this book is arranged in a way that will
provide the reader with recognisable and, we hope, intellectually
justifiable coordinates. The chapters are divided into two main parts.

Part I is concerned with the core of our geographical world – the
economy, polity and society – and of the way in which theories of
these interconnecting 'worlds' can aid our geographical enquiries.
There is of course a long-established tradition within the social sciences that has singled out the economy, polity and society as the
key sources of power and of power relations, of holding 'primacy'
in explanations of the human condition. After all how our geographical world is constituted cannot be understood without recourse to explaining the way in which economic, political and social
relations structure the very time-space fabric of our everyday lives.
As Ron Martin notes in his chapter on economic theory and human geography, since the 1970s a series of disruptions have taken
place to the constitution of the space economy and of our thinking
about it, as reflected in what has been commonly identified as a
new and qualitatively different phase of capitalist development, associated with, among other things, the advent of new informational
and communication technologies, more differentiated and individualised patterns of consumption, and the renegotiation of boundaries and relations between economic markets and nation-states and
public and private spheres of economic activity. These changes have
stimulated a bewildering array of theoretical activities that challenge
traditional ways of thinking about the space economy. In navigat-
ing the reader through a critique of such retheorising, including

regulation theory and postmodernism, this chapter argues that if we are to understand the way in which such changes and shifts are altering the meaning and operation of the capitalist economy then the key tasks must be to construct a contextual economics and economic geography in which socio-spatial embeddedness is moved centre-stage rather than demoted to a secondary contingent role.

Interrelated but not simply reducible to the economic reconstitution of the capitalist world economy have been important changes to the constitution of politics and to the most powerful territorial form that politics takes, the nation-state. Processes of both globalisation and locally based politics are challenging the meaning of sovereignty upon which rests an important locus of state power. As Graham Smith argues in his chapter on political theory and human geography, such challenges to state sovereignty mean that as geographers we need to rethink our theories of the citizen-state and how such notions as citizen-identity and citizen-rights are undergoing redefinition as a result of what he calls a new spatiality to politics. This he illustrates with regard to a variety of social movements engaged in renegotiating the social and geographical boundaries of citizenship, ranging from ethnoregional movements through to environmental movements. Within a global context such social movements, he argues, are symptomatic of differing socio-spatial contexts linked to particular social transformations that are now underway in the first, second and third worlds.

In the final chapter in Part I, Derek Gregory explores the terrain of social theory and its relationship to geographical enquiry. Our geographical enquiries, it is claimed, need to move into richer and less narrowly defined arenas of thinking about and interpreting our and other peoples' worlds. This means acknowledging the problematic nature of Eurocentric-based theory-building, which neither Geography as spatial science nor Marxist geography managed to escape successfully. Through the geometric gaze of geography as spatial science, both places and their peoples were interpreted within a theoretical schema that emphasised generality through homogeneous abstraction and of optimal detachment from everyday struggles and concerns. Indeed the geographers' engagement with Marxism was in part a response to a spatial science unable to engage with a world of social injustice. But the tendency to latch on to classical Marxism, one which analysed landscapes of capital accumulation produced by social processes in material spaces, in part reflected an engagement with Marxism that seemed insensitive to rich intellectual traditions that emphasised the importance of culture, morality and politics. What this means is that we need to rethink our social theory in which engagements with historical materialism, structuration theory and feminist theory offer, in different ways and to varying degrees, richer building blocks for more engaging and committed geographies.

In Part II of this book, systematic consideration is given to selected perspectives on geography that cross-cut economic, political and social sources of power. Of these geographical perspectives, it is the physical environment that is most explicitly concerned with the material conditions that anchor economic, political and social power. Geography, of course, has had a long-established although not always untroubled concern with the relationship between the natural world and society. Yet as Tim Bayliss-Smith and Susan Owens argue in their contribution, because of its particular location at the interface of the physical and social sciences academic geography is well placed to claim the high ground within the social sciences for environmental-based research. A number of environmental debates within the social sciences are taken up. Consideration is first paid to what is meant by 'the environment'. This is followed by an examination of environmentalism as social movement, the modern origins of which, while traceable back to the nineteenth century, have become increasingly a feature of what Inglehart calls a postmaterialist culture, one that, as Smith notes in his chapter, is symptomatic of a myriad of new forms of social opposition, the most novel being 'act local, think global'. Environmental problems and the conflicts surrounding them cannot, however, be treated in a geographically undifferentiated way, a claim the authors illustrate with regard to two substantive 'third world' and 'first world' examples. Finally, the role of formal techniques in environmental-based research, most notably environmental-impact assessment, are considered and their utility examined.

The next two contributions focus on the interrelationship between the differential distribution of economic, political and social power and questions of culture and development. In the first of these chapters Linda McDowell examines one of the fastest growing branches of our subdiscipline, cultural geography. She begins by examining the legacy of one of the doyens of the subject, Carl Sauer, and of the continuing impact of his works on reading and interpreting landscapes in terms of a material conception of culture. Yet cultural landscapes are also imbued with a variety of rich meanings that lend themselves to interpreting culture and the places they represent with symbolic meanings and as texts to be interpreted. The explosion of interest in cultural studies by geographers has also been accompanied by a focus on place and the shared meanings and images that an association with place holds for communities at a variety of geographical scales, from the local neighbourhood up to the nation-state. As this chapter also illustrates, within Western industrialised societies new socioeconomic practices such as novel life styles, forms of work and patterns of consumption have ruptured traditional meanings of place, giving rise to the reconstitution of the individual's sense of identity with community and place, and to the emergence of a new cultural politics reflective of what a number of commentators have signalled as postmaterialist values.

In her concern with development studies, Morag Bell latches on to the way in which geography and the other social sciences have tended to conceive and theorise the third world through a Eurocentric lens, in which the third world has been imbued with a mistaken homogeneity as captured in such spatial dualisms as north–south, core–periphery and developed–developing. What a postcolonial critique of such societies must take on board, argues Bell, is a sensitivity to difference, to moving away from treating the third world in terms of racial, cultural, economic or political stereotyping. If we are to contribute to understanding such pervasive problems of poverty and environmental catastrophe, then as geographers we need to be sensitive to how peoples and the places in which they live differ in their cultural, economic and political practices, produce their own localised geographies, and engage in often radically different strategies for improving their material conditions. As this chapter also notes, the politics of Third-World empowerment, as reflected in the emergence of a multiplicity of new social movements, notably environmentalism and feminism, invites geographers to embark upon agendas of social research that both broaden and recast our conceptions of others.

The next two chapters – on 'the region' and 'the urban' – take as their starting point the importance of geographical differentiation in mapping out the constitution of human relations. The argument developed in the first of these chapters is that regional geography is central to the practice of doing human geography, not least because it poses questions about the world in a way that enables us, as geographers, to be sensitive to the differing contexts in which people live out their lives and interact with the environment. Nigel Thrift structures his chapter around the ideas of three major social thinkers, beginning with Vidal de la Blache and Karl Marx, both of whom have had a major impact on geographical thinking about regions. In also drawing upon the ideas of Fredric Jameson and his engagement with postmodernism, this chapter teases out the connections between a particular strand of current thinking on space and locality and situates these ideas in relation to Vidal and Marx. This enables Thrift to consider how to construct a regional geography for our times, a task that, he argues, must be sensitive to a world in which regions are in flux in ways different from nineteenth-century France or England. Our regional geographies of 'the present', he argues, must be particularly sensitive to ways in which places are associated with the displacement of bounded spaces as a consequence of globalisation, of how the imagination of community and sense of place is being restructured, in which the media plays a vital mediative role, and of the problem of understanding the meanings behind 'community'.

In her chapter on 'the urban', Susan J. Smith argues for a place for urban studies but one which needs to acknowledge that, as most societies are now urbanising societies, the city is an interrelated part of a complex web whose conceptual and spatial boundaries are not easily distinguishable. Yet as an arena for intellectual enquiry, urbanism is still about different conceptions and interpretations of what the city is and should be. This she considers in relation to two differing normative approaches to understanding the city. First, in considering the city from the neo-Marxist perspective, she argues that we need to go beyond simple 'production-oriented' and 'consumption-based' approaches by also recognising that urban life is also gendered and racialised in ways that cannot simply be read off from either the spatial differentiation of capital accumulation or by focusing on a class-based urban politics of consumption. Second, in examining the impact of the New Right, she notes that from the vantage point of this ideology there is a far greater tendency to portray urban problems as more distinctively urban and manageable, by, for instance, depicting urban problems as a symptom of state intervention and as simply a consequence of falling living standards. For the New Right, rectifying urban problems entails policies that free up the market in combination with emphasising the centrality of policing as a means of social control. Yet such debates in urban studies have more recently been usurped by considerations of the impact of postmodernism and of the way in which it finds expression in built form, how consumption is organised and social life conducted, and in the way in which our personal identities – 'the self' – are being renegotiated.

What the foregoing chapters signal is a sensitivity to 'history' and to the importance of bringing 'history back in' to our geographical studies. While most 'good' geographies of 'the contemporary' take cognisance of the way in which historical processes illuminate 'the present', this does not mean that there is no place for a distinctive subdiscipline that focuses on geographical studies of the past. Yet, as Chris Philo argues in the final chapter, historical geography, or what he would prefer to call 'geographical history', has undergone a welcome sea change. Rather than just focusing on the materiality of 'geographical facts', on the objects of 'the visible landscape', historical geography has increasingly moved towards a concern with the immateriality of historical phenomena, as reflected in a concern for urban and rural protest movements, the operations of central and local states and the spatial diffusion of innovations. Thus the central project of historical geography should be to bring to studies of historical happenings a sensitivity to place, space, distance, location and region. In focusing on a substantive example, geographies of 'the mad business' – the nineteenth-century institutions that housed those designated as 'mad' and the 'mad-doctoring' profession responsible for their treatment – Philo illustrates the complexity of geographies in the location and design of 'mad houses' and in the formation and organisation of this profession. This particular glimpse at a 'geographical history' raises questions about the nature of knowledge and of power, which this chapter goes on to explore in relation to Michel Foucault's concern to tease out 'the spatialising of history' or geographical history.

References

Baynes, K., J. Bohman and T. McCarthy (1987) *After Philosophy: End or Transformation?* (Cambridge, Mass.: MIT Press).

Best, S. and D. Kellner (1991) *Postmodern Theory: Critical Interrogations* (London: Macmillan).

Billinge, M., D. J. Gregory and R. L. Martin (eds) (1984) *Recollections of a Revolution: Geography as Spatial Science* (London: Macmillan).

Clifford, J. and G. Marcus (1986) *Writing Culture: The Poetics and Politics of Ethnography* (Berkeley: University of California Press).

Cloke, P., C. Philo and D. Sadler (1991) *Approaching Human Geography: An Introduction to Contemporary Theoretical Debates* (London: Chapman).

Dear, M. (1988) 'The Postmodern Challenge: Reconstructing Human Geography, *Transactions of the Institute of British Geographers, NS*, vol. 13, pp. 262–74.

Geertz, C. (1983) *Local Knowledge: Further Essays in Interpretive Anthropology* (New York: Basic Books).

Gregory, D. J. (1978) *Ideology, Science and Human Geography* (London: Macmillan).

Gregory, D. J. and R. Walford (eds) (1989) *Horizons in Human Geography* (London: Macmillan).

Harraway, D. (1991a) 'A Cyborg Manifesto: Science, Technology and Socialist-Feminism in the Late Twentieth Century', in D. Harraway, *Simians, Cyborgs and Women: The Reinvention of Nature* (London: Routledge and Kegan Paul), pp. 149–82.

Harraway, D. (1991b) 'Situated Knowledges: The Science Question in Feminism and the Privilege of Partial Perspective', in D. Harraway, *Simians, Cyborgs and Women: The Reinvention of Nature* (London: Routledge and Kegan Paul), pp. 183–220.

Harvey, D. (1969) *Explanation in Geography* (London: Edward Arnold).

Harvey, D. (1973) *Social Justice and the City* (London: Edward Arnold).

Harvey, D. (1989) *The Condition of Postmodernity: An Enquiry into the Origins of Cultural Change* (Oxford: Basil Blackwell).

Johnston, R. J. (1983) *Geography and Geographers: Anglo-American Geography Since 1945* (London: Edward Arnold).

Johnston, R. J. (ed.) (1993) *The Challenge for Geography: A Changing World: A Changing Discipline* (Oxford: Basil Blackwell).

King, L. (1976) 'Alternatives to a Positive Economic Geography', *Annals of the Association of American Geographers*, vol. 66, no. 2, pp. 293–308.

Kobayashi, A. and S. Mackenzie (eds) (1989) *Remaking Human Geography* (London: Unwin Hyman).

Latour, S. (1987) *Science in Action* (Milton Keynes: Open University Press).

Lefebvre, H. (1991) *The Production of Space* (Oxford: Basil Blackwell).

Ley, D. (1989) 'Fragmentation, Coherence and Limits to Theory in Human Geography', in A. Kobayashi and S. Mackenzie (eds), *Remaking Human Geography* (London: Unwin Hyman), pp. 227–44.

Macmillan, B. (ed) (1989) *Remodelling Geography* (Oxford: Basil Blackwell).

McLennan, G. (1989) *Marxism, Pluralism and Beyond: Classic Debates and New Departures* (Cambridge: Polity).

Peet, R. and N. J. Thrift (eds) (1989) *New Models in Geography,* vols 1 and 2 (London: Unwin Hyman).

Penley, C. and A. Ross (eds) (1991) *Technoculture* (Minneapolis: University of Minnesota Press).

Rouse, J. (1987) *Knowledge and Power: Toward a Political Philosophy of Science* (Ithaca: Cornell University Press).

Rousseas, S. (1979) *Capitalism and Catastrophe: A Critical Appraisal of the Limits to Capitalism* (Cambridge University Press).

Smith, N. (1990) 'Afterword: The Beginning of Geography', in N. Smith, *Uneven Development: Nature, Capital and the Production of Space*, second edn (Oxford: Basil Blackwell), pp. 160–78.

Soja, E. (1989) *Postmodern Geographies: The Reassertion of Space in Critical Social Theory* (London: Verso).

Spivak, G. C. (1988) *In Other Worlds: Essays in Cultural Politics* (London: Routledge and Kegan Paul).

Stoddart, D. R. (1987) 'To Claim the high Ground: Geography for The End of the Century', *Transactions of the Institute of British Geographers, NS*, vol. 12, pp. 327–36.

Young, R. (1990) *White Mythologies: Writing History and the West* (London: Routledge and Kegan Paul).

Part I

The Core of Human Geography

2
Economic Theory and Human Geography

RON MARTIN

> No existing theory explains the main economic events [since] 1979. . . . Nor could it have predicted them. Reality has outgrown existing theories. . . . To give us a functioning economic theory we need a new synthesis that simplifies. But so far there is no sign of it. And if no such synthesis emerges we may be at the end of economic *theory*. There may then be only economic *theorems*, that is formulae and formulations that describe this or that problem rather than present economics as a coherent system.
>
> P. Drucker, *The New Realities*

Exordium: Economic Geography at the Cross Roads

Although economic geography has existed as an identifiable subdiscipline for close on a century, it is only since the Second World War that its intellectual history has been closely shaped by economics. Nevertheless, by the mid-1980s economic geography appeared to have matured into a stable and well-structured field of academic endeavour, organised around two primary and interrelated *research programmes*, focusing respectively on industrial location dynamics and the process of uneven regional development, and using concepts and theories from neoclassical, Keynesian and Marxian economics. Not surprisingly, given the quite different 'world views' that characterise these three main competing schools of modern economic thought (see Wolff and Resnick, 1987; Cole, Cameron and Edwards, 1991), this theoretical trigemony within economic geography produced contrasting and conflicting analyses of the space economy. However, underpinning these diverse and contrasting accounts there were certain shared assumptions, principles and aspirations, which, even if rarely acknowledged, served to impart an underlying unity to economic geography as it evolved from the mid-1950s to the mid-1980s.

Above all the modern capitalist economy was seen as an *industrial* system with patterns and trajectories of industrial location and regional development that seemed to be, and were certainly assumed to be, well-behaved and predictable. This perceived order provided the warrant for essentialist or 'deep-logic' interpretations of the economic landscape, in which the processes shaping the space economy were attributed to deep-seated behavioural mechanisms or irresistible developmental forces. This economic essentialism in turn aided the widespread ambition of constructing general, universal laws of industrial location and regional development. In this way modern economic geography became distinctly objectivist in orientation, involving the prioritisation of 'scientific' knowledge over subjective knowledge based on introspection, perception and intuition. And in prosecuting these assumptions and aspirations, economic geography tended to structure itself according to the same 'scientific' principles it sought to portray in the economic landscape.

In the last few years, however, the theories, premises and principles of modern economic geography have been progressively called into question. A distinct sense of reappraisal, uncertainty and exploration has come to pervade the discipline, and both of its major research programmes are undergoing reformulation. What I want to argue in this chapter is that this upheaval can be traced to three principal and interrelated sources of disruption. The first is substantive and paratonic in nature, and has to do with what many believe is the advent of a new and qualitatively different phase of capitalist economic development, to the advent of 'new economic realities' (see, for example, Hall and Jacques, 1989; Drucker, 1989; Reich, 1991). These shifts pose some major problems for our accepted theories of the space economy, and for what a reconstructed economic geography should look like. Second, to compound this issue, economics itself is likewise in turmoil, largely for the same reason. There is a crisis *in* and *of* economics (Wiles and Routh, 1984; Drucker, 1989). None of the main schools of economics – neoclassical, Keynesian or Marxian – adequately explains the events and changes of the past two decades, and as these mainstream paradigms have come under siege so numerous revisions, reformulations and alternative perspectives have been advanced. But, third, as if these challenges were not enough, in some quarters of both economics and economic geography the very epistemological and ontological bases of theoretical enquiry are being contested. Viewed from this so-called 'postmodern' critique we are witnessing not just a movement from one phase of capitalist economic development to another, but also an associated movement from one epistemological tradition to another. At the core of this challenge is the general question of how we view and represent the world, of the relationship between our concepts and 'reality', in whatever sense the latter is taken.

The impact of these disruptions has been to open up not only major enquiries into the meaning and of significance of current shifts and trends in the economy, but also about the theoretical approaches, research methodologies and conceptual categories we use, and even about our subject matter. In many ways modern economic geography stands at a decisive crossroads with respect to both its mode of theorising and its empirical content. My aim in the remainder of this chapter is to explore some of the contours and implications of this *methodenstreit* in more detail, to provide a critical reading of some of the signposts, as it were.

The Changing Economy

It is now widely agreed that something dramatic has been happening to the advanced capitalist economies since the early 1970s, to say nothing of course of the (former) socialist economies. There has been much less consensus, however, as to the precise nature and significance of the changes that have occurred, and are continuing to take place. The problem is that in a period of rapid and far-reaching change it is by no means straightforward to assess what stage we are at in the process, to identify the trends and shifts involved and to separate the fundamental from the ephemeral. As a result there have been quite different opinions as to what the fundamental shifts are, as well as different interpretations of them.

Without doubt one of the most profound changes is the advent of a new information-based 'techno-economic paradigm' (Schiller, 1986; Dosi, *et al.*, 1988). Whereas the postwar paradigm was based on low-cost oil, electrical machinery, energy-intensive materials and mass production and consumption, the bases of the new paradigm are information and communication technologies, microelectronics, computerisation, knowledge-intensive products and consumption patterns that are much more differentiated and individualised. This new technology system is transforming the technical, corporate and social organisation of production, as well as patterns of demand, consumption and distribution. A second shift has been the acceleration in the 'tertiarisation' of economic development. Although in many advanced capitalist countries services surpassed manufacturing in terms of output and employment as early as the 1950s and 1960s, the pace of this structural shift has quickened dramatically since the 1970s. Private-sector producer, consumer, financial, personal and cultural–leisure services have all expanded at the same time that manufacturing has stagnated or, in many cases, de-industrialised (Petit, 1986). The structures of production and consumption, and the social, class, gender and spatial divisions of labour, are being recast as a result. A third significant development is the trend towards what has been called 'hyper-consumptionism' or even 'over-consumptionism'. The mass-consumption culture of the post-war period has exploded into a new culture of consumption that is simultaneously more individualised, internationalised and multi-dimensional. The introduction of the 'instant credit economy', the increasing assertiveness and acquisitiveness of a new middle class, changes in tastes and lifestyles, the revolution in information technology, the media and advertising, the increasing differentiation of products, and the rise of a whole new 'culture industry' based on the commodification of the visual, aesthetic and symbolic, all of these have stimulated new patterns and landscapes of consumption (especially the phenomenon of malls) in which instant gratification, positionality and image are now as important as use value (Zukin, 1991). The fourth major shift is that of globalisation. Since the early 1970s the internationalisation of industry, services and capital has intensified dramatically. In some respects the world economy is becoming truly transnational or global (Simai, 1990). The dynamic, successful firm is becoming increasingly a globally dencentralised 'enterprise web' of profit centres, business units, spin-offs, licensees, suppliers and distributors. Likewise, more and more products are now typically international composites, and both corporate ownership and control are becoming globally diffused. Even more profound, however, has been the emergence of global banking and globally integrated money markets, of a supranational economy of 'stateless

a fifth chape

yet
chape

'monies' that have their own dynamics (Wachter, 1986; Ohmae, 1990; O'Brien, 1992). Finally, a new mode of economic regulation has swept through the developed and developing countries alike over the past decade and a half, involving a fundamental renegotiation of the links and boundaries between states and markets, between the public and private spheres of the economy. Countries at all stages of economic development have sought to liberalise and privatise their economies in an attempt to increase their competitiveness and flexibility in the new global market place (Letwin, 1988; Rosow, 1988).

These and other formative developments have not, of course, suddenly appeared overnight, but have been evolving for some time. The point, however, is that such trends have accelerated sharply over the past two decades, restructuring and transforming the economic landscape in the process. Although these changes have in part been crisis-induced, stimulated by the slowdown of the world economy since the early 1970s, equally the new realities are themselves destabilising as the old structures of economic accumulation and regulation are disrupted and outmoded by the new. It may even be that this instability is not simply a transitory phenomenon associated with restructuring, but is in fact a central feature of the new era, that disorder, rapid change and uncertainty are now the hallmarks of advanced capitalist economic development, indeed of the global economy as a whole. Geographically the economic landscape has certainly been changing dramatically. Old industrial spaces have declined and are being restructured, while new industrial spaces have taken over as the leading centres of economic growth (see, for example, Martin and Rowthorn, 1986; Henderson and Castells, 1987; Peet, 1987; Massey and Allen, 1988; Scott, 1988; Harvey, 1989a; Rodwin and Sazanami, 1989, 1991). Whereas some industries and services appear to be undergoing spatial dispersal and locational decentralisation, others seem to be concentrating or reconcentrating geographically. Similarly, in many large and older cities, at the same time that selected economically derelict areas have been transformed into newly built spaces of consumption, spectacle and commerce, the continued economic and social plight of other districts has been thrown into even sharper relief. Yet further, as national, regional and local economies become increasingly internationalised and integrated into transnational and global networks of production, competition, investment and corporate strategy, so they are also becoming progressively functionally disarticulated internally (Castells, 1989). If the postwar capitalist space economy was relatively stable and predictable, it is now much more *un*stable and *un*predictable, and without question far less manageable politically.

All this presents economics and economic geography with major challenges. Over the past few years a vast literature has appeared that is devoted to mapping out the new realities, and new empirical specialisms have proliferated within both disciplines. For example, within economic geography industrial restructuring, small and new firm development, corporate organization, multinationalisation, high-technology activity, service-sector growth, and the new social and spatial divisions of labour have all received considerable empirical attention. But the challenge goes much further than this: it is not simply a question of documenting and describing the new economic landscape, important though that task is. The key issue is how we explain and account for the new realities.

My argument here is that *the changes and shifts under way are changing the meaning and operation of the capitalist economy*. Thus the convergence of discrete technologies, especially computing, tele-communications and information processing, is increasing the or-ganisational and productive flexibility of businesses of all kinds of sizes. Information and communications technologies now pro-vide the common denominator for an ever-growing share of the production of goods and services, and as a consequence are redefining the social, cultural and institutional bases of the economy. Further-more the production of the means of communication has taken on a quite new significance in relation to production in general, and hence to the whole process of uneven development. At the same time, the growth of services has altered consumption norms and hence the traditional links between production and consumption. And given the generally lower productivity of services, tertiarisation has major implications for national economic growth and for the whole productivity–wage–consumption nexus, as well as the social distribution of productivity gains. It is not just that services now outweigh manufacturing in the economy; it is also that in some cases the distinction between the two is becoming increasingly blurred, while in others services have become an autonomous source of growth, demand, capital accumulation and economic regulation, no longer simply linked to or dependent on industrial growth but hav-ing their own structural dynamic. The concept of the industrial economy that has for so long permeated economics and economic geography no longer provides an adequate account of actual reality. The new capitalism, moreover, is one in which the 'symbol' economy of money and credit now dominates the real economy of goods and services. Money and finance have become 'securitised', traded and speculated in for profit without being linked to the production of goods and services, yet exerting a fundamental influence on the latter. This new system of 'money-manager capitalism' (Minsky, 1989) is possibly now the single most important force shaping the nature and structure of uneven development. And as almost every factor of production – technology, money, investment, information – moves ever more rapidly across borders, the very meaning and role of the 'national' economy, to say nothing of the 'regional' and 'local' economy, are being redefined.

This is not the first time capitalism has undergone a wide-ranging upheaval. Periodically economic reality has outgrown prevailing theories, throwing the latter into confusion and stimulating wide-ranging debate and reappraisal. The problem then is one of reconstruction, of whether the dominant research programmes prove to be 'progressive', responding with new theories and concepts more appropriate to the changed economic conditions and institutions; or whether the response is more one of attempting to salvage and revive 'degenerating' programmes by means of ad hoc amendments, revisions and extensions. Such a critical moment has occurred (at least) twice before in economics. The 'economic revolutions' of the 1870s (from classical to neoclassical economics) and the 1930s (from neoclassical to Keynesian economics) were both in part 'progressive' responses to the emergence of new conditions and circumstances that rendered the prevailing orthodoxy obsolete. Economic geography, being relatively underdeveloped, was on those occasions unaffected. The current conjuncture has once more thrown economics into disarray, and this time economic geography as well. All three mainstream schools of economic theory have recognised that reality has changed, although of course they agree neither on the specific nature and significance of the changes, as they see them, nor on their import for the future of capitalism. All have reexamined the adequacy of their traditional formulations and each is searching for an explanation of the new economy as seen through its own ideological prism.

Of course, not unexpectedly, there are defenders of the faith who reject the idea that new circumstances require new theories. The chief exponents of the use of Marxian political economy in geography exemplify this reaction. Though fully conscious that their theoretical perspective is challenged by the new capitalism, these theorists have been at some pains to counter this offensive. They acknowledge that capitalism is changing in unexpected and fundamental ways not predicted by Marxist theory, but at the same time insist that despite these changes the validity of that theory remains unblemished. Thus David Harvey has argued that the multifarious changes that are under way are confined to the 'surface appearance' of capitalism, and thus should not be mistaken for a basic alteration of its underlying 'structural laws of motion', which 'still continue to operate as immutable truths within the confusing fragmentations and perplexing twists of the present conjuncture' (Harvey, 1989a; see also Harvey, 1989b). The argument is that the new realities represent another of capitalism's periodic attempts to secure a new spatial and technological 'fix', and that since we still live in a world dominated by capitalism – in fact, in one that is witnessing the reassertion and extension of the 'capitalist imperative' (Storper and Walker, 1989) – the fundamental principles of Marxist political economy are neither negated nor weakened by the 'surface' shifts and changes that are occurring.

But the resurgence and extension of capitalism does not of itself provide automatic support for the continued relevance and superiority of mainstream economic perspectives, whether Marxian, neoclassical, Keynesian or any other. As economic geographers we are faced with a basic conundrum. On the one hand we are concerned to formulate theories of uneven regional development that are explicitly historical in orientation, that attempt to uncover the mechanisms and processes that shape the evolution of the space economy over historical time. But on the other hand, as the economy itself develops and changes historically so does its specific mode of functioning, which thus throws into doubt the likelihood of constructing theories that remain valid for any extensive period of time. What is at issue, in other words, is the 'historicity of concepts' (Sayer, 1987). As the nature and organisation of capitalism changes, so does the content of concepts such as 'markets', 'capital', 'labour', 'firm', 'competition', 'demand', 'money', 'regional development' and so on. To expect the same concepts and theories to apply to different epochs of capitalist economic development is to move in a charmed circle of excessive abstraction, to do violence to the very realities our concepts and theories are meant to help us understand. The new capitalism cannot be adequately represented and explained by existing conceptual categories and theoretical frameworks. At the very least the new realities have exposed serious flaws and gaps in our theories, and thus the need for a substantial rethinking.

New Perspectives for New Realities

Notwithstanding their arch-defenders, as the mainstream perspectives have come under siege so there have been corresponding moves to revise and reformulate them. A whole new corpus of post-Keynesian economics has emerged (see for example, Eichner, 1986; Sawyer, 1988; Lavoie, 1992) that gives greater recognition to money, history, uncertainty and institutions in shaping economic development, together with a new-Keynesian microeconomics that focuses on imperfect competition and market rigidities (Gordon, 1990; Mankiw and Romer, 1992). While this has been happening, on the neoclassical side a revamped microeconomics of rational expectations and a new supply-side macroeconomics have been combined with elements of public-choice theory to form a new-classical school (Phelps, 1990), an apologetic for free-market capitalism that has proved popular with recent neoliberal governments in many countries. Similarly, in the Marxist camp there are Ricardian reconstructions that utilise Sraffian economics in an effort to derive a surplus-based theory that by-passes the Marxist labour theory of value and associated concepts of class struggle and exploitation (for example Pack, 1985; Steedman, 1988); and game-theoretic and rational-choice versions that attempt to rebuild Marxist theory on a foundation of methodological individualism (Roemer, 1981; Elster, 1985; Roemer, 1986). And in addition to these different reformulations several other schools of economics have appeared or reappeared, including neo-Sraffian (Schefold, 1989; Bharadwaj and Schefold, 1992), organisational (Williamson, 1985, 1986), evolutionary (Clark and Juma, 1987; Hodgson, 1993), neo-Schumpeterian (Oakley, 1990), neoinstitutional (Tool, 1988; Hodgson, 1988; Eggertsson, 1990), and a new sociological economics (Block, 1990; Zukin and DiMaggio, 1990).

Economic geographers have begun to draw upon and engage with some of these new approaches, in particular elements of the post-Keynesian, Sraffian, rational-choice Marxist and organisational schools (for a flavour of these developments see, respectively, Clark, Gertler and Whiteman, 1986; Sunley, 1992; Sheppard and Barnes, 1990; *Economic Geography*, 1992; Scott, 1988). However the primary focus has been on deriving a general, synoptic theorisation of the new realities, a new large-scale master concept of the capitalist space economy that identifies the 'big structures and processes' at work and demonstrates the interconnectedness of ostensibly unrelated and diverse patterns of change and transformation. Several such macrointerpretations have gatecrashed the geographical literature in the past few years in the form of 'epochal' or 'transition' models. Most of these see the primary changes in capitalist development as marking the shift to a new production system: 'neo-Fordism' (Aglietta, 1979), 'post-Fordism' (Murray, 1989; Elam, 1990), 'flexible specialisation' (Piore and Sabel, 1984), 'the new competition' (Best, 1990), 'lean production' (Womack *et al.*, 1990), and 'mass customisation' (Pine, 1992) are the main concepts mobilised to expound this characterisation of contemporary economic change. Others see it more as a transition in the structure and organisation of economic accumulation in a general sense: 'disorganised capitalism' (Offe, 1986; Lash and Urry, 1987), 'post-industrial society' (Hirschorn, 1984; Block, 1990; Rose, 1991), 'flexible accumulation' (Harvey, 1989a, 1989b), 'postmodernism' (Jameson, 1991; Crook *et al.*, 1992), 'money manager capitalism' (Minsky, 1989) and 'postcapitalist society' (Drucker, 1993) are among the main models that adopt this interpretation. Although these models differ in various ways, all claim not only to have uncovered the key features of the new reality, but also to provide a general account of its underlying logic.

There is no doubt that these models have contributed to our understanding of recent and contemporary economic change and that they have added a whole new conceptual and empirical lexicon to economic geography. Yet the very attractions and aspirations of this search for an 'encompassing' interpretative framework have simultaneously exposed the major weaknesses of such an ambition (Martin, 1989; Thrift, 1989; Sayer, 1989a, 1989b). All of the models tend to overgeneralise, either by collapsing a complex range of trends and shifts into a single concept or logic, or by synecdochically projecting what are certain key dimensions of the new economy into a statement of the totality. The result tends to be an interpretative framework in which both the old and the new realities are highly stylised and idealised, a problem reinforced by the use of 'oppositional typologies' to distinguish the new forms of economic organisation from the old, and by the flourish of negativised rhetoric embodied in such prefixes as 'post-' and 'dis-' that are enlisted to describe the new economic system. Such models thus tend to impose a facade of coherence upon what in fact is a much more confused, complex and unstructured reality. Within geography a further serious issue has been the over-eagerness to 'read off' spatial stereotypes from these macro-characterisations, so that the particular form or process of regional development highlighted or implied by a given model has all too often been viewed as if it were *the* spatial symbol of the new economic landscape throughout the capitalist world. In fact, even as used and adapted by economic geographers most of these transition models actually have surprisingly little to say about the geographical constitution of the new realities at the global, national, regional or local scales.

These problems are well exemplified by the post-Fordist and flexible-specialisation accounts, currently the two most influential of the new cognitive frameworks in economic geography. The post-Fordist perspective, drawing on French regulation theory, sees the contemporary restructuring of the capitalist space economy in terms of a shift from one 'regime of accumulation' and associated 'mode of regulation' called Fordism to another called (not very originally) post-Fordism (for overviews, see Boyer, 1990; Dunford, 1990; Jessop, 1990a; Lipietz, 1992). In a similar way the flexible specialisation school argues that we are passing over a second 'industrial divide' to a new logic of production and economic organisation in which flexibility is the key imperative, and new specialised 'industrial districts' the primary spatial expression (see Piore and Sabel, 1984; Scott, 1988; Sabel, 1989; Storper and Scott, 1989; Pyke, Becattini and Sengenberger, 1990; Scott and Storper, 1992). However, although highly suggestive, neither approach has yet been able to provide a viable regional political economy.

In the case of regulation theory, both its historical accuracy concerning the nature and breakdown of 'Fordism' and its claim that flexible accumulation is replacing mass production are questionable (Brenner and Glick, 1992; Sayer, 1989a, b). Secondly, although regulation theory operates with the concept of the 'integral economy', the approach is ultimately productionist and fails to deal seriously with the role of services in the accumulation and regulation processes of modern capitalism. Thirdly, notwithstanding the pivotal role attached to institutional forms in holding together symmetrical systems of production and consumption, these are not in fact examined in any detail: thus far the approach has not succeeded in theorising the 'mode of regulation' and its historical evolution, or how the mode of regulation actually links consumption and production (Tickell and Peck, 1992). In particular, regulation theorists have still not adequately addressed the problem of the state, one of the most significant elements of the mode of regulation, and instead have tended to 'read off' the state from the nature of the accumulation regime (see Jessop, 1990b, for a critique). Fourthly, regulation theory is distinctly macroeconomic in orientation, a model in which the national economy is prioritised as the key unit of analysis and both local and global economic and regulatory processes are subordinated to those of individual nation-states. Although regulation theory supposedly seeks to address the central question of 'how economic and social dynamics vary over space and time' (Boyer, 1990, p. 29), the constitution and integration of accumulation and regulation at different spatial scales remains largely untheorised. Finally, despite its claims to the contrary, the approach remains trapped in the functionalism that permeates its Marxist crisis-theoretic foundations. Too many shortcomings, inconsistencies and ommisions exist, then, for the regulation approach to be considered a coherent body of economic theory, or a new paradigm for economic geography. It is, rather, a 'normative scaffolding of knowledge' in which the purpose is less to provide a precise theory and more one of building ideal types or frameworks to be used to assess and investigate the 'stylised facts' of economic organisation and development (Teague, 1990).

Nor, as it currently stands, does flexible specialisation theory fare any better (Jessop, 1992). On close inspection the theoretical underpinnings of the flexible specialisation thesis are in fact surprisingly orthodox in orientation. In effect, flexible specialisation theory represents a resurrected and reworked version of Marshall's notion of 'agglomeration economies', brought up to date by the application of concepts about transactions costs from Williamson's (1985, 1986) organisational economics. Both of these streams of theory follow standard neoclassical logic in conceptualising local economies as collections of atomistic competitors, whereas what is required is an approach grounded in a conceptual analysis of the firm as a strategic entity. Equally, although analysts of industrial districts repeatedly stress the contextual significance of communal noneconomic institutions and systems of collaboration, trust and cooperation, these remain largely untheorised (Harrison, 1992). Moreover, like its regulation counterpart, flexible specialisation theory has several fundamental lacunae. First, not enough concrete examples exist to support the general propositions advanced by the theory. Not only is the empirical generality of new industrial districts of flexibly specialised production much exaggerated, they differ considerably in structure, organisation, insertion into the national and international divisions of labour, and so on: for example, in some cases the specialisation is sectoral, while in others it is functional. How far it is possible to generalise across such diverse types is open to debate (Amin and Robinson, 1990). Secondly, the theory conflates essentially different industrial and commercial strategies: there are several different forms of and paths to 'flexibility', not all of which are necessarily incompatible with mass production, nor necessarily as pervasive, novel or progressive as the theory alleges them to be (Gertler, 1988; Pollert, 1991). Thirdly, by focusing on the so-called 'new' industrial spaces, the theory tends to suppress and ignore the equally crucial developments and dynamics of 'old' industrial spaces (Martin, 1991; Gertler, 1992), and has barely recognised service-based regional economies. And fourthly, the theory neglects the wider international context of regional and local economic development (Gertler, 1992), and especially the powerful tendencies towards accelerating capital and market integration at the global scale that run counter to the notion of self-contained, locally integrated economies.

Similar problems and limitations characterise the other models and approaches. None are sufficiently developed to offer a convincing new theoretical foundation for economic geography. Instead they yield *ideal types*, which have to be rescued either by a 'severe stylisation of the facts' or by devising ad hoc hybrid forms to fit actual empirical experience. This is not to suggest, as some have done (for example, Callinicos, 1989), that the economic landscape these new meta-narratives and master concepts seek to grasp is merely a fiction of their own creation. Rather, it is to point up the fact that they fail to provide any real theoretical purchase on the key processes and realities involved, on technological change and its assimilation, on services and their role in accumulation, on globalisation, or on state intervention and regulation. These issues are precisely those about which economics still has relatively little to say.

Take, for example, the issue of globalisation. Although some initial formulations of a new 'global political economy' (Gill and Law, 1988; Wallace, 1990) and a new 'international economics' (Krugman, 1986; Porter, 1990) are beginning to appear, there is as yet no coherent theoretical framework that adequately integrates the various transnationalisation and internationalisation processes that are reconfiguring the geographies of capital, money, production, trade and technologies across the world economy. To be sure, all three main schools of economic theory have sought to accommodate the globalisation challenge. Thus Marxian political economy sees the global economic system in terms of the same developmental dynamics, laws of motion and crisis tendencies that characterise the national capitalist economy. This model of 'global capitalism' reaches its most totalising but certainly not most convincing expression in 'world systems theory' (Wallerstein, 1979, 1984, 1991). Similarly, a new 'global neoclassicism' by-passes the nation-state altogether and sees the global economy in terms of the competitive equilibration of integrated worldwide financial and product markets; while the new 'international Keynesianism' pictures the global economy as a system of interdependent national economies between which aggregate demand, income and investment are maldistributed and malregulated, to the detriment of the system as a whole. But to assume, as these forms of 'global' economics do, that the same concepts used to analyse the national economy can be simply projected onto the global system is to assume that the latter is essentially no different in structural complexity and operation from the former, that concepts and theories are scale-independent. For their part geographers recently have made much of the global–local interplay (for example, Cooke, 1986; Dunford and Kafkalas, 1992), yet paradoxically even they have so far failed to articulate a coherent or convincing analytical framework for linking different material and conceptual scales. This absence is especially apparent at the present time, as transnationalisation and internationalisation rapidly disrupt our conventional notions of geographical scale, rendering any simple hierarchical division of functional economic space into local, regional, national and international levels increasingly ambiguous.

Likewise, there is a glaring need to devote much greater theoretical attention to services in economics and economic geography. Despite the central role these now play in the capitalist economy, many economists and geographers continue to deny that the enormous shift towards services has changed any of the forces and categories fundamental to industrialism. Either the centrality of services is dismissed as a myth (Cohen and Zysman, 1987), or, if their empirical significance is acknowledged, it is assumed that services operate according to the same economic laws and logic that characterise manufacturing, and hence can be explicated using the same theories and concepts (the position adopted by many economic geographers). Neither posture is self-evidently true. The nature and forces of production, the form of the capital–labour relation and of that between labour and product, the materiality and fungibility of the product, and the relationship between production and consumption, are all sufficiently different – not simply in degree but kind – from manufacturing as conventionally defined, that most services cannot simply be swept under the conceptual carpet of 'industrialism'. Not only have services changed the nature of capitalist accumulation, they have also changed the process and mode of economic regulation. Neither economics nor economic geography seems to have fully grasped this fact. However, constructing a new economics and a new economic geography that give explicit consideration to the conceptualisation of services will be far from straightforward. The sheer diversity of service activities, ranging from public services at one extreme through the wide spectrum of personal, consumer, distributive and producer services, to global financial services at the other, must raise fundamental questions about the applicability of any single body of economic or geographic theory.

Major theoretical gaps also exist with respect to technological change and the role of the state. Within both economics and economic geography, technological change and the state are generally treated not as endogenous socio-institutional forces in the process of capitalist development, but as exogenous variables. Although recently there has been a flood of literature documenting the history of technological change and its relationship to national and regional economic growth, it has essentially remained outside any formal body of theory. What attempts have been made to theorise the historical and spatial dynamics of technological change have drawn mainly on Marxian, Schumpeterian or product-life-cycle economics. Although these perspectives certainly recognise the centrality of technological change, they treat it rather mechanistically, for example as the inevitable outcome of capitalist competition or as a wave-like phenomenon stimulated by the periodic bunching of key innovations, and do not capture the full nature and dynamic of technology as a social, institutional and cultural process. With respect to the state, most of the time its part in shaping the economic landscape is ignored or marginalised, subordinated to the structural imperatives of capitalist development. In those instances where state intervention is addressed, it tends to be in terms of the impact of this or that specific policy rather than the role of the state in a more fundamental systemic sense. Given the importance of the state as regulator, producer, purchaser and redistributor, any attempt to construct a realistic regional theory must bring the state into the foreground. The contemporary restructuring of state intervention in the shift to the new capitalism reinforces this need. For contrary to the perceived wisdom of certain circles, the state is not simply 'withering away', undermined by economic and spatial decentralisation within and globalisation without, but rather continues to exert its own substantial influence on the nature, evolution and geography of global capitalism (Hirst and Thompson, 1992; Martin, 1993).

These examples are sufficient to emphasise the need for economic geographers to widen their empirical and analytical concerns beyond their longstanding preoccupation with industrial development. Indeed, despite all the reappraisal and reformulation of the past few years, economic geography still remains overwhelmingly *industrial* geography. As a result, for the most part, interpretations of the new economic realities have been seen through a particular and rather restricted lens: the post-Fordist and flexible specialisation theses amply illustrate this myopia. The new realities extend far beyond the realm of industrial production, and it is very unlikely that the concepts, theories and perspectives devised to explain the latter are appropriate for grasping the full complexity of the former. Nor is it persuasive to argue that, recent developments and changes notwithstanding, manufacturing remains the paramount source of capitalist economic propulsion. The geographies of money, information, technology, consumption, services and state regulation are all of equal importance; and each raises its own theoretical problems and issues.

Postmodernist Epistemology and the Economic Landscape

The challenge, however, is not just one of finding new theoretical frameworks more appropriate to changing economic realities, whatever the orientation of these new approaches. It is also one of confronting the postmodern critique concerning the nature of 'adequate' explanations, concerning the limitations of all theoretical and conceptual schemes. If the changing nature of the capitalist economy has undermined the relevance of established economic and geographic theory, postmodernism threatens the very epistemological foundations upon which such theory is based. What is in question in certain quarters of both economics and economic geography is not simply *which* theory, but the very *idea* of theory itself.

Modernism rests on the belief that through the application of science and reason the world can be understandable and controllable, that beneath the seeming chaos and vagaries of social and economic life there are detectable universal tendencies and commonalities. The role of social science is to uncover this underlying, external reality: in this way the workings of society and the economy can be rationalised and managed. Postmodernism contests these assumptions and ambitions. Instead, we are urged to see the world as a plurality of heterogeneous spaces and temporalities, of differences and contingencies rather than similarities and necessities: complexity, indeterminacy, contextuality and uncertainty are the new watchwords. Given its antiessentialist world-view, postmodernist epistemology involves the rejection of totalising categories, grand theories, 'metanarratives' and rationalist explanation in favour of context-rich micronarratives, local knowledge and particular explanations. This in turn means abandoning the modernist canon that objective truth is in principle attainable; rather, for postmodernists there is no singular or absolute truth, but multiple 'truths' and 'stories' (see Pignansi and Lawson, 1988). The task of explanation therefore becomes one of discourse analysis and deconstruction, of revealing the discursive structures, ideological beliefs and textual strategies that we use, consciously or unconsciously, to establish the content and persuasiveness of our different knowledge claims.

Together these motifs would appear to strike at the very edifice of modern economics and economic geography (see McCloskey, 1986, 1988; Klamer *et al.*, 1988; Phelps, 1990; Samuels, 1990; Ruccio, 1991). At one level postmodernism has been used to mount methodological and epistemological critiques of mainstream modernist canons and theories, to attack their scientific, essentialist and verificationist foundations. Secondly, it has promoted considerable interest in economics as discourse, in the systems of language, rhetoric and persuasion that economists deploy in their theories, models and paradigms. And thirdly, it has begun to challenge the content and core categories of the subject. Within economic geography there is likewise a growing interest in the metaphorical tropes and discursive practices that permeate different theories and explanations of the economic landscape. In addition, the postmodern turn in economic geography is also rooted in a belief that one of the hallmarks of the new capitalism is greater economic, social and spatial diversity, a widespread fragmentation that allegedly undermines the scope for general theorising. The postmodern celebration of the synchronic and spatial over the diachronic and temporal, and its prioritisation of the fragmented over the general, have been seized upon by some geographers to push the local and the unique (back) on to the research agenda. Spatial particularity, local context and the specificity of place have assumed prominence as the analytical referents of what in effect is a new-found focus on 'areal differentiation' (see Barnes, 1989; Cooke, 1986, 1989; Gregory, 1987; Soja, 1989; *Society and Space*, 1987).

It has to be said, however, that much 'postmodern thinking' in both economics and economic geography has been more an exercise in doxography – the liturgical citation of the opinions and ideas of the 'hot' French postmodernist and deconstructionist philosophers (Foucault, Derrida, Lyotard and so on) and the once 'cool' but now rediscovered and equally 'hot' Wittgenstein and Nietzche – than of the construction of an identifiable 'postmodern' economics (Dow, 1990, 1991) or economic geography (Barnes and Curry, 1992). This is not, perhaps, surprising, since there is no coherent or consistent 'postmodern' social theory or paradigm as such to draw upon (Best and Kellner, 1991; Rose, 1991). Some postmodern theorists, like Lyotard and Foucault, focus on developing new categories of knowledge and new, radical modes of thought and discourse. Others view the postmodern epistemological project to be primarily deconstructionist, to reveal the deficiencies of modernist theories and practices. Still others, like Jameson and Harvey, utilise modernist (primarily Marxist) theory to analyse and account for postmodern economic, social and cultural forms. Although postmodern theorists have cast valuable light on the new technologies, on the hyperconsumerism and the cultural and informational commodification that characterise the new capitalism of our times, thus far none have provided an adequate analysis or conceptualisation of the economy or of its relationships with the state and globalisation. Indeed, most postmodern theorists want to decentre the economy altogether, in order to focus on micropolitical and microcultural phenomena. Not surprisingly therefore, the postmodern turn in economics and economic geography has not gone uncontested (for the case of economics, see Coats, 1988; Maki, 1988; Rappaport, 1988; Rosenberg, 1988; in geography see Harvey, 1987; Harvey and Scott, 1989). Yet, although the prospects for an integrated postmodern methodology or theory within economics and economic geography seem limited, if not self-contradictory, there are nevertheless issues that spiral out of the postmodernism debate that impinge on both the conduct and the content of economics and economic geography, and which resist easy dismissal or facile incorporation into existing paradigms. Three interrelated issues in particular deserve discussion.

The first is that the postmodern challenge compels us to give much closer critical examination to the meaning of 'economic reality' and its relationship to the various theoretical models and modes of discourse we use. As a mode of discourse, economic geography, like economics upon which it draws, is inescapably bound up with the structure and content of the language it uses and by the worldviews or ideologies that underpin different discursive systems. The space economy is characterised by enormous complexity, heterogeneity and variability. This diversity permits multiple interpretations and explanations. As a result there are multiple specifications of 'reality' to choose from, and our choices are profoundly influenced by ideological dispositions and linguistic formations. Ideologies, the belief systems by which we perceive and interpret the arrangements that order our lives, are 'social constructions' of reality. They are the conceptual frameworks by which order is imposed upon and moral legitimacy accorded to the raw stuff out of which social understanding is forged (Heilbroner, 1990). Economics and economic geography are thus inescapably ideological. Different theories are based on different belief systems, and as such construct different images or 'readings' of 'the economy'. The different approaches used by economic geographers embody different world views with respect to the workings of the capitalist economy, the nature of uneven development, the role of location in economic decision-making, and so on. Much of the 'conceptual' content of different explanations in fact consists of metaphorical and rhetorical strategies through which certain representations and aspects of reality are selected while others are blocked out. Furthermore, our choice of theory is shaped by our own ideology, which in turn depends on our own social embeddedness within the very structure we are trying to conceptualise.

This recognition of an inextricable ideological content to economic geography challenges the 'objective' facticity of the space economy. It forces us to acknowledge the ambiguity of our research object: that although the 'space economy' is existentially independent of any individual researcher, our knowledge of it is necessarily ideologically and discursively constituted. Facts are discourse-specific.

Even if all economists and economic geographers were philosophical realists, believing that the real exists independent of our idea of it, there is still the inevitable necessity of having to choose between alternative and competing specifications of the 'real', and those choices are profoundly influenced by our ideological predispositions. This also implies that disputes between alternative explanations and approaches cannot be decided simply through rational demonstration since each theory, in accordance with its own construal of reality, predetermines the very empirical categories, or 'facts', and testing criteria to be used to assess its validity. The choice between competing schools of thought is thus inherently rhetorical and ideological, and these aspects of our theories need to be revealed and critically examined. Construed as discourse, then, economic geography acquires an essential interpretative or *hermeneutic* element. However, all this does not mean a retreat into a postmodernist bedlam of conflicting and irreconcilable theories or assertions as to the nature of the space economy and its 'proper' explanation. It is one thing to reveal the central (and often obfuscatory) role that ideology and metaphor play in our explanations; but it does not follow, as McCloskey (1986) incorrectly asserts in the case of economics, that this is all there is and that we must abandon epistemology and methodology altogether. The recognition of economic geography as discourse, as ideology, should impart a self-consciousness to the discipline, but not a self-destructiveness.

A second issue is that postmodernism directs our attention to the inconclusivity and relativism of our explanations and analyses. Relativism describes the view that truth is paradigm- or theory-dependent. For the relativist there is no single overarching explanatory framework, or theoretical monism, but rather a non-reducible plurality of conceptual schemes and paradigms. Postmodernists, however, go further and push relativism to its extremes: there is no decidability of meaning, and all that is possible is multiplicities of fragmented, partial and equally valid knowledges. Within economic geography this postmodernist emphasis on relativism and pluralism has surfaced in the attack on realist theorising and in the focus now accorded to spatial particularity and local uniqueness (see Hudson, 1988). The problem with this view is that what begins as a legitimate concern with diversity and difference can all too easily turn into a nihilistic pluralism that substitutes contingency for causation and the specific for the systematic. While it is right to highlight the importance of difference and specificity in the space economy, it does not follow that generalisation and synthesis are thereby ruled out. To subscribe to the contrary carries the danger of a retrogressive withdrawal from theory into empiricist descriptive recitations of locally specific characteristics, into a 'flat ontology' realism (Bhaskar, 1990) of the sort that has characterised much 'locality research' in the past few years and of which Harvey (1987) is rightly critical.

The impression given by the 'radical relativist turn' in economic geography that according prominence to spatial specificity, particularity and difference imposes a severe if not fatal constraint on the prospects for and propriety of applying integrative explanatory concepts, is misleading. An extreme postmodern position that denied any possibility of constructing or using general concepts to explain the spatially varying process of economic development would be contradictory. For such a picture would itself be tantamount to postulating an alternative 'grand narrative' or general conception of locally specific logics of economic accumulation and production, and would therefore imply some vision as to why and how such spatial diversity and specificity exists. To deny any role for generalising theory and concepts, as Hudson and others appear to want to do, is to argue that all local events and changes in the space economy are ultimately wholly contingent and unique: in effect to argue for *spatial exceptionalism*. But beyond mere assertion, without some prior identification and theorisation of larger-scale structures and processes, however shadowy that prior theorisation might be, there is no way of knowing what constitutes a special local instance to which specific processes apply, or when and what particular contingencies should be taken seriously.

Thus although the new relativism certainly poses some searching questions for realism, it is incorrect to view these two epistemics as irreconcilably opposed. Whilst realist approaches to the analysis of the economic landscape involve a structural conception of essential mechanisms and causal powers, there can be no definitive attempt to fix the nature of those mechanisms and powers once and for all. Rather, realist arguments are transcendental in character, having to do with what reality must be like for certain features of general experience and aspects of human agency to be possible. Realists have to accept both the relativity of all knowledge and the *differentiated* nature of real processes. Economic processes operate at a variety of different levels of abstraction, which from a geographical point of view also means at different spatial scales. Thus a realist approach has to support the idea that a plurality of levels operate in the socio-economic domain, and that within each level a number of factors, processes and mechanisms are usually in play (Lawson, 1989). Local economic events are to be explained, therefore, in terms of the nesting and interplay of both locally specific and more general national and international structures, with the relative importance and interaction of these different spatial domains of causal powers varying from area to area. Real plurality of this sort necessitates conceptual pluralism, given the nature of the economy and epistemic relativity: no one theory can or should be expected to 'reveal' the complex totality. In principle this approach avoids both the pitfalls of crude totalising determinism of an economic reductionist kind and the unconstrained pluralism of postmodernism: it combines the search for deep-structure explanations with the recognition that such explanations are nevertheless differentiated from place to place. Epistemologically speaking, relativism must be openly embraced by realist theorists.

A third and closely related implication of the postmodernism debate is that economic events are necessarily contextual, that is embedded in spatial structures of social relations, and that our explanations should seek explicitly to incorporate this fact. Mainstream schools of economic theory do not deal adequately, if at all, with the issue of social context and embeddedness. Indeed, the prevailing assumption has been that economic behaviour has become more autonomous with the march of industrialism and modernisation (see Granovetter, 1985). Neoclassical theory represents a distinctly undercontextualised model of economic production and distribution, based as it is on an atomised-actor conception of economic behaviour. Marxian political economy, on the other hand, construes economic action in terms of mechanical, macrostructural class conflict while relegating the complex specifics of socioinstitutional embeddedness to the status of mere epiphenomena. And, as we have already noted, even regulation theory, with its emphasis on the mode of regulation, fails to provide any adequate conceptualisation of institutional structures and processes. To the extent that attempts have been made to sensitise these theoretical perspectives to social relations and institutional conditions, the latter are merely seen as arising from and facilitating the underlying economic logic and imperatives of the system.

Among the various alternative approaches that economic geographers have recently suggested for dealing with context in the economic landscape, the most prominent is the Sraffian neo-Ricardian model of commodity production (see Barnes, 1989). The attraction of this form of economics, it is argued, is that it provides a non-value, non-essentialist theory of economic reproduction. It portrays the economy as a circular system in which at every stage commodities are produced by other commodities, so that there is never an ultimate source of value. As a result 'we must wait to learn how things are valued in different places and at different times; we must look at the context' (Barnes, 1989, p. 145). According to its exponents, Sraffian economics allows economic geographers to examine the specific geographical context within which the technical, social and institutional conditions of production are embedded. This dependency on context, the argument continues, means that the Sraffian economic model is compatible with methodological pluralism: in one context a structuralist approach may be appropriate, in another it may be more relevant to emphasise human agency, while in yet another both structure and agency may be important. However, whilst laudable in its intentions, Sraffian economic geography does not offer the advance its protagonists claim. To argue that the strengths of the Sraffian perspective derive from what it leaves unsaid rather than from what it says, might understandably strike as odd. In addition to its various shortcomings as a theorisation of economic production (its lack of economic mechanisms, its simplistic treatment of technology, its lack of historical dynamic, to name but some), and the fact that it *does* have a theory of value (namely a cost-of-production concept), it highlights socio-spatial context only by invoking it as an extraeconomic explanatory adjunct.

Thus constructing a contextual economics and economic geography, in which socio-spatial embeddedness is moved centre-stage rather than demoted to a secondary contingent role, remains a key task. The recent revival and reformulation of Veblenian evolutionary institutional economics may well offer some scope in this direction (see Tool, 1988; Wisman and Rozansky, 1991; North, 1992). Evolutionary institutional economics – not to be confused with the neoclassically inspired, efficiency-orientated 'new institutional economics' (see Williamson, 1985; Eggertsson, 1990) – seeks explicitly to integrate institutional analysis into the study of the economy and its performance. At its most general level, neo-Veblenian institutional economics posits a systemic, holistic and evolutionary view of the economy, in which technology is the motor force for evolutionary economic change, human behaviour is a social product, institutions are the basic unit of analysis, and where the social context is characterised by power, conflict and vested interest. It focuses on the processes of change inherent in the set of institutions that we call the economic system, where by institutions is meant those forms of social organisation which, through the operation of custom, tradition or legal constraint, tend to create and reproduce durable and routinised patterns of behaviour. Methodologically and conceptually, institutional economics is perforce contextual, realist and relativist: institutional structures operate at a variety of levels, and both vary and interact in different ways across time and space. Thus there can be no universal theory of institutional structures and evolution, of economic behaviour and performance: rather explanations will be relative to time and place. Some have gone so far as to argue that, given these attributes, institutionalist economics is in fact intrinsically 'postmodern' in character (Brown, 1991). Whether this view is accepted or not, economic geography could benefit appreciably by incorporating and adapting the developments currently taking place within evolutionary institutional political economy.

There can be little doubt, therefore, that in various ways the 'postmodern challenge' is making economic geographers think much more closely about how they explain and theorise. Although it does not itself provide a satisfactory vision of the economy, nor programmatic guidance as to the construction or content of economic or geographic theory, it does compel us to assign greater epistemological significance to the pluralistic character of the contemporary space economy, not just in the sense of acknowledging the diversity of its surface forms but also in the sense of incorporating that diversity explicitly into our conceptual categories and modes of explanation. It also compels us to question the authority and positionality of our knowledge claims. All economic thought is a power-saturated process that is used to explain, intervene in and perpetuate a sphere of social activity that is itself a system of power relations. We need therefore to be sensitive to the politics of inclusion, exclusion and centrism that permeate our attempts to model and represent the livelihoods of others. Both economics and economic geography, for example, continue to be dominated by an Anglo-American and male-centric view of capitalist development. In these and other respects we should seek to decentre our theoretical and conceptual frameworks.

Postlude: Towards a Multidimensional, Multiperspectival and Multivocal Economic Geography

My aim in this chapter has been to chart a selective but hopefully sufficiently representative path through the shifts and challenges currently affecting economic geography. It is not my intention by way of conclusion to launch into detailed summative or promissory statements about where we should go from here. It is appropriate, however, to point to one or two aspects of the sort of agenda that is implied by the foregoing discussion. As we enter a new historical terrain of capitalist development there is growing evidence that we need new concepts and theories to make sense of the new realities. It is neither sufficient nor convincing to attempt to force the new realities into the conceptual schemas of mainstream economic perspectives, schemas which in any case may not have been particularly relevant even to the 'old' realities. The various attempts to revise and reformulate those mainstream theories in response to changing circumstances have not proved adequate to the task. To be sure, those revisions are not without value. But they are as much a sign of the decay of the core paradigms as of their successful adaptation to changing empirical circumstances. We desperately need new cognitive maps of the economic landscape, to say nothing of new political strategies for intervening in that landscape. This is not to argue for the establishment of a new master concept or narrative of industrial-location dynamics or regional development. Instead the agenda should be for a reconstruction of economic geography that is much more *multidimensional*, *multiperspectival* and *multivocal*.

A multidimensional economic geography would seek to provide an analysis of the various levels or domains of economic process and the ways in which those domains interact to produce a specific configuration of spatially uneven development. It would have to consider at least four such levels: the microeconomy of individuals and firms; the macroeconomy of the nation-state; the economy of transnational capital and finance; and the global or world economy. Each of these spheres or levels is a partially dependent variable. None totally controls the others; yet none is fully independent from the others either. Economic geography must therefore encompass all four; it must seek to conceptualise the connections between these levels, and how and why their interaction and relative importance varies across, and shapes the differences between, different regions and localities: how, in other words, the meaning of economic events

varies with geographical scale, and how the latter, itself as socioeconomic artifact, is made and remade. A multidimensional economic
geography is thus non-reductive and contextual: the socioinstitutional
embeddedness of economic processes means that the 'space economy'
is both *complex artifact* and *structural context*. There can be no
single unifying theory or totalising principle for integrating or syn-
thesising this complexity. A multidimensional economic geography is, therefore, also multiperspectival, open to a broad range of
theories and perspectives on the domains of spatial economic reality and how they are constituted and interact. Any given perspective or theoretical vantage point is selective, and unavoidably mediated
by one's own pregiven world view, assumptions, values and interests
(or what Schumpeter once referred to as 'pre-analytic cognition').
A multiperspectival economic geography is thus relativist and
hermeneutic. It should also, therefore, be multivocal: that is concerned to recognise and accord explicit theoretical and substantive
significance to the different social groups that make up the 'economy',
of incorporating the specific experiences and roles of particular
groups or communities rather than suppressing or subsuming them
under supposedly 'neutral' categories and 'general' types. The need
to grind a gender corrective into our analytical lens is a primary
case in point (Seitz, 1992).

This is not, however, to sanction a postmodernist multiplicity of
fragmented microperspectives and interpretations. The sort of
microexplanations and mappings championed by some postmodern
theorists unquestionably provide a corrective to the overgeneralising
and totalising tendencies of modern economics and economic geography. But of themselves they do not provide a viable framework for understanding the economy and its spatial organisation.
We still need theories that endeavour to conceptualise, describe and
interpret macrosocioeconomic processes, particularly those that are
central to the evolving trajectory of capitalist development (for
example technological change, tertiarisation, cultural commodification, state regulation, globalisation and so on). Without such macro-
theories we lose sense of the systemic features and relations that
structure the contemporary space economy, and how different social
groups and communities relate to and are affected by the wider
system. A reconstructed economic geography cannot, therefore,
abandon the macro for the micro, but must seek to integrate the
two. By 'integration' here I do not mean the search for some all-
embracing masterscript or synthesis, of the sort whose loss is grieved

by Drucker in the opening quote to this chapter, but *articulation*. That is, a method of enquiry and explanation that recognises that the complex and changing features of the space economy are not determinable within the parameters of a single overarching, theoretical framework, but which instead involves the differential articulation of concepts, assumptions and principles of varying degrees of abstraction situated in different planes of analysis and drawn from different theoretical systems and analytical perspectives. Such an orientation would create the much-needed space for a more anthropological, interpretative and contextual approach to economic geography, and would avoid the empiricism that derives from an exclusive emphasis on appearances, the essentialism and reductionism that derive from an exclusive emphasis on a specific form of deep-structure economics, and the subsumptionism of the 'particular' versus the 'general'.

Acknowledgements

Earlier versions of this chapter were presented as seminars at the Departments of Geography at the Universities of Cambridge and Oxford. I have tried to incorporate the many useful comments made on those occasions. I also wish to thank Peter Sunley (Geography, University of Edinburgh) and Tony Lawson (Economics, University of Cambridge) for their constructive criticisms.

References

Aglietta, M. (1979) *A Theory of Capitalist Regulation: The US Experience* (New York: Basic Books).
Amin, A. and F. Robinson (1990) 'Industrial Districts and Regional Development: Limits and Possibilities', in F. Pike, G. Becattini and W. Sengenberger (eds), *Industrial Districts and Inter-Firm Co-operation in Italy* (Geneva: Institute for Labour Studies), pp. 185–219.
Barnes, T. J. (1989) 'Place, Space and Theories of Economic Value: Contextualism and Essentialism in Economic Geography', *Transactions, Institute of British Geographers, NS*, vol. 14, pp. 299–316.
Barnes, T. J. and M. R. Curry (1992) 'Postmodernism in Economic Geography: Metaphor and the Construction of Alterity', *Society and Space*, vol. 10, pp. 57–68.
Best, M. H. (1990) *The New Competition: Institutions of Industrial Restructuring* (Cambridge: Polity).
Best, S. and D. Kellner (1991) *Postmodern Theory: Critical Interrogations* (London: Macmillan).

Bharadwaj, K. and B. Schefold (eds) (1992) *Essays on Piero Sraffa: Critical Perspectives on the Revival of Classical Theory* (London: Routledge and Kegan Paul).

Bhaskar, R. (1990) *Reclaiming Reality: A Critical Introduction to Contemporary Philosophy* (London: Verso).

Block, F. (1990) *Postindustrial Possibilities: A Critique of Economic Discourse* (Berkeley: University of California Press).

Boyer, R. (1990) *The Regulation School: A Critical Introduction* (New York: Columbia University Press).

Brenner, R. and M. Glick (1992) 'The Regulation Approach: Theory and History', *New Left Review*, vol. 192, pp. 45–119.

Brown, D. (1991) 'An Institutionalist Look at Postmodernism', *Journal of Economic Issues*, vol. 25, pp. 1089–103.

Callinicos, A. (1989) *Against Postmodernism: A Marxist Critique* (Cambridge: Polity).

Castells, M. (1989) *The Informational City: Information Technology, Economic Restructuring and the Urban-Regional Process* (Oxford: Basil Blackwell).

Clark, G. L., M. S. Gertler and J. Whiteman (1986) *Regional Dynamics: Studies in Adjustment Theory* (London: Allen and Unwin).

Clark, N. and C. Juma (1987) *Long-run Economics: An Evolutionary Approach to Economic Change* (London: Pinter).

Coats, A. W. (1988) 'Economic Rhetoric: The Social and Historical Context', in A. Klamer, D. McCloskey and R. M. Solow (eds), *The Consequences of Economic Rhetoric* (New York: Cambridge University Press).

Cohen, and Zysman (1987) *Manufacturing Matters: The Myth of the Postindustrial Economy* (New York: Basic Books).

Cole, K., J. Cameron and C. Edwards (1991) *Why Economists Disagree: The Political Economy of Economics* (London: Longman).

Cooke, P. (1986) *Global Restructuring: Local Response* (London: ESRC).

Cooke, P. (1989) *Localities* (London: Unwin-Hyman).

Crook, S., J. Pakulski and M. Waters (1992) *Postmodernization: Change in Advanced Society* (London: Sage).

Dosi, R., C. Freeman, R. Nelson, S. Silverberg and L. Soete (eds) (1988) *Technical Change and Economic Theory* (London: Frances Pinter).

Dow, S. (1990) 'Is There Such a Thing as Postmodern Economics?', mimeo, Department of Economics, University of Stirling.

Dow, S. (1991) 'Postmodernism and Economics', in J. Doherty, E. Graham and M. Malek (eds), *Postmodernism and the Social Sciences* (London: Macmillan).

Drucker, P. (1989) *The New Realities* (Oxford: Heinemann).

Drucker, P. (1993) *Post-Capitalist Society* (Oxford: Butterworths).

Dunford, M. (1990) 'Theories of Regulation', *Society and Space*, vol. 8, pp. 297–322.

Dunford, M. and G. Kafkalas (eds) (1992) *Cities and Regions in the New Europe* (London: Bellhaven).

Economic Geography (1992) 'Rational choice, Collective Action and Technological Learning', *Economic Geography*, vol. 68, no. 1 (theme issue).

Eggertsson, T. (1990) *Economic Behaviour and Institutions* (Cambridge University Press).

Eichner, A. S. (1986) *Towards a New Economics* (London: Macmillan).
Elam, M. (1990) 'Puzzling out the Post-Fordist Debate: Technology, Markets and Institutions', *Economic and Industrial Democracy*, vol. 11, pp. 9–37.
Elster, J. (1985) *Making Sense of Marx* (Cambridge University Press).
Gertler, M. (1988) 'The Limits to Flexibility: Comments on the Post-Fordist Vision of Production and its Geography', *Transactions, Institute of British Geographers, NS*, vol. 13, pp. 419–32.
Gertler, M. (1992) 'Flexibility Revisited: Districts, Nation-States and the Forces of Production', *Transactions, Institute of British Geographers, NS*, vol. 17, pp. 259–78.
Gill, S. and D. Law (1988) *The Global Political Economy* (London: Harvester Wheatsheaf).
Gordon, R. J. (1990) 'What Is New-Keynesian Economics?', *Journal of Economic Literature*, vol. 28, pp. 1115–71.
Granovetter, M. (1985) 'Economic Action and Social Structure: The Problem of Embeddedness', *American Journal of Sociology*, vol. 91, pp. 481–510.
Gregory, D. J. (1987) 'Areal Differentiation and Postmodern Human Geography', in D. J. Gregory and R. Walford (eds), *Horizons in Human Geography* (London: Macmillan), pp. 67–96.
Hall, S. and M. Jacques (1989) *New Times: The Changing Face of Politics in the 1990s* (London: Lawrence and Wishart).
Harrison, B. (1992) 'Industrial Districts: Old Wine in New Bottles?', *Regional Studies*, vol. 26, pp. 469–84.
Harvey, D. (1987) 'Three Myths in Search of a Reality in Urban Studies', *Society and Space*, vol. 5, no. 4, pp. 53–65.
Harvey, D. (1989a) 'The Geographical and Geopolitical Consequences of the Transition From Fordism to Flexible Accumulation', in G. Sternlieb (ed.), *The New American Economic Geography* (New York: Rutgers University Press).
Harvey, D. (1989b) *The Condition of Postmodernity* (Oxford: Basil Blackwell).
Harvey, D. and A. J. Scott (1989) 'The Practice of Human Geography: Theory and Empirical Specificity in the Transition from Fordism to Flexible Accumulation', in B. Macmillan (ed.), *Remodelling Geography* (Oxford: Basil Blackwell), pp. 217–30.
Heilbroner, R. (1990) 'Economics as Ideology', in W. J. Samuels (ed.), *Economics as Discourse: An Analysis of the Language of Economics* (Boston: Kluwer), pp. 101–16.
Henderson, J. and M. Castells (eds) (1987) *Global Restructuring and Territorial Development* (London: Sage).
Hirschorn, (1984) *Beyond Mechanization: Work and Technology in a Postindustrial Age* (Cambridge, Mass: MIT Press).
Hirst, P. and G. Thompson (1992) 'The Problem of Globalization: International Economic Relations, National Economic Management, and the Formation of Trading Blocs', *Economy and Society*, vol. 21, no. 4, pp. 357–96.
Hodgson, G. (1988) *Economics and Institutions: A Manifesto for a Modern Institutional Economics* (Cambridge: Polity).

Hodgson, G. (1993) *Economics and Evolution: Bringing Life Back into Economics* (Cambridge: Polity).

Hudson, R. (1988) 'Uneven Development in Capitalist Societies: Changing Spatial Division of Labour, Forms of Spatial Organization of Production and Service Provision, and their Impact on Localities', *Transactions of the Institute of British Geographers*, vol. 13, pp. 484–96.

Jameson, F. (1991) *Postmodernism, or The Cultural Logic of Late Capitalism* (London: Verso).

Jessop, B. (1990a) 'Regulation Theories in Retrospect and Prospect', *Economy and Society*, vol. 19, pp. 153–216.

Jessop, B. (1990b) *State Theory: Putting Capitalist States in Their Place* (Cambridge: Polity).

Jessop, B. (1992) 'Post-Fordism and Flexible Specialisation: Incommensurable, Contradictory, Complementary, or Just Plain Different Perspectives? in Ernst, H. and Meier, V. (eds), *Regional Development and Contemporary Industrial Response* (London: Belhaven), pp. 25–43.

Klamer, A., D. McCloskey and R. M. Solow (eds) (1988) *The Consequences of Economic Rhetoric* (New York: Cambridge University Press).

Krugman, P. (ed.) (1986) *Strategic Trade Policy and the New International Economics* (Cambridge, Mass: MIT Press).

Lash, S. and J. Urry (1987) *The End of Organised Capitalism* (Cambridge: Polity).

Lavoie, M. (1992) *Foundations of Post-Keynesian Economic Analysis* (London: Edward Elgar).

Lawson, T. (1989) 'Abstraction, Tendencies and Stylized Facts: A Realist Approach to Economic Analysis', *Cambridge Journal of Economics*, vol. 13, no. 1, pp. 59–78.

Letwin, O. (1988) *Privatising the World: A Study of International Privatisation in Theory and Practice* (London: Cassell).

Lipietz, A. (1992) *Towards a New Economic Order: PostFordism, Ecology and Democracy* (Cambridge: Polity).

Maki, U. (1988) 'How to Combine Rhetoric and Realism in the Methodology of Economics', *Economics and Philosophy*, vol. 4, pp. 89–109.

Mankiw, N. G. and D. Romer (eds) (1992) *New Keynesian Economics* (2 vols) (London:).

Martin, R. L. (1989) 'The Reorganization of Regional Theory: Alternative Perspectives on the Changing Capitalist Space Economy', *Geoforum*, vol. 20, pp. 187–201.

Martin, R. L. (1991) 'Flexible Futures and Post-Fordist Places', *Environment and Planning*, vol. 22, pp. 1276–80.

Martin, R. L. (1993) 'Stateless Monies, Global Financial Integration and National Autonomy: The End of Geography?', in S. Corbridge, R. L. Martin and N. J. Thrift (eds), *Money, Power and Space* (Oxford: Basil Blackwell), pp. 253–78.

Martin, R. L. and R. E. Rowthorn (eds) (1986) *The Geography of Deindustrialisation* (London: Macmillan).

Massey, D. and J. Allen (eds) (1988) *Uneven Re-Development: Cities and Regions in Transition* (London: Hodder and Stoughton).

McCloskey, D. (1986) *The Rhetoric of Economics* (Brighton: Wheatsheaf).

McCloskey, D. (1988) 'The Consequences of Rhetoric', in A. Klamer,

D. McCloskey and R. M. Solow (eds), *The Consequences of Economic Rhetoric* (New York: Cambridge University Press).

Minsky, H. P. (1989) 'Financial Crises and the Evolution of Capitalism: The Crash of '87 – What Does it Mean?', in M. Gottdiener and N. Komninos (eds), *Capitalist Development and Crisis Theory: Accumulation, Regulation and Spatial Restructuring*, (London: Macmilan), pp. 391–403.

Murray, R. (1989) 'Fordism and Post-Fordism', in S. Hall and M. Jacques *New Times: The Changing Face of Politics in the 1990s* (London: Lawrence and Wishart), pp. 38–53.

North, D. C. (1992) *Institutions, Institutional Change and Economic Performance* (Cambridge University Press).

Oakley, A. (1990) *Schumpeter's Theory of Capitalist Motion: A Critical Assessment and Exploration* (London: Edward Elgar).

O'Brien, R. (1992) *Global Financial Integration: The End of Geography* (London: Pinter Publishers).

Offe, C. (1986) *Disorganized Capitalism: Contemporary Transformations of Work and Politics* (Cambridge: Polity).

Ohmae, K. (1990) *The Borderless World* (New York: Harper Business).

Pack, S. J. (1985) *Reconstructing Marxian Economics: Marx Based upon a Sraffian Commodity Theory of Value* (New York: Praeger).

Peet, R. (1987) *International Capitalism and Industrial Restructuring* (London: Allen and Unwin).

Petit, P. (1986) *Slow Growth and the Service Economy* (London: Frances Pinter).

Phelps, E. S. (1990) *Seven Schools of Macroeconomic Thought* (Oxford University Press).

Pignansi, L. A. and H. Lawson (eds) (1988) *Dismantling Truth: Reality and Science in Postmodern Times* (London: Weidenfeld and Nicolson).

Pine, J. (1992) *Mass Customisation* (Cambridge Mass.: Harvard University Press).

Piore, M. and C. Sabel (1984) *The Second Industrial Divide* (New York: Basic Books).

Pollert, A. (ed.) (1991) *Farewell to Flexibility?* (Oxford: Basil Blackwell).

Porter, M. E. (1990) *The Competitive Advantage of Nations* (London: Macmillan).

Pyke, F., G. Becattini and W. Sengenberger (eds) (1990) *Industrial Districts and Inter-Firm Co-operation in Italy* (Geneva: Institute for Labour Studies).

Rappoport, S. (1988) 'Economic Methodology: Rhetoric or Epistemology?', *Economics and Philosophy*, vol. 4, pp. 129–49.

Reich, R. B. (1991) *The Work of Nations: Preparing Ourselves for Twentieth Century Capitalism* (London: Simon and Schuster).

Rodwin, L. and H. Sazanami (eds) (1989) *Deindustrialization and Regional Economic Transformation* (Boston: Unwin Hyman).

Rodwin, L. and H. Sazanami (eds) 1991) *Industrial Change and Regional Economic Transformation* (London: Harper Collins).

Roemer, J. (1981) *Analytical Foundations of Marxian Economic Theory* (Cambridge University Press).

Roemer, J. (ed.) (1986) *Analytical Marxism* (Cambridge University Press).

Rose, M. A. (1991) *The Post-Modern and the Post-Industrial* (Cambridge University Press).

Rosenberg, A. (1988) 'Economics is Too Important to be Left to the Rhetoricians', *Economics and Philosophy*, vol. 4, pp. 129–49.

Rosow, J. M. (ed.) (1988) *The Global Market Place* (New York: Facts on File).

Ruccio, D. F. (1991) 'Postmodernism and Economics', *Journal of Post-Keynesian Economics*, vol. 13, pp. 495–510.

Sabel, C. (1989) 'Flexible Specialization and the Re-emergence of Regional Economies', in P. Hirst and J. Zeitkin (eds), *Reversing Industrial Decline?* (Oxford: Berg), pp. 17–70.

Samuels, W. J. (ed.) (1990) *Economics as Discourse: An Analysis of the Language of Economics* (Boston: Kluwer).

Sawyer, M. (ed.) (1988) *Post-Keynesian Economics* (Aldershot: Edward Elgar).

Sayer, A. (1989a) 'PostFordism in Question', *International Journal of Urban and Regional Research*, vol. 13, pp. 666–95.

Sayer, A. (1989b) 'Dualistic Thinking and Rhetoric in Geography', *Area*, vol. 21, no. 4, pp. 301–5.

Sayer, D. (1987) *'The Violence of Abstraction: The Analytical Foundations of Historical Materialism* (Oxford: Basil Blackwell).

Schefold, B. (1989) *Mr Sraffa on Joint Production, and Other Essays* (London: Unwin-Hyman).

Schiller, H. (1986) *Information and the Crisis Economy* (Oxford University Press).

Scott, A. J. and Storper, M. (1992) 'Regional Development Reconsidered', in Ernste, H. and Meier, V. (eds), *Regional Development and Contemporary Industrial Response* (London: Belhaven), pp. 3–24.

Scott, A. J. (1988) *New Industrial Spaces* (London: Pion).

Seitz, J. A. (1992) 'Gender and Economic Analysis', in N. De Marchi (ed.), *The Methodology of Economics* (Boston: Kluwer).

Sheppard, E. and T. Barnes (1990) *The Capitalist Space Economy: Geographical Analysis after Ricardo, Marx and Sraffa* (London: Unwin-Hyman).

Simai, M. (1990) *Global Power Structure, Technology and World Economy in the Late Twentieth Century* (London: Pinter).

Society and Space (1987) 'Reconsidering Social Theory', *Society and Space*, vol. 5, no. 4 (special issue).

Soja, E. (1989) *Postmodern Geographies: The Reassertion of Space in Critical Social Theory* (London: Pion).

Steedman, I. (ed.) (1988) *Sraffian Economics* (Aldershot: Edward Elgar).

Storper, M. and A. Scott (1989) 'The Geographical Foundations and Social Regulation of Flexible Production Complexes', in J. Wolch and M. Dear (eds), *The Power of Geography: How Territory Shapes Social Life* (Boston: Unwin-Hyman).

Storper, M. and R. Walker (1989) *The Capitalist Imperative: Territory, Technology and Industrial Growth* (Oxford: Basil Blackwell).

Sunley, P. (1992) 'An Uncertain Future: A Critique of Post-Keynesian Economic Geographies', *Progress in Human Geography*, vol. 16, no. 1, pp. 58–70.

Teague, P. (1990) 'The Political Economy of the Regulation School and the Flexible Specialization Scenario', *Journal of Economic Studies*, vol. 17, no. 5, pp. 32–54.

Thrift, N. J. (1989) 'New Times and New Spaces? The Perils of Transition Models', *Society and Space*, vol. 7, pp. 127–9.

Tickell, A. and J. A. Peck (1992) 'Accumulation, Regulation and the Geographies of Post-Fordism: Missing links in Regulationist Research', *Progress in Human Geography*, vol. 16, pp. 190–218.

Tool, M. (ed.) (1988) *Evolutionary Economics: Foundations of Institutionalist Thought* (London: Sharp).

Wachter, H. M. (1986) *The Money Mandarins: The Making of a Supranational Economic Order* (New York: Pantheon Books).

Wallace, I. (1990) *The Global Economic System* (London: Unwin-Hyman).

Wallerstein, I. (1979) *The Capitalist World Economy* (Cambridge University Press).

Wallerstein, I. (1984) *The Politics of the World Economy: The States, the Movements, the Civilizations* (Cambridge University Press).

Wallerstein, I. (1991) *Geopolitics and Geoculture: Essays on the Changing World System* (Cambridge University Press).

Wiles, P. and G. Routh (1984) *Economics in Disarray* (Oxford: Basil Blackwell).

Williamson, O. E. (1985) *The Economic Institutions of Capitalism: Firms, Markets, Relational Contracting* (London: Macmillan).

Williamson, O. E. (1986) *Economic Organization: Firms, Markets and Policy Control* (Brighton: Wheatsheaf).

Wisman, J. D. and J. Rozansky (1991) 'The Methodology of Institutionalism Revisited', *Journal of Economic Issues*, vol. 25, pp. 709–37.

Wolff, R. and S. Resnick (1987) *Economics: Marxian versus Neoclassical* (Baltimore: Johns Hopkins University Press).

Womack, J., D. Jones and D. Roos (1990) *The Machine that Changed the World* (New York: Rawson).

Zukin, S. (1991) *Landscapes of Power: From Detroit to Disneyland* (Berkeley: University of California Press).

Zukin, S. and P. DiMaggio (eds) (1990) *Structures of Capital: The Social Organization of the Economy* (Cambridge University Press).

3

Political Theory and Human
Geography

[handwritten: political peo vs. geopolitics?]

GRAHAM SMITH

[handwritten: interesting because the rise of neoliberalism which seeks to contract the role of govt.]

Since the 1970s there has been a revival of interest in political theory
in geography. At the heart of this renaissance is a concern about
the underlying character of modern political life and of the way in
which space is important to how politics is constituted and practiced.
As a consequence political geography, that branch of geography whose
legitimacy rests ōn its claim to be the most directly concerned with
'the political', has undergone a much welcomed sea change. This is
not to suggest that traditional political geography was unconcerned
with political theory. We only need to recall the works of such
influential turn-of-the-century political theorists as Halford Mackinder
(heartland theory), Friedrich Ratzel (author of *lebensraum*) and Peter
Kropotkin (idea of decentralised, self-sufficient and ecologically
balanced communities) to remind ourselves of the subject's rich,
influential and diverse intellectual heritage. Compared, however, with
the subject's more inward-looking recent past, in which there was
little concern with or advance in political theory, today political
geography recognises that pivotal to comprehending our modern world
is a theoretically informed subject that acknowledges the centrality
of power and of power relations to understanding our political world
(Driver, 1991; Smith, 1985). As one of the coeditors of *New Models
in Geography* argues: 'If political geography was once a "moribund
backwater". . ., 20 years later it is a lively eddy in the stream of
political economy' (Peet, 1989, pp. 262–3). It is the contention of
this chapter that the central task now facing this 'new political geography' is to address itself to the hitherto neglected ways in which
current transformations affecting the nation-state, acknowledged as

[handwritten left margin: Friedrich Ratzel / Peter Kropotkin]

54

the single most important political agent in the territorial organisation of the world, is undergoing challenges more profound than at any time in modern history. This should not only carry important implications for the future shape of political geography but also for the study of human geography more generally.

Mapping the Political Condition

Striking at the heart of this challenge to the nation-state is the notion of political sovereignty and of its relationship to the idea of political community. We have become accustomed to mapping and interpreting our political world based on a theory of sovereignty which holds that it is the political community of the state that exercises supreme authority over a particular territorial jurisdiction and that it is the most appropriate reflection of how political space should be organised, bounded and, within much of political geography, theorised (for example, Johnston, 1989). Of course who exercises power over the state's territorial jurisdiction is far less straightforward, but it is generally held in theories of sovereignty to be the state and its agencies. This conception of sovereignty, it is argued, is reinforced by the symbiotic relationship a state has with its national citizenry and the sense of political community this relationship reflects. Moreover, according to the theory of sovereignty, beyond the territorial and identific boundaries of the nation-state the world is compartmentalised into other sovereign states in which the state must accept that it will be one among many states with, in principle, equal rights to self-determination. What has attracted the attention of a handful of political theorists but has as yet received little consideration by geographers is the way in which these conceptions of sovereignty and their association with the nation-state are now under challenge (see, for example, Camilleri and Falk, 1992; Held, 1991; McGrew and Lewis, 1992; Walker and Mendlovitz, 1990; White, 1991).

These challenges to the sovereign nation-state emanate both 'from above' (from global processes) and 'from below' (within civil society from decentralised, community-based and localised forms of collective action). On the one hand there is a sense that the world is becoming increasingly interconnected as a consequence of the transformative impact on localities of new forms of global production and of the greater hypermobility of capital, from developments in information technology and global communications, and from the emergence of more internationalised divisions of labour. One impact of these globalising processes has been to question and further erode the autonomous powers of the nation-state. This is most starkly seen in the way in which the sovereign powers of the nation-state are passing to new supraregional organisations and transnational institutions. Increasingly it would seem, the fate of localities is being determined not by the nation-state but by decisions, activities and events beyond the state's territorial jurisdiction.

On the other hand a multitude of challenges to the nation-state emanate from the very localities over which it claims political sovereignty. These challenges are most starkly manifest in the recent upsurge of ethnic nationalism based on the same principle of national self-determination that legitimates the very political formations from which many ethnic regions wish to renegotiate their geopolitical relations. Within late-modern democracies in particular, 'sovereignty' as a principle of state authority is also being challenged by a wide range of collectivised forms of social action, albeit in often more subtle and indirect ways. Underlying these challenges is a sense that the 'common political good', upon which the authority of the sovereign democratic state rests, should not simply be interpreted as the prerogative of the nation-state. Conceptions, in other words, of what is democracy are not simply viewed by such politicised challengers as coterminous with the nation-state. And nor is the nation-state necessarily judged as the most appropriate vehicle to deal with a variety of both global and local issues that impinge upon our everyday lives. In part this questioning of the relevance of the nation-state is linked to the conflation of many 'global' and 'local' issues that is captured in the slogan 'think global, act local'. An increasing global consciousness about the environment, world peace and Third-World poverty has led to a growth in transnational social movements, such as Greenpeace, Live Aid and the peace movement, all of which transcend and bypass the nation-state. Within our local communities and cities new sorts of social movements have emerged, associated with the politics of ecology, women, gays and a range of counter-cultural groupings for whom politics is not in the first instance centred on what the welfare state can provide or linked to issues of distribution, but of defending endangered ways of life and of championing alternative ways of articulating their rights as citizens through new forms of local community and group action that either bypass or negate the usual channels of institutional state politics.

The thesis I want to develop can for the moment be summarised as follows. It is that these challenges 'from above' and 'from below' are not only questioning the appropriateness of the nation-state as political community but are also reflective of what I want to refer to as a new spatiality to politics. These global and local processes of spatiopolitical reshaping can be conceptualised as follows.

First, processes of globalisation are facilitating greater integration and interconnectedness between states and localities. Such processes reflect a multiplicity of linkages and interconnections in which events, decisions and activities in one part of the globe can come to have significant consequences in places quite distant from these actions. What, however, makes these processes historically novel is the impact of both their geographical scope (processes that embrace most of the globe and operate worldwide) and spatial intensity (in which the levels of interaction, interdependence and interconnectedness between states and places are becoming greater). Understood as such, globalisation is challenging the sovereignty of the nation-state as well as the nation-state's ability to make decisions autonomously both with regard to its place within the world economy and over the every day social, political and cultural life of localities.

Secondly, localised forms of collective political action are also challenging the nation-state. In some instances such political actions are bound up with the impact of globalising processes and of the way in which localities are increasingly subject to relentless but uneven globalisation. Yet while localised senses of communal identity are as a consequence undergoing intense social change they are not necessarily leading to what Appadurai (1990) rather clumsily calls the '"deterritorialisation" of local socio-political life'. Rather a variety of political and cultural forms of resistance have emerged, some of which are novel in scope.

Thirdly, these twin challenges to the nation-state raise fundamental questions about whether the nation-state is the most appropriate form of 'political community' in the modern world. In particular it questions a theory of sovereignty that has long since claimed that the meaning of citizenship and of the rights, obligations and identity that citizenship assumes is most appropriately bound up with the nation-state. Citizenship, in short, and the issues it raises by different social movements, seems increasingly less appropriate and capable of reflecting the principle of sovereignty as simply residing with and spatially bound to the nation-state. Within late-modern democracies we see this in the ways in which communities are reexamining how best to effect local security, autonomy, rights and identities for their citizens. Such developments are also reflective of the way in which so-called new social movements are engaging in creating new political spaces for new geographies linked to a celebration of identities of difference.

The rest of this chapter sketches out this new spatiality to politics. By drawing upon world-systems theory, I begin by considering the thorny concept of globalisation. The limits to this particular interpretive mapping are noted. I then move on to consider what I see as three crucial perspectives to understanding the challenges that currently confront the nation-state but which I claim are not adequately dealt with by world-systems theory. These are: the impact of globalisation as a multidimensional phenomenon, the relationship between the nation-state and democracy, and the emergence of local collective actions in the form of so-called 'social movements'. These movements, I suggest, while disparate in their aims and strategies all share a common desire to establish new political spaces out of the sociospatial transformations currently linked to globalisation.

Globalisation and World-Systems Theory

The most widely accepted paradigm in which 'globalisation' and its impact on localities is considered is within a corpus of literature known as world-systems theory. Such an approach is also particularly germane to recent developments in political geography because world-systems theory has been influential – albeit in a largely uncontested way – in claiming the high ground for constructing 'the new political geography'. What world-systems theory offers is a framework for locating our understanding of the nation-state and of the politics of localities within a global context, thus moving away from statecentric approaches that separate what is going on 'at the global level' from 'the local/domestic arena'. Indeed such a framework is based on the premise that what is happening at the global level has a direct bearing in shaping the nature of local forms of collective political action. As one of its main advocates in political geography argues 'it [the global] is the scale that "really matters"' (Taylor, 1993, p. 45).

As world-systems theorists rightly remind us, globalisation needs to be located in a much longer history than the present moment. It is inextricably bound up with the making of the capitalist world economy, whose crystallisation can be traced back to sixteenth-century Europe and which expanded to become truly global in scope by the late nineteenth century. From the outset 'capitalism was . . . an affair of the world economy and not of nation-states . . . capital has never allowed its aspirations to be determined by national boundaries in a capitalist world economy' (Wallerstein, 1979, p. 19). It is thus capitalism that underpins the logic of an interdependent and interstate world system in which economic and social processes in one part of the world are systematically related to processes in other parts. Within the capitalist world economy, states therefore play a pivotal role in ensuring its survival, for 'the fundamental role of the state as an institution in the capitalist world-economy is to augment the advantage of some against others in the market . . . that is to reduce the freedom of the market' (Wallerstein, 1979, p. 291). Thus the interstate system and global competition between states can only be understood within the structural context of market relations in which states, with varying degrees of success, compete within a global world economy in order to secure capital accumulation.

The impact of globalisation is highly uneven, for the spatial logic of capitalism has favoured and continues to favour some places over others. Accordingly Wallerstein (1979 and 1984) and his colleagues distinguish between nation-states on a tripartite basis in relation to their location within the world economy, between countries of the core, semiperiphery and periphery, although the position of each state is not immutable to socio-locational change. Such spatio-economic differentiation is held to be of crucial significance in ensuring the survival of the capitalist world economy for competition between nation-states is considered as providing the motor for the system's reproduction. Nation-states then function within a capitalist world economy in which 'the precise effects of these global processes can be reduced or enhanced by the politics of the nation-state in which it is located' (Taylor, 1993, p. 45). Ultimately a state's location within the world economy shapes much of its citizenry's social wellbeing. What benefits accrue to individuals as members of a given state (their citizenship rights and entitlements), while mediated by the state, are in the final analysis considered to be reflective of 'the always existing (if continually shifting) hierarchies both within the world-system as a whole and within each sovereign state' (Wallerstein, 1991, p. 171).

At the global level these 'hierarchies' are in large measure deemed to be both a reflection of a state's location within the capitalist world economy and a product of the interrelationship between the capitalist world economy and local communities engaged in emancipatory struggles. These antisystemic movements, so called because of the universal way in which they challenge the spatial logic of capitalism, have varied in their degrees of success in winning and consolidating state power (Arrighi *et al.*, 1990). However all are constrained by the structures of the capitalist world economy. During the first two thirds of the twentieth century, two emancipatory movements predominated and gained state power, namely those espousing socialist and nationalist-libertarian aims. Having acquired state power these movements affected the extension of certain social benefits to their citizenry. One consequence in the 'core states' (or 'first world') was the establishment of social welfarism and the welfare state. In what became labelled as 'the Second World', it created socialist states committed to improving the social welfare of its citizenry, albeit at the expense of their civil and political rights. In 'periphery states' (or the third world) movements of national liberation, in achieving sovereign statehood for their peoples, secured some development and an improvement in life chances, at least for an educated urban stratum. Yet the revolutionary ideals of these movements, once in power, were not fully realised. During the 1980s all three worlds had to come to terms with the slowdown in the capitalist world economy. As Taylor argues (1991, p. 216), 'In the "First World" the social democrats finally accepted the conservative critique of their welfare states, in the "Second World" the command economies failed, culminating in the 1989 upheavals, and in the "Third World" the material crisis undermined all the nationalist hopes of freedom as IMF conditions of austerity replaced formal imperialism'. Moreover the inability of these movements to succeed in their emancipatory projects not only created a multitude of marginalised, socially excluded groups – such as the peasantry, women, ethnic minorities and migrant populations – but gave rise to new social movements whose targets have become the 'old movements in power'. This includes feminist and environmental movements in the First World, antibureaucratic state movements in the Second World and a variety of forms of social movements in the Third World ranging from Muslim fundamentalist to peasant/farmers' movements.

Although bold in concept and attractive in its integrative – holistic approach, there are limits to world-systems theory as a framework for understanding the linkages between globalisation, the nation-state and local struggles. In particular, questions have been raised over its economically reductionist and functionalist character (for example, see Kearns, 1988; Smith, 1989) Three dimensions require further elucidation: the multidimensional nature of the challenge of globalisation, the relationship between the nation-state and democracy, and the resurgence of recent social movements.

The Challenge of Globalisation

The major strength of world-systems theory – the pivotal role ascribed to globalisation as synonymous with an integrated capitalist world economy – is also its main weakness. World-systems theorists are right to emphasise the way in which economic interdependency is increasingly fashioning a world of nation-states who in their universal commitment to economic growth, are inextricably bound up with the workings of a global economy that limits their national economic policy choices. But there is more to globalisation than simply reducing it to the logic of the capitalist world economy, in which competition between nation-states for scarce resources predominates. Globalisation is broader and more multidimensional in scope and is subject to a more latent dynamic intensity in the nature of its interconnectedness, which world-systems theory does not bring out. Three aspects are particularly crucial.

Firstly, there is the role played by such key non-state actors as transnational corporations and institutions in the globalisation of production and finance (Agnew and Corbridge 1989; Thrift, 1989). Although Wallerstein acknowledges that one distinctive aspect of the world economy since the 1960s has been the rise of multinational companies, their activities are explicated largely in relation to their location within the system of nation-states. But the ways in which multinational activities plan and execute their corporate investment decisions is increasingly unrelated to their place of origin. In short, just as multinational companies respect no national boundaries so individual states have become increasingly incapable of regulating the activities and policies of companies with multiple national locations but no unambiguous 'home country' to which profits will automatically flow (Dale, 1984). States may and do challenge this process of relentless globalisation through pursuing, for instance, policies designed to protect their own markets, but in a world in which multinational companies have become increasingly powerful within the global market place, interstate competition for the location of production has meant that in their desire to secure the means of economic growth the sovereign state has become vulnerable to such corporate interests.

Secondly, there is the role played by power-bloc formations in the process of globalisation. Geopolitical systems of 'collective security' have been crucial in challenging state sovereignty. In understanding the role of such power-bloc formations in shaping globalisation, we must acknowledge that the nature of interstate relations that they reflect are not simply reducible to the workings of the capitalist world economy. As Skocpol reminds us, 'Throughout modern world history [the inter-state system] represents an analytically autonomous level of transnational reality – interdependent in its structure and dynamics with world capitalism, but not reducible to it' (Skocpol 1979, p. 22). This is particularly evident with regard to the Cold War (1945–89). What it reflected were two geopolitical blocs, based around the US and the Soviet Union, whose formations cannot be understood simply in terms of economic power but rather also reflected forms of political–military power whose legitimacy rested on particular normative views of the world order (Smith, 1993; Kaldor, 1991). Without acknowledging that the world system is also formed by a global system of nation-states in which political and military power are important and which cannot be exhaustively reduced to economic power and economic interdependency, it is unlikely that we can understand why the Soviet Union remained as a superpower at the centre of the world geopolitical stage for most of the last half of the twentieth century. Because of its economic reductionism, world-systems theory allocated it at most geopolitical space on the margins of the 'core'. Yet of particular significance in understanding the relationship between such geopolitical power-bloc formations and globalisation was that important economic implications followed, most notably for intrabloc interdependency, as reflected in the ways in which economic organisations such as the IMF, GATT and the World Bank formed an integral part of Western global capitalism, or Comecon in relation to the socialist world. Both systems of collective security facilitated intrabloc integration through a complex network of bilateral and multilateral agreements concerning the location of both military–industrial bases and certain weapons systems, and through the flow of advanced military technology. In short the whole spatial logistics of war were planned and implemented by joint and integrated military command structures that undercut individual state authority. Both forms of regional collective security therefore served to restrict state sovereignty. In the socialist bloc superpower hegemony was more direct, but in both 'camps' the individual state's sovereign claim to exercising a monopoly over the use of force within the global arena was less apparent than at any time in modern history.

The end of the Cold War, while bringing to a close two particular and unprecedented global forms of 'collective regional security', does not mean that we are simply returning to a form of state security of the sort that dominated Europe in the nineteenth century. New forms of regional security are emerging with worldwide (the United Nations) and regional (for example the European Union) institutions taking on and becoming more global in internationalising security relations. Moreover a whole variety of non-state actors, such as multinational companies and arms dealers, are bound up with a war business that states find increasingly difficult to monitor and spatially control.

Finally, there is a further aspect to globalisation, captured in the notion of 'a global culture' (Featherstone, 1991), that is undeveloped in Wallerstein's account of world systems (his 1991 book not withstanding). Although deeply problematic in what it entails, it is generally associated with the spread of Western values and lifestyles. It is however important to distinguish between earlier and modern forms of cultural imperialism. Earlier and more geographically restricted forms were usually extensions of national sentiments and ideologies associated with such hegemonic political formations as the British or Russian Empire. We also see this form associated in the present moment with the spread of a more globally penetrative US cultural hegemony. What, however, adds a distinctive dimension to today's imperialisms is their specific non-national character, associated in particular with the growth of transnational and supranational institutions. Cultural imperialisms, in short, have become less placebound and more placeless. Thus essential to the functioning of transnational corporations in a competitive world market is their ability to use a communicative technology containing a suitably packaged imagery and a host of symbols to sell their services. Although particular *lingua francas* are still required to secure place-specific market niches, nonetheless new systems of telecommunications and computerised information networks enable such enterprises to speak a commonly understood universal language in which the buffers of local culture make little difference. Not surprisingly then there is a growing sense that states are losing control of their national cultures to privately owned print, the electronic media, and the imagery and styles of mass advertising (Hall, 1991). In short, what has been created is a global culture that operates at several geographic scales simultaneously: as a cornucopia of standardized commodities, as a patchwork of denationalised ethnic or folk motifs, as a series of generalised "human values and interests", as a uniform "scientific" discourse of meaning, and finally as the interdependent system of communications which forms the material base for all the other components and levels' (A. Smith, 1990, p. 176).

Yet this 'culture of globality' can also stimulate differing forms of local resistance not only from the nation-state (invariably a 'defensive nationalism'), but also from a variety of ethno-regional and linguistic movements as well as religious movements such as Islamic fundamentalism. Indeed, for such 'imagined communities', to use Anderson's (1991) term, collective identities possess the capacity to retain localised meanings of place and community, and to reassert their sense of difference, often in starkly political terms.

The Nation-State, Sovereignty and Democracy

One of the problems of world-systems theory is the tendency to see the nature of state regimes as largely a function of their location within the world economy (Giddens, 1985). Among other things, this marginalises the role that autonomous local and national actors, differing political cultures and geopolitics play in determining the nature of state formations (Bendix, 1964; Mann, 1986, 1988). Yet whatever the nature of state formations and the validity of their near-universal claims to being democratic, there is a sense that increasingly the model to which many postcolonial states in both the Third World and more recently in the Second World aspire is the model of the Western liberal–democratic nation-state. This conception of the superior nature of liberal democracy and of the state as the most appropriate form of representative government is most boldly reflected in 'the end of history thesis' in which, in the wake of the collapse of state socialism (at least in its European heartland), the Western liberal–democratic state is considered to have finally triumphed over alternative political projects of modernity (Fukuyama, 1992).

Yet as new states are busily proclaiming themselves into existence on the basis of their commitment to liberal democracy, within liberal democracies themselves the theory of sovereignty upon which the liberal–democratic state is based is undergoing re-evaluation. In its simplest form such a theory broadly assumes that the nation-state is the most appropriate and effective means of ensuring representative government and of protecting the interests of its citizenry. Since the late 1970s in particular, this notion of territorial congruence between state and democracy has been widely questioned and is reflected in a series of overlapping debates concerning normative conceptions of democracy. Central to this discourse of democracy have been the debates between the so-called 'New Right' and 'New Left', which have provided an impetus for claiming a more central role for issues of citizenship within human geography (S. Smith, 1989). The New Right argues that liberal democracy has spawned massive growth in public bureaucracies that has overwhelmed the space for private initiative and the exercise of individual responsibility. What ails liberal democracy is 'overloaded government'. Part of the solution is 'to roll back the state', to give citizen voters more space to regulate their own activities. In contrast The New Left emphasises the problems associated with the potentially 'Janus-faced' character of the modern state. On the one hand the state is not an autonomous force, a neutral arbiter. The state is inescapably locked into the maintenance and reproduction of capitalism, distorting decision outcomes in favour of particular interests (Clark and Dear, 1984; Johnston, 1989). Accordingly the whole basis of its claim to legitimacy and citizen allegiance is in doubt. Individuals then need to be protected against the state. On the other hand the interventionist state is necessary in order to protect the most vulnerable. In short emphasis is on democratic accountability, on the devolution of power and on the state serving the differing aspirations and needs of its citizenry.

What these debates highlight is the way in which the social and spatial frontiers of citizenship and their relationship to the liberal–democratic state are undergoing re-evaluation. Such changes reflect a series of polarising trends (Heater, 1990, Roche, 1992). Firstly, there is a tension between a liberal tradition that focuses on the right to be free of interference from, or oppression by, the state versus a conception of citizenship that provides opportunities to serve the community. The New-Right project of countering the growing infrastructural powers of the state (for example, welfarism, growing centralised bureaucracy) is based on the necessity of diffusing power away from the state, in which emphasis is put on citizen responsibility ('the active citizen') and on the need to protect the individual against the intrusive and inefficient state ('the citizen's charter'). In contrast, communitarian citizenship emphasises the state's civic duties and moral responsibility to provide collective services in the fields of health, education and welfare. It is the erosion of these social rights and their spatial implications that have attracted particular geographical interest (for example, see Mohan, 1988).

Secondly, there is a tension between the idea of the private and public citizen, of a clash between two kinds of freedom: the freedom from civic concerns in order to pursue a private life; and the need to participate democratically in order to ensure the social reproduction of political freedom. There is a sense that liberal democracies have become less participatory, with a political system geared towards the articulation of demands 'from below', which the state, having expanded its socioterritorial functions, can no longer provide. The 'overloaded state' and its inability to promote the social and economic needs of its citizenry can lead, so this thesis goes, to a disillusionment with institutional politics that is manifested in electoral apathy and the marginalisation of particular places from formal politics (for example parts of inner cities, deprived regions). This transference of citizen commitments away from 'the public' to the 'private' concerns of everyday individual life can also be linked to an ascendant political culture of 'possessive individualism', in which personal satisfaction is measured in relation to the privatised world of individual consumption. This retreat into the private poses as much a threat to the integrity of the sovereign state as do protest movements.

Finally, there is the relationship between 'postindustrial society' and 'the unitary polity'. Here the central question is whether the variety and range of entitlements demanded by an increasingly multilayered society, where identities overlap in a complex array of sociospatial settings, can be adequately expressed through or represented by a single, universal status of citizenship. During formative democratic state-building, as Marshall's path-breaking treatment of the sequential expansion of civil, political and then social citizenship shows, the question of who was and who was not a citizen was bound up with struggles against a 'politics of closure' in which class was central (Barbalet, 1988). In modern-day liberal democracies, however, the 'politics of closure' takes on a variety of sociospatial forms, cross-cutting and often marginalising class

divisions. Social closure, affecting various 'subordinate' groups –
be they ethnic and racial groups or women – do not simply reflect
a class division of labour but rather are more likely to reflect differential access to places of living and of the workplace in which a
variety of factors mediate, and in which eligibility for civil, political and social rights follow complex and differentiated patterns of
exclusion. What such complexities signal is the problem of whether
democracy is best served by creating an homogeneous citizen-body
or of treating the particular needs of 'subordinate groups' separately.
Crudely, the choice has tended to be between 'assimilation', whereby
incorporation occurs through the process of equalisation by the loss
of separate identity, or integration, in which a 'subordinate group'
is accepted as of equal worth and dignity to the majority but has
privileges or rights and is able to celebrate being different.

The Political Geography of Social Movements

The major problem with world-systems treatment of contemporary
social movements as antisystemic movements is that, in surveying
the world from the grand edifice of world-systems theory, all social
movements are in the final analysis derivative of the capitalist world
economy and of the way in which state actions are constrained by
their location within a world economy in which capitalism holds
sway. Rather, any understanding of the recent resurgence of such a
plurality of social movements, and of the disparate but near-universal
challenges to state sovereignty that they represent, must acknowledge that such forms of collective political action are a product of
a panoply of forces that cannot be adequately explained either in
terms of one particular strategy or agenda or without recourse to
contextualising ways in which the very localities in which social
movements arise and unfold differ.

Contemporary social movements embrace a multitude of often
overlapping forms of 'oppositional politics', but all in one way or
another take issue with the way in which within particular localities
politics is presently constituted. Some directly question the sovereign integrity of the nation-state by appealing to a different geographical scale of consciousness in strikingly novel ways (for example
peace and ecological movements) while others seize upon more
established and traditional concerns (for example peasant and workers'
movements, nationalist movements). Thus although what constitutes

a social movement is open to a variety of interpretations, for our purposes we can define it as 'a collective actor constituted by individuals who understand themselves to have common interests and, for at least some significant part of their social existence, a common identity' (Scott, 1990, p. 6). Furthermore we can suggest that four ingredients are central. Firstly, social movements are both products and agents of socio-spatial transformations. In being primarily concerned to change or defend society, they can be differentiated from collectivities such as voluntary associations or clubs. Secondly, they must appeal to some form of collective identity or consciousness. One aspect here that speaks directly to the core of human geography is the relationship of such a consciousness to locality, be it local community (for example inner-city dwellers), workplace (for example labour), region (for example nationalism), or even global (for example environmental, antinuclear). Thirdly, a social movement engages or has the potential to engage in mass mobilisation as its prime source of social sanction, and hence of power. This further distinguishes a social movement from collective actors such as pressure groups. And finally, as Touraine (1985) argues, membership is drawn from subordinate groups who constitute a social movement precisely because they translate their exclusion and alienation into concrete social action.

What becomes apparent is that the nature of social movements and the issues they embrace are going to be highly dependent on a whole variety of socioeconomic and political processes, not least the differential impact of globalisation, political culture, socioeconomic development and the nature of the state (authoritarian/liberal–democratic) to which they are bound. Their ability to mobilise places and communities into political action is also going to be dependent upon the availability of local resources (for example organisational capabilities, time budgets) and opportunities, and of the calculated personal costs and benefits envisaged by their potential constituent members (Rucht, 1991). Nowhere are these differences and the agendas they reflect likely to be more differentiated than in relation to the now commonplace distinction between First, Second and Third Worlds. What distinguishes these 'three worlds' both from their recent past and from each other is the nature of their current geographical transitions, of which social movements can be considered as both symptoms and bearers. These geographical transformations can be loosely identified as the transitions from an industrial to a postindustrial society (First World), from a socialist to a postsocialist society (Sec-

[margin note: ingredients of social movements]

ond World) and from a colonial to postcolonial society (Third World). Contextualising social movements in this way does not mean that each can be simply explained with reference to a single set of particular sociospatial structural changes or that these transitions are neatly coterminous with 'each world'. Yet as Laclau and Mouffe made clear when examining the emergence of First and Third World contemporary social movements, compared with the First World where a multiplicity of points of tensions exist in the constitutive nature of collective actions, 'in the countries of the third world, imperialist exploitation and the predominace of brutal and centralised forms of domination tend from the beginning to endow the popular struggle with a centre, with a single and clearly defined enemy' (Laclau and Mouffe, 1985, p. 131). A similar view is also echoed by Slater (1991). Consideration here, however, is given to why and in what forms social movements in postindustrial and postsocialist worlds are challenging state sovereignty.

From Industrial to Postindustrial Society

In advanced capitalist society, researchers have in various ways linked important structural changes over the past three decades to the emergence of a new politics associated in particular with novel forms of collective action. This transformation has been causally linked with the transition from Fordist to post-Fordist methods of more flexible accumulation (Harvey, 1989), with the transformation of value systems associated with a fundamental shift from material to 'postmaterialist' values (Inglehart, 1977; White, 1991), and as a symptom of a potential legitimation crisis of late capitalism linked to a defensive resistance to processes of social and cultural change (Habermas, 1987). According to Offe (1985) the newness of social movements lies in a disillusionment with 'the comprehensive growth-security alliance' prevalent in Western democracies in the post-Second World War era. It was an 'alliance' that failed to pass on equitable benefits of economic growth. Thus the fledgling social movements of the 1960s – the antinuclear, environmental, student, women's and peace movements – tended to highlight alternative values to that of economic growth and geopolitical security that emphasised the quality of life, individual self-realisation, participation, peace and conservation. In short they not only pointed to the unacknowledged costs of economic growth, mass consumption and Cold-War geopolitical security, but in signalling a particular normative view of society they constituted a new type of movement, differing in their grievances and aspirations to the more traditional labour movement. In short these new social movements seek a different relationship to the physical environment, to the opposite sex, to the workplace and to urban consumerism.

Elements of continuity, however, should not be underemphasised. The origins of many social movements labelled as 'new' can be traced back to the nineteenth century (for example secessionist, environmental, feminist). They also reflect an alienation from the existing system of production and antagonism towards globalising processes of economic development that threaten both local cultures and the environment. Today's social movements, then, have not developed in a historical vacuum but rather they have been 'thrown into an already existing world' (Kosik, 1976). Their newness lies in four elements. Firstly, their geographical scale of community and political action is not confined to the political specificity of the nation-state. Rather they are concerned with the rearticulation of political space and the concomitant reconstruction of community at the global, regional and local levels (Dalby, 1991). Secondly, new social movements (NSMs) are not based on class politics or on a simple division of labour. Rather, as the literature on NSMs emphasises, as class politics have become more marginal to postindustrial society and as newer forms of collective political action are more multilayered and socially pluralistic, so the utility of class analysis to understanding their motives, interests and rationality is limited (Scott, 1990). Thus geography needs to go beyond just focusing on the social relations of production and on the workplace and industrial region and take on board the way in which new forms of collective political actions are opening up space for new kinds of geographies. Thirdly, the aims of NSMs differ. Unlike more traditional social movements that historically saw the state as both a means towards actualising their aims and an instrument through which to assert power, NSMs are ambivalent towards the usual routes to political participation (for example elections, formation of political parties), which led to the institutionalisation of old social movements into the state system. Their aim is not to control or seize state power. However this does not mean that they are not prepared to use some of the opportunities offered by institutional politics (for example public enquiries, actions in the courts). Rather they prefer instead to focus on small-scale, decentralised and 'community-level' local politics. As Moos (1989) shows with regard to the gay community of Los Angeles' West Hollywood district, this can even be linked to gaining political power in the local state. Finally, by challenging the established routines of 'doing politics' new social movements offer the possibility of new projects, and new ways of viewing the world and organising social life. Strategies for change are orientated towards participating in changing values and developing alternative lifestyles (Eyerman and Jameson, 1991).

NSMs are also far more socially wideranging and their origins and developments more diverse than Offe's focused account would suggest. Rather, what distinguishes the NSMs is their preoccupation with three interrelated aspects of modernity (Camilleri and Falk, 1992). Firstly, the experience of sociospatial uprootedness and the breakup of traditional communities linked to globalisation and social change has given rise to a powerful quest for the rediscovery of historical and cultural identities. Striking at the heart of this is rediscovery is the age-old need for a sense of place and community. Within the city it has manifested itself in the revival of ethnic identities in inner cities and in the growth of the neighbourhood movement. Secondly, the NSMs focus on the technological risks to humanity and nature that now form an integral part of postindustrial society. These concerns range from potential catastrophes associated with particular technologies (for example nuclear power) and forms of pollution associated with modern lifestyles (for example cars, plastics) and their global and possibly irreversible consequences. And thirdly, NSMs are a product of the failure of a state driven by economic growth and technical rationality to effectively evaluate and internalise the social, cultural and environmental ramifications of modernity. Although the scale of the significance of NSMs in changing the political architecture of 'local' and 'global' politics is still unclear, they nonetheless pose a challenge to the political economy of modernity, of which the sovereign state is a functional part.

From Socialist to Postsocialist Society

Social movements in the Second World are a relatively new phenomena largely associated with the collapse of state socialism and with the novel transition to postsocialist societies. Consequently it is primarily because social movements were born in localities undergoing structural changes set in motion by state-initiated but failed attempts to reform socialism that it is important to treat them separately. They can neither be considered as NSMs in the Western sense nor, as the reductionist logic of world systems would have it when considering the 1989 popular revolutions in Eastern Europe, as antisystemic (capitalist) movements (Taylor, 1991). Indeed what the 1989 and 1991 revolutions in Eastern Europe and the former USSR highlighted were popular movements antithetical not to capitalism and its functioning but to actually existing socialism (see Smith, 1993).

What brought about the dramatic rise in social-movement activity in the former Soviet Union and Eastern Europe from the late 1980s were three developments. Firstly, what credibility socialism still possessed in these countries was quickly disappearing as a result of the inability of this particular utopian ideology to legitimately claim to represent an alternative and superior route to modernity than that of capitalism. In the absence of participatory politics and civil rights, the centralised state relied heavily on economic growth, and the redistributive techniques of central planning associated with providing a welfare state and commitment to eradicating social inequalities between both regions and town–country, as the basis for continuing political legitimacy. By the mid-1980s, not least because of the Cold War and the economic costs of 'imperial overstretch' (Kennedy, 1988), the Soviet hegemon could guarantee neither. Secondly, there was the more gradual impact of social change associated with the move towards a more urbanised society, and in particular with the the the rise of a new urban-based intelligentsia (Lewin, 1991). It was from the ranks of these diploma holders, frustrated by the whole project of neo-Stalinism, that 'the Gorbachev generation' came to challenge the previous dominant social formation of party functionaries within as well as outside formal institutional state politics. Without, however, a third factor – the new structure of opportunities introduced by the Gorbachev regime in the form of *glasnost* and democratisation – the rise of mass-based and effective social movements could not have occurred. By permitting 'the opening up of civil society' the new reform-minded Soviet state in effect provided the socioterritorial bases for its destruction as it allowed civil society in both its internal and external empires to participate in sociopolitical change.

The most striking feature of the social movements was that their boundedness was largely ethnoregional and heavily 'national in content'. They were in effect anticentre and prosovereign. Thus in Eastern–Central Europe the 1989 revolutions were primarily directed against five decades of externally imposed Soviet socialism. In the non-Russian republics of the Soviet multiethnic empire, social movements also took on a heavily anti-Russian stance in which Russification, socialism and Sovietisation were seen as inextricably bound up with colonial infringement of sovereign rights. The 'popular movements' that emerged throughout many of the non-Russian republics and in Eastern Europe were therefore primarily 'umbrella organisations' bringing together a variety of groups and organisations – ethno-regional, ecological, feminist, religious, human rights, peace – that shared a common belief that their social salvation lay in territorial sovereignty if not in outright independent statehood (Smith, 1990; Sedaitis and Butterfield, 1991).

Securing greater sovereignty was also viewed as the most effective path to rejoining the capitalist world economy. This in part was reflected at least in Eastern Europe in what Habermas (1990) calls 'the rectifying revolutions' of 1989, where one finds the popular desire to reconnect with the inheritance of constitutional democracy, and socially and politically with the styles of commerce and life associated with capitalism. Information technology, particularly television, was crucial in this regard, not only because of the role it played in the 1989 revolutions in facilitating a domino effect between the capital cities of Eastern Europe, but also because of the positive imagery it presented of life under late capitalism. To be sure, there were movements more wary of the benefits that would accrue from embracing capitalism. Some Green movements were a case in point, as was the new labour movement. But even this movement was divided over the merits of marketisation, in which local economic conditions played a crucial part. During the coalfield strikes between 1989 and 1991, for instance, miners in Ukraine, where coalfields were less competitive, machinery outdated and many seams all but exhausted, remained suspicious of the benefits of marketisation, whereas for Russia's Kuzbass miners, whose coalfields were richer and more productive and potentially more competitive, there was support for the further 'rolling back' of the state (Rutland, 1991).

Few would question that the contributions of the social movements to the events of 1989 and 1991 were emancipatory, based on an urge towards establishing political democracies. The events were, as Garton-Ash so eloquently puts it, 'the springtime of societies aspiring to be civil'. These movements were mainly an urban phenomenon in which the intelligentsia were the most active. Where the intelligentsia were least powerful, the transition towards liberal democracy and capitalism has proven to be more problematic, as in the case of peasant-dominated Romania and Bulgaria (Wertheim, 1992). The more universal problem that has arisen, however, is that the emancipatory state has not automatically followed emancipatory movements. This is for two principal reasons. Firstly, the claim to sovereignty is based on a Wilsonian-type notion of self-determination in which national and state boundaries are held to be co-terminous. This 'nation-state' belief has tended to manifest itself as intolerance by the dominant nation towards 'outsiders' inside its sovereign borders (for example the Hungarian minority in Romania, anti-Turkish policies in Bulgaria, Russians in Latvia) and in extraterritorial claims (for example Serbia, Ukraine, Armenia) based on a nationalist belief that national and sovereign spaces should be congruent. Thus in some states, movements that were formerly emancipatory, having gained power are in the process of denying or limiting the rights of ethnic minorities through citizenship legislation. Secondly, entry into the capitalist world economy, particularly for states competing on its margins, is giving rebirth to the idea of the strong state, of the need to effect central control and thus to redefine citizen rights in order to secure the conditions suitable to attracting foreign capital and economic growth. Neither uncertain electoral outcomes nor an uncontrolled labour force – in societies that have little or no collective memory of either – is easily compatible with such statist goals.

Conclusions

In this chapter I have sketched out one of the central agendas of concern in political theory, the future of the nation-state and of the way in which both 'global' and 'local' processes are transforming the meaning of sovereignty. These processes, I have also suggested, are inextricably bound up with a spatiality to politics in which global processes have implications for the politics of places and of the way in which the place of politics, at least in late-modern democracies, is being increasingly conducted in 'postnational terms' and in 'postnational spheres'. Such processes carry important implications for our conceptual and normative understanding of the spatiality of both citizenship and democracy.

References

Agnew, J. and S. Corbridge (1989) 'The new geopolitics: the dynamics of
geopolitical disorder', in R. Johnston and P. Taylor (eds), *World in
Crisis? Geographical Perspectives* (Oxford: Basil Blackwell), pp. 266–88.
Anderson, B. (1991) *Imagined Communities*, 2nd edn (London: Verso).
Appadurai, A. (1990) 'Disjuncture and Difference in the Global Cultural
Economy', in M. Featherstone (ed.), *Global Culture, Nationalism,
Globalization and Modernity* (London: Sage), pp. 295–310.
Arrighi, G. *et al.* (1990) *Antisystemic Movements* (London: Verso).
Bendix, R. (1964) *Nation-building and Citizenship: Studies of our Changing
Social Order* (New York: Wiley).
Barbalet, J. (1988) *Citizenship, Rights, Struggle and Class Inequality* (Milton
Keynes: Open University Press).
Camilleri, J. and J. Falk (1992) *The End of Sovereignty? The Politics of a
Shrinking and Fragmenting World* (Aldershot: Edward Elgar).
Clark, G. and M. Dear (1984) *State Apparatus, The Structures and Languages
of Legitimacy* (London: Allen and Unwin).
Dalby, S. (1991) 'Critical geopolitics: discourse, difference, and dissent',
Environment and Planning D. Society and Space, vol. 9, pp. 261–83.
Dale, R. (1984) 'Nation state and international system: The world-system
perspective', in G. McLennan *et al.* (eds), *The Idea of the Modern State*
(Milton Keynes: Open University Press).
Driver, F. (1991) 'Political Geography and State Formation', *Progress in
Human Geography*, vol. 15, no. 3, pp. 268–80.
Eyerman, R. and A. Jameson (1991) *Social Movements. A Cognitive Ap-
proach* (Oxford: Polity Press).
Featherstone, M. (ed.) (1991) *Global Culture. Nationalism, Globalization
and Modernity* (London: Sage).
Fukuyama, F. (1992) *The End of History and the Last Man* (London:
Hamish Hamilton).
Giddens, A. (1985) *The Nation-state and Violence* (Oxford: Polity Press).
Habermas, J. (1987) *The Theory of Communicative Action*, vol. 2, (Cam-
bridge: Polity).
Habermas, J. (1990) 'What Does Socialism Mean Today? The Rectifying
Revolution and the Need for New Thinking on the Left', *New Left
Review*, no. 183, pp. 3–22.
Hall, S. (1991) 'The local and the global: globalization and ethnicity, in
A. King (ed.), *Culture, Globalization and the World-system* (London:
Macmillan), pp. 19–39.
Harvey, D. (1989) *The Condition of Post-Modernity* (Oxford: Basil
Blackwell).
Heater, D. (1990) *Citizenship. The Civil Ideal in World History, Politics
and Education* (London: Longman).
Held, D. (1991) 'Democracy, the Nation-State and the Global System', in
D. Held (ed.), *Political Theory Today* (Cambridge: Polity), pp. 197–235.
Inglehart, R. (1977) *The Silent Revolution: Changing Values and Political
Styles among Western Publics* (Princeton NJ: Princeton University Press).
Johnston, R. (1989) 'The Individual and the World Economy', in

R. Johnston and P. Taylor (eds), *World in Crisis? Geographical Perspectives* (Oxford: Basil Blackwell), pp. 200–28.

Kaldor, M. (1991) *The Imaginary War* (Oxford: Basil Blackwell).

Kearns, J. (1988) 'History, Geography and World-systems Theory', *Journal of Historical Geography*, vol. 14, pp. 281–92.

Kennedy, P. (1988) *The Rise and Fall of the Great Powers* (London: Fontana).

Kosik, K. (1976) *Dialectics of the Concrete* (Dordrecht: Reidal).

Laclau, E. and C. Mouffe (1985) *Hegemony and Socialist Strategy. Towards a Radical Democratic Politics* (London: Verso).

Lewin, M. (1991) *The Gorbachev Phenomenon. A Historical Interpretation*, 2nd edn (Berkeley: University of California Press).

Mann, M. (1986) 'The autonomous power of the State: Its Origins, Mechanisms and Results', in J. Hall (ed.), *States in History* (Oxford: Basil Blackwell), pp. 109–36.

Mann, M. (1988) *States, War and Capitalism* (Oxford: Basil Blackwell).

McGrew, A., P. Lewis *et al.* (eds) (1992) *Global Politics. Globalization and the Nation-State* (Oxford: Polity).

Mohan, J. (ed.) (1988) *The Political Geography of Contemporary Britain* (London: Macmillan).

Moos, A. (1989) 'The Grassroots in Action: Gays and Seniors Capture the Local State in West Hollywood, California', in J. Wolch and M. Dear (eds), *The Power of Geography. How Territory Shapes Social Life* (Boston: Unwin Hyman).

Offe, C. (1985) 'New Social Movements: Challenging the Boundaries of Institutional Politics', *Social Research*, vol. 52, no. 4.

Peet, R. (1989) 'Introduction', in Peet, R. and N. Thrift (eds) (1989) *New Models in Geography. The Political Economy Perspective*, vol. 1 (London: Unwin Hyman), pp. 257–66.

Roche, M. (1992) *Rethinking Citizenship. Welfare, Ideology and Change in Modern Society* (Oxford: Polity).

Rucht, D. (ed.) (1991) *Research on Social Movements. The State of the Art in Western Europe and the USA* (Boulder: Westview).

Rutland, P. (1991) 'Labour Movements and Unrest in 1989 and 1990', *Soviet Economy*, vol. 6, no. 1, pp. 345–84.

Scott, A. (1990) *Ideology and the New Social Movements* (London: Unwin Hyman).

Sedaitis, J. and J. Butterfield (eds) (1991) *Perestroika from Below. Social Movements in the Soviet Union* (Boulder: Westview).

Skocpol, T. (1979) *States and Social Revolutions* (Cambridge University Press).

Slater, D. (1991) 'New Social Movements and Old Political Questions. Rethinking State–Society Relations in Latin American Development', *International Journal of Political Economy*, vol. 21, no. 1, pp. 32–65.

Smith, A. (1990) 'Towards a Global Culture?', in M. Featherstone (ed.), *Global Culture. Nationalism, Globalization and Modernity* (London: Sage), pp. 171–92.

Smith, G. (1985) 'Political Geography', in R. Robins (ed.), *Introducing Political Science. Themes and Concepts in Studying Politics* (London: Longman), pp. 126–47.

Smith, G. (1989) 'Privilege and Place in Soviet Society', in D. Gregory and R. Walford (eds), *New Horizons in Human Geography* (London: Macmillan), pp. 320–40.

Smith, G. (1990) *The Nationalities Question in the Soviet Union* (London: Longman).

Smith, G. (1993) 'Ends, Geopolitics and Transitions', in R. Johnston (ed.) *The Challenge For Geography. Changing World, Changing Discipline* (Oxford: Basil Blackwell), pp. 76–99.

Smith, S. (1989) 'Society, Space and Citizenship: A Human Geography of the "New Times"?', *Transactions, Institute of British Geographers, NS*, vol. 14, no. 2, pp. 144–56.

Taylor, P. (1991) 'The Crisis of the Movements: The Enabling State as Quisling', *Antipode*, vol. 23, no. 2, pp. 214–28.

Taylor, P. (1993) *Political Geography, World-Economy, Nation-State and Locality*, 3rd edn (London: Longman).

Touraine, A. (1985) 'An Introduction to the Study of Social Movements', *Social Research*, vol. 52, no. 4.

Thrift, N. (1989) 'The Geography of the International Economic Disorder', in R. Johnston and P. Taylor (eds), *World in Crisis? Geographical Perspectives* (Oxford: Basil Blackwell), pp. 16–68.

Walker, R. and R. Mendlovitz (eds) (1990) *Contending Sovereignties: Redefining Political Community* (Boulder: Lynne Rienner).

Wallerstein, I. (1979) *The Capitalist World-Economy.* (Cambridge University Press).

Wallerstein, I. (1984) *The Politics of the World-Economy, The States, The Movements and The Civilisations* (Cambridge University Press).

Wallerstein, I. (1991) *Geopolitics and Geoculture. Essays on the Changing World-System* (Cambridge University Press).

Wertheim, W. (1992) 'The State and the Dialectics of Development', *Development and Change*, vol. 23, no. 3, pp. 257–82.

White, S. (1991) *Political Theory and Postmodernism* (Cambridge University Press).

4
Social Theory and Human Geography

DEREK GREGORY

Take the construction of the Ark. What does he do? He builds it in gopher-wood. Gopher-wood? Even Shem objected, but no, that was what he wanted and that was what he had to have. The fact that not much gopher-wood grew nearby was brushed aside. No doubt he was merely following instructions from his role-model; but even so. Anyone who knows anything about wood – and I speak with some authority in the matter – could have told him that a couple of dozen other tree-types would have done as well, if not better; and what's more, the idea of building all parts of a boat from a single wood is ridiculous. You should choose your material according to the purpose for which it is intended; everyone knows that. Still, this was old Noah for you – no flexibility of mind at all. Only saw one side of the question.

Julian Barnes, *A history of the world in 10½ chapters*

Mountains and Islands

In this chapter I explore some of the relations between human geography and social theory. I do not want to be drawn into any boundary disputes over the first of those terms – there have been too many deadening proclamations about the 'nature' or 'spirit and purpose' of geography – but I do need to say something about the second because I do not use it as a synonym for sociology or even social science. Instead I propose to treat social theory as a series of overlapping, contending and contradictory discourses that seek, in various ways and for various purposes, to reflect explicitly and more or less systematically on the constitution of social life, to make social practices intelligible and to intervene in their conduct and consequences. This is a bare-bones characterisation, but it does not limit social theory to any one discipline and it makes three closely connected claims that I hope will breathe life into the discussion that follows.

To speak of social theory as a discourse is to enter a complicated arena, but as a first approximation discourse refers to all the ways in which we communicate with one another: to that vast network of signs, symbols and practices through which we make our world(s) meaningful to ourselves and to others. It is a term that draws attention to the embeddedness of intellectual inquiry in social life: to the contexts and casements that shape our local knowledges, however imperiously global their claims to know, and to the practical consequences of understanding (and indeed being in) the world like this rather than like that. As I understand and use it, therefore, social theory is not a commentary on social life but rather an *intervention in* social life. It is not a series of ideas conjured up by the gods of abstraction and hurtled like a thunderbolt through the clouds to illuminate a murky landscape below: social theory is always and everywhere grounded, constructed at particular sites to meet particular circumstances, and deeply implicated in constellations of power, knowledge and (as I will try to show) spatiality. This does not mean that it is immobile. On the contrary, social theory is in constant motion, moving from one place to another, and in its travels it becomes freighted with a host of different assumptions that sometimes do not (and often should not) survive the journey intact. This implies a particular way of using social theory, in which its ideas have to be worked with − patiently, carefully, rigorously − in each of its different ports-of-call: not 'tested' in some isolated laboratory, not 'applied' from outside, but *worked with*.

In much the same way I insist that social theory is about making social life intelligible because this does not immediately privilege one, nominally 'scientific', set of working practices over and against another. 'Science' is a weasel word. Within the humanities and the social sciences it is much used (and abused) as a term of approbation or condemnation, made to stand for a system of knowledge to which we are enjoined to aspire or from which we are supposed to recoil. But these are, as often as not, knee-jerk responses. They are rarely based on a close scrutiny of the received model of natural science, on an investigation of scientific practices in the laboratory, in the field or in the journals, on what it is scientists actually *do*, but rely instead on what philosophers have had to say about these matters. This has started to change, in sometimes startling ways, partly because the privileges that 'Philosophy with a capital P' ascribes to itself have come under increasing scrutiny (Baynes, Bohman and McCarthy, 1987), and partly because a new sociology of science – perhaps even an ethnography of science – has shown through a series of detailed case studies that the hard sciences are much less 'objectivist' than either their protagonists or their critics have usually claimed (Woolgar, 1988). The sciences have much more in common with other social practices – for good or ill – than most of us have ever imagined and they do not escape the mutual imbrications of power and knowledge by wrapping a cloak of objectivism around themselves (Rouse, 1987). For these reasons, I am suspicious of any discourse that gathers to itself privileges and closures that sustain a supremely self-confident claim to a singular and universal 'truth' independent of subject position. All our knowledges are *situated* (Haraway, 1991, pp. 183–201).

This is all very schematic, I realise, and I have deliberately made no discriminations between different traditions of social theory. But my purpose is not to offer a general prospectus but to think instead about the wider implications of the contemporary interest in social theory and human geography. One of its most obvious consequences, I suggest, is that an interest in place, space and landscape – traditionally one of the central concerns of human geography – has become one of the focal concerns of the humanities and the social sciences as a whole. I do not think this means that the discipline is dissolving, but I do think it implies that the *discourse* of geography has become much wider than the discipline. This is not the result of the dialogue between social theory and human geography alone, of course, and there are several other ways in which traditionally geographical concerns bear directly on wider conversations: most obviously, and probably most importantly, on those debates surrounding political ecology and the cultural politics of 'nature' which, in their turn, have considerable implications for mainstream social theory which, with one or two exceptions, has shown remarkably little interest in such matters (Eckersley, 1990; Merchant, 1990).

In my view, these complicating developments open up both social theory and geographical inquiry and ought to be welcomed. The

intellectual division of labour has always been an untidy affair –
which is in part why there have been so many new disciplines and
interdisciplinary projects brought into being – and yet it is not
completely arbitrary. It is always possible to provide (historical)
reasons for drawing the boundaries this way rather than that. But
once those boundaries have been established they usually become
institutionalised. All the apparatus of the academy – teachers, courses,
journals, texts, academic societies – is mobilised to mark and, on
occasion, to police them. But these disciplinary divisions do not
correspond to any natural breaks in the intellectual landscape:
social life does not respect them and ideas flow across them. It is
this busy cross-border traffic I have in mind when I talk about
'discourse'.

Now in this sense the discourse of geography is not confined to
any one discipline, nor even to the specialised vocabularies of the
academy. We all routinely make sense of places, spaces and landscapes in our everyday lives – in different ways and for different
purposes – and these 'popular geographies', personal and public,
are as important to the conduct of social life as are our understandings
of (say) biography and history. When we are required to think critically and systematically about social life and social space, however, we usually need to distance ourselves from those commonplace,
taken-for-granted assumptions. We can never suspend them altogether,
and our reflections will only make sense, to ourselves and to other
people, if they retain some connection with the ordinary meanings
that are embedded in the day-to-day negotiations of lifeworlds. But
we need to interrogate those 'common sense' understandings: we
need to make them answer to other questions, to have them speak
to other audiences, to make them accountable to other actors. This
is more than a matter of challenging the 'matter-of-factness' of
things, though that is extremely important. It is also necessary to
tease out the intricate web of conditions and consequences in which
they are implicated: to show how practices and processes connect
and collide in complexes of action and reaction in place and over
space, often far beyond our immediate horizons, and in doing so
constantly transform the tremulous geographies of modernity.

This concern is what geographer David Harvey, among others,
once described as the 'geographical imagination', and in his remarkable inquiry into *Social justice and the city* he attempted to
connect this critical sensibility to what sociologist C. Wright Mills
had previously identified as the 'sociological imagination'. Neither

of these terms was protected by a disciplinary fence, let me say, and neither Harvey nor Mills was seeking to advance their own disciplines over and against others. They were both sharply critical of the prevailing orthodoxies in geography and sociology. What they each sought to do, in their own way, was to emphasise the ethical and political responsibility of accounting for the connections between place and space (Harvey, 1973) and biography and history (Mills, 1959). When these twin projects are juxtaposed (and this was, I think, Harvey's primary purpose), the challenge becomes one of solving the equations simultaneously because for the most part human geography showed little interest in social processes and, conversely, sociology paid little attention to theorising the spatialisation of social life. This is a complicated matter, but in general social theory has always been more interested in time than in space, though the relations between social theory and the historical disciplines have often been contentious, and it is only recently that it has ventured into what Neil Smith calls 'deep space':

> The twentieth century has ushered in the discovery of deep space, or at least its social construction, and yet it is only as the century draws to a close that this fundamental discovery is becoming apparent. . . . Deep space is quintessentially social space; it is physical space infused with social intent (Smith, 1990).

The *Star Trek* language is not altogether out of place, partly because the horizons of science (and, for that matter, science fiction) provide important orientations; partly because the sheer physicality of social space is of cardinal significance; and partly because these discoveries are beginning to chart regions where few have gone before.[1]

In what follows I want to explore this new intellectual landscape. My account will take the form of a sketch-map, a partial and provisional historical geography of ideas drawn (in the main) from work in Britain and North America. But I need to sound two notes of caution. First, there are other geographies and other geographical traditions, and it would be both arrogant and misleading to assume that the English-language work to be discussed here is somehow exemplary of (or even worse, in advance of) other contributions. That said, the professionalisation of the discipline has combined with its internationalisation in ways that often marginalise those other voices or subsume them within a hegemonic discourse whose terms have largely been dictated by the Western academy. Second, and in counterpoint, the history of modern geography has often been cast in loosely geographical terms. In its origins, towards the end of the eighteenth century, it is supposedly a 'European science' (though 'Eurocentric' would be a more accurate description); in the closing decades of the nineteenth century it was formally admitted to the Western academy, often through its close association with nationalism and imperialism, and distinctive schools of geography were associated with particular national traditions ('the French School', 'the German School'); and in the twentieth century, as those seeds were transplanted on the other side of the Atlantic, individual places have been used as markers in the intellectual landscape ('the Chicago School', 'the Berkeley School', and more recently still even 'the Los Angeles School'). But the global scale of many of the problems that concern geographers today has combined with the global circulation of information – with its attendant inequalities, restrictions and deformations – to make many of these parochialisms increasingly problematic. No doubt we have retained many of them – as I have already indicated, many of those in the Western academy still assume they occupy (and ought to occupy) a central place in these discussions – and I suspect that we have also invented new ones: the contemporary pursuit of high theory has not noticeably diminished the ethnocentrism of our inquiries, since so many of those formulations have been the product of Western thinkers responding to Western predicaments. We constantly need to be reminded of the strangeness of our assumptions, therefore, the oddness of our own points of view. But the fact remains: 'local knowledge' simply isn't local anymore. As James Clifford puts it,

> A conceptual shift, 'tectonic' in its implications, has taken place. We ground things, now, on a moving earth. There is no longer any place of overview (mountaintop) from which to map human ways of life, no Archimedian point from which to represent the world. Mountains are in constant motion. So are islands: for one cannot occupy, unambiguously, a bounded cultural world from which to journey out and analyse other cultures. Human ways of life increasingly influence, dominate, parody, translate and subvert one another (Clifford, 1986, p. 22).

But this is to anticipate: let me begin my history in a period when geography was still perched, like Noah's Ark, on top of a mountain.

Spatial Science and the World-as-Exhibition

In the middle of the twentieth century the discipline of geography
was remodelled as 'spatial science' and defined in terms of a distinctive focus on spatial organisation and spatial order.[2] This way
of looking at things closely corresponds to what Mitchell (1988,
1989), following Derrida and Heidegger, has identified as 'the world-
as-exhibition'. This has a much longer history than any formal spatial
science and includes within its horizon of meaning much of Western philosophy and metaphysics, science and social thought. It can
be traced back at least as far as the seventeenth and eighteenth centuries, but it achieved a particular force in the closing decades of
the nineteenth century, when it became embedded in the spatialities
of what Mitchell calls a 'colonising' system of power. Although he
is most concerned with the inscription of this specifically European constellation of power-knowledge on late nineteenth-century
Egypt, it is important to understand that the world-as-exhibition had
already colonised Europe and, indeed, was subsequently repatriated
to the metropolis in a visibly heightened form. In the most general
terms, it depended on a conception of order that was produced by
and resided in a structure that was supposed to be somehow separate from what it structured: a framework that seemed to precede
and exist apart from the objects it enframed.

> [This] ordering creates the impression that the gaps between things
> are an abstraction, something that would exist whether or not
> the particular things were put there. This structural effect of some-
> thing pre-existent, non-particular and non-material is what is ex-
> perienced as 'order' (Mitchell, 1989, p. 79).

This may seem at once blindingly obvious (what other, non-abstract
conception of order could there be?) and maddeningly obscure (what
is this 'structural effect' that Mitchell so awkwardly invokes?). But
in a way that is precisely Mitchell's point: this way of conceiving
order is so much taken for granted, made to seem so natural, that
we have lost sight of quite other ways of making the world intelligible.
   I want to suggest that in the decades following the Second World
War the same conception of order was made focal to Anglo–American spatial science.[3] It was articulated most clearly by Peter Haggett
in his seminal review of *Locational analysis in human geography*,
first published in 1965 when this so-called 'new geography' was

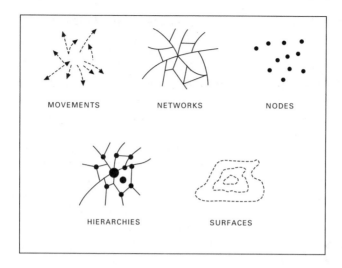

MOVEMENTS   NETWORKS   NODES

HIERARCHIES   SURFACES

FIGURE 4.1   *Abstract Geometries and Spatial Science*

SOURCE: after Haggett, 1965.

near its zenith. 'Order depends not on the geometry of the object we see,' he affirmed, 'but on the organizational framework in which we place it.' For Haggett, it was the framework itself that was geometric, and over the next twenty-five years or so he sought to recover a geometrical tradition – a concern for 'spatial structure' – that used to be a commonplace of classical Greek geography and to install it in a central place within the modern discipline. Locational analysis was thus organised around the decomposition of a regional system into a series of abstract geometries: movements, networks, nodes, hierarchies and surfaces (Figure 4.1). In an elegant essay reflecting on this project Haggett (1990, p. 5) described his vision of geography as a 'distant mirror', a way of seeing the world from a distance, which vividly recalls the strategies of all those European travellers in Mitchell's Egypt who could only 'form a picture' of what they saw – who could only render the world intelligible – by placing themselves on 'viewing platforms' (Telegraph Hill outside Cairo or the Great Pyramid at Giza) which provided them with what Mitchell (1988) calls 'optical detachment': a position from which they could see without being seen. The parallel with the surveillant eye of spatial science is, I think, exact (Gregory, 1994).

There are all sorts of connections between these visual metaphors and the ways in which 'knowledge' is conceived within modernity: how often do you say 'I see' when you mean 'I understand'? But I want to draw particular attention (another visual metaphor) to the scientific gloss – 'the optics' – involved in this way of setting up the world-as-exhibition within human geography. For those who have been most concerned to do so, including Haggett, have usually invoked the language of the sciences to advance their particular conception of order. This strategy was, I think, symptomatic of the postwar constellation of science and technology that contained at its core an ideological nucleus that virtually eliminated the distinction between the technical and the practical (cf. Habermas, 1971, 1978).[4] In many ways spatial science was the formal realisation of what Habermas would call a purely technical interest within the sphere of geography. It promised to enlist both physical geography and human geography in joint explorations of spatial structure – to dissolve the divisions (if not the distinctions) between the two – and to equip the expedition with the baggage of the natural sciences. Haggett repeatedly drew parallels between modern physics and modern geography in order to fix the position of his project. In his view, 'two of the greatest intellectual achievements of twentieth-century science', relativity theory and quantum mechanics, were 'concerned with spatial structures', and he used this congruence of interest to locate his own geography midway between 'the elegant worlds of the galaxy and the atom' (Haggett, 1990, pp. 23, 184).

Those worlds are not without their wonders, of course, and the intellectual curiosity of modern physicists is by no means bounded by the observatory or the laboratory. Here, for example, is Niels Bohr talking with another physicist, Werner Heisenberg, about their visit to Kronberg Castle in Denmark:

Isn't it strange how this castle changes as soon as one imagines that Hamlet lived here? As scientists we believe that a castle consists only of stones and admire the way the architect put them together. The stones, the green roof with its patina, the wood carvings in the church, constitute the whole castle. None of this should be changed by the fact that Hamlet lived here, and yet it is changed completely. Suddenly the walls and the ramparts speak a quite different language (Heisenberg, 1972, p. 51).

Haggett cites this passage too; but it was that 'different language' that concerned many of the critics of spatial science. Indeed the most succinct expression of the distance between the two was probably his own decision to strip the place-names from the maps in *Locational analysis* and replace them with Greek symbols: a manoeuvre that literally re-placed them in an abstract – geometric, generalisable – space.

The more developed versions of spatial science were not uniquely determined by the geometric gaze, however, but focused on partial or general models of an economic landscape or 'space-economy'. The spatial order that they supposed to be immanent in the human landscape was usually derived from a particular version of economic theory called neoclassical economics, and in particular from transcodings of its abstract calculus of supply and demand into an equally abstract 'friction of distance'. Ironically, however, this manoeuvre only strengthened the connections with the physical sciences. Although there were important differences between its proponents, the marginalist revolution in economics in the 1870s had depended on concepts and methods drawn directly from the physical sciences. There was never any secret about this, and Walras (one of the mandarins of marginalism) described his 'pure' economics as a 'physico–mathematical' science. In fact, so open and systematic was the piracy that Mirowski (1988, 1989) mischievously suggests that the entire episode is more properly described as the marginalist 'annexation': except, of course, that it was more than a passing episode. The heir to marginalism was neoclassical economics, which continues to be modelled on a mid-nineteenth-century, post-Newtonian physics and which, as Mirowski remarks, has in consequence been left stranded by the retreat of atomistic determinism and much else besides from twentieth-century physics. One hundred years later it was possible to read the same ironies in the texts of spatial science. In some cases the models were derived directly from physics – usually models of spatial interaction and spatial diffusion – and in other cases – usually models of location and spatial behaviour – they were mediated by neoclassical economics. But in both cases the world they exhibit was enframed by – and hence structured by – the logic of highly constrained physical metaphors.

If this produced a human geography that was conceptually estranged from the social, it was also one that in quite other ways impinged directly upon the social through both its teaching and its research programmes. I say this because these representations of the world were more than intellectual abstractions: they shaped the way in which those who accepted them and used them thought about, made sense of and acted in the world. Let me make this more concrete. At the heart of neoclassical location theory was a preoccupation with *rational* action and *rational* landscapes – which is why its models were supposed to have such important policy implications – but that seemingly innocent adjective was given a highly specific meaning. It was a form of rationality oriented towards the allocation of means to ends: that is to say, a strictly 'cognitive–instrumental' rationality whose gradual institutionalisation culminated in what Max Weber called the 'iron cage' of capitalist modernity.[5]

This story has been told many times and in many ways, but these narratives have rarely noticed the tacit involvement of spatial science in the rationalisation of social action. Perhaps the standard histories of geography are silent because the origins of this particular version of enframing did not lie solely in academic geography. Foucault (1979, 1980) suggests that a dispersed and anonymous system of spatial sciences emerged in Europe in the eighteenth century as part of a generalised medico–administrative system of knowledge that was deeply implicated in the formation of a modern 'disciplinary society' and its constitutive technologies of surveillance, regulation and control. Human geography had no formal place in Foucault's genealogy of the human sciences, but it would not be difficult to show that by the middle decades of the twentieth century, through the sort of intellectual changes that I have been describing here, human geography had centralised and formalised that project. In other words, the disciplinary knowledge of spatial science was systematically connected to disciplinary power. In modelling itself upon the physical sciences this vision of human geography effectively endorsed ('naturalised') the existing structures of social life: indeed they were left in almost complete darkness. Its spectacular illuminations of the world-as-exhibition, now increasingly powered by the graphical displays of geographical information systems (GIS) and other political technologies, continue to be strategic moments in the contemporary 'colonisation' of the lifeworld (cf. Poster, 1990). This is to move from Foucault to a later Habermas (1987), and there are real difficulties in doing so. But at this general level the connections between disciplinary power, the colonisation of the lifeworld and the instrumental rationalities of spatial science seem to me compelling. Fortunately they have not gone unchallenged.

The Contours of Marxism

The critique of spatial science was many-stranded, but it should be clear from what I have said so far that social theory was (and continues to be) a vital means of dissent: that it helped to question the 'matter-of-factness' of these supposedly objective, disinterested representations of the world. There were other versions of social theory that would have been compatible with the programmes of spatial science, such as the structural functionalism developed by Talcott Parsons and his successors, but the interest in social theory was driven almost entirely by critical intentions. I cannot discuss all those challenges here: they certainly did not speak with one voice, and they brought their own particular problems with them. In what follows I want to concentrate on objections derived from political economy, and in particular from historical materialism, which began to be registered towards the end of the 1960s.

I realise that this explosion of interest in Marxism may seem strange to many, perhaps most readers today, but human geography was probably the last of the humanities and social sciences to take Marxism seriously: and it remains the case, I think, that no serious work can be done in these fields without coming to terms with Marx's writings. In the case of geography, it should also be said that these developments cannot be disentangled from the political culture of which they were a part: these were the years of student protest movements in Europe and North America; of a growing concern over civil rights and social justice; and of demonstrations against the war in Vietnam.[6] And yet one cannot reduce this politico–intellectual movement to its context: the move to Marxism was also shaped by the intellectual momentum of the dominant research programme that preceded it. Harvey, who played such a prominent role in the reorientation and radicalisation of human geography, was plainly disenchanted with spatial science – with its inability 'to say anything really meaningful about events as they unfold around us' – but he also retained a strong commitment to a *scientific* geography that could analyse the *structure* of the space-*economy* (Harvey, 1973). This triple emphasis helps to account for his interest in Marx's own writings and what I take to be his proximity to a tradition of more or less 'classical' Marxism developed in Britain by Maurice Dobb and Eric Hobsbawm, both of whom were primarily interested in the economic trajectory of the capitalist mode of production, rather than (say) the cultural materialism of E. P. Thompson and Raymond Williams that was to attract a later generation of Anglophone geographers. What this emphasis does not explain, however, is Harvey's seeming indifference to the development of a Francophone school of structural Marxism, which was also exercised by the scientific status of Marx's work and which sought to theorise the contradictory coexistence of multiple structures within capitalism.[7] But these conceptual innovations were hostile to the historicism that was embedded within Harvey's work – to the powerful 'logic' to historical eventuation that threads through many of his early essays in Marxist geography – and considerably less interested in bracketing the movements of other (political and cultural) levels in order to theorise the movements of the capitalist economy. In sum, the economy remained at the centre of this newly radical geography, as it had of spatial science.

But it was now theorised in strikingly different terms. Political economy registered an important advance over the models of spatial science because it socialised those abstract geometries. Spatial structures were no longer generated by point-process models in mathematical spaces and geography's grids were no longer indifferent to what Mitchell (1988) calls 'the particular things [that] were put there.' Instead, human geography now analysed landscapes of capital accumulation that were produced by social processes in concrete spaces; it mattered desperately what those 'things' were. These changes also set those landscapes in motion: just as Marx had described capitalist modernity as a world in which all that is solid melts into air, so the frozen lattices of spatial science began to fracture, heave and capsize. Equilibrium was now seen as problematic, even illusory; crisis and contradiction were connected to the production and reproduction of space; and regional transformations were no longer merely topological operations but the complicated outcomes of social processes and social struggles (see Massey, 1984). There were exceptions of course, and spatial analysis by no means disappeared. But in most cases geographical dynamics were largely removed from the laboratories of the physical sciences and placed on the crowded fields of human history. While there were other actors involved – including those establishing a humanistic geography that, in some versions at least, overlapped with various traditions of historical materialism – there is no doubt that the unprecedented interest in historical materialism played a central role in that process of relocation. This was more than an intellectual achievement; it had the liveliest of political implications. Once geography was freed from the naturalising cast of spatial science and once the delinquent particularities of the world were loosed from its carceral language of 'deviation' and 'residual', it was possible to think of social practices in other ways and to imagine other scenarios.[8]

I hope this will not be misunderstood. It *is* possible to represent some of those social processes in mathematical terms, and the development of analytical political economy and its translation into human geography gives the lie to those who have tried to treat political economy as the innumerate's response to spatial science (Sheppard and Barnes, 1990). Nevertheless the critique of spatial science cast a long shadow and few of the early engagements between political economy and human geography were analytical in quite this sense. Part of the attraction of Marx's work for Harvey was undoubtedly its analytical rigour, and I think it fair to say that his early, exuberant explorations of historical materialism were not altogether free of a residual positivism. Like many others, however, Harvey had become sceptical of mathematical modelling – of its analytical rather than dialectical form – and suspicious of the unidentified calculus of spatial analysis. It was this spatial formalism and its implied claim for an autonomous and self-sufficient spatial science that perturbed Harvey and many others, and Marx's critique of commodity fetishism was extended to a critique of what came to be called 'spatial fetishism'. In other words, spatial science was charged with severing spatial structures from the bundles of social relations that were embedded within them. The result was a widespread withdrawal from the analysis of spatial structure altogether. In consequence, most of the early engagements between political economy and human geography were distinctly one-sided. Historical materialism was projected more or less directly into human geography, so that studies of the uneven development of capitalism conducted under its sign were inevitably limited by the uneven development of Marxism itself, and in particular by its emphasis on history rather than geography. For this reason, when Harvey (1982) so carefully delineated *The limits to capital* he was marking not only the bounding contours of capitalist development – the ways in which capitalism was constrained by the sedimented landscapes that were laid down through successive cycles of accumulation – but also an important lacuna in Marx's master-work.

To be sure, Marxism is not closed around Marx's own writings, but with the exception of lone figures such as Walter Benjamin and Henri Lefebvre, twentieth-century Western Marxism maintained the same strategic silence about the spatiality of capitalism. It is perfectly true that Louis Althusser accentuated the uneven development of capitalism and it is equally true that human geography could have learned much from the complex, differentiated topography that his structural Marxism described. But his project was concerned with the *temporalities* of capitalism, with the different and often discordant rhythms of its economic, political and ideological levels, not with their *spatialities*. It is hardly surprising, therefore, that Soja (1989) should see the subsequent mapping of human geography into Western Marxism as a 'provocative inversion' because it involved a basic restructuring of the largely spaceless problematic of historical materialism. Many writers would now agree that the production of space has assumed a particular salience in the late twentieth-century world: that the emergent forms of high modernity (perhaps even of postmodernity) depend upon tense and turbulent landscapes of accumulation whose dynamics are so volatile and whose space-economies are so disjointed that one can glimpse within the dazzling sequences of deterritorialisation and reterritorialisation a new and intensified fluidity to the politico–economic structures of capitalism (Harvey, 1989); that the hypermobility of finance capital and information cascading through the circuits of this new world system, surging from one node to another in nanoseconds, is conjuring up unprecedented landscapes of power in which, as Castells (1983) put it, 'space is dissolved into flows', 'cities become shadows' and places are emptied of their local meanings; and that ever extending areas of social life are being wired into a vast postmodern hyperspace, an electronic inscription of the cultural logic of late capitalism, whose putative abolition of distance renders us all but incapable of comprehending – of mapping – the decentred communication networks whose global webs enmesh our daily lives. In sum, and as Jameson (1990) has argued particularly forcefully, 'a model of political culture appropriate to our own situation will necessarily have to raise spatial issues as its fundamental organizing concern.'

This image is a composite of course, and there are important (and often sharp) disagreements between its authors. As these descriptions suggest, however, Soja sees this 'reverse mapping' as provocative for other reasons too. Whereas Harvey's early engagements with historical materialism drew upon classical Marxism, and his later writings continue to work towards the construction of an historico–geographical materialism that remains remarkably close to Marx's original work, many of these other formulations are supposed to be contributions to a 'Western Marxism' whose concerns have considerably enlarged the agenda of political economy. And yet Western Marxism is not easy to define with any precision. It is sometimes described as 'the Marxism of the superstructure', presumably to emphasise its interest in philosophical reflection and in the political, cultural and aesthetic dimensions of capitalism, but since so many of its leading architects were concerned to displace the classical model of base and superstructure this is at best misleading. In any case it must be obvious from the preceding paragraph that much of this recent work remains closely interested in the global dynamics of the capitalist economy, and most particularly in the new international divisions of labour and the emergence of new regimes of capital accumulation. If this loosely collective project is part of Western Marxism, then it is being conducted at one or more removes from most of the original luminaries. One might glimpse the faint outlines of Horkheimer and Adorno's grim dialectic of enlightenment or Marcuse's one-dimensional society, even Habermas's colonisation of the life-world: but these are highly generalised affinities that have rarely been developed in any systematic fashion. The interest in culture and cultural politics is real enough, and this may well owe something to the traditions of a somewhat diffuse Western Marxism, but many of these developments have drawn on traditions outside its traditional heartland, beyond the boundaries of continental Europe. Where this new cultural geography makes use of historical materialism, it typically looks to the work of Anglophone art critics and historians such as John Berger and Timothy Clark or cultural critics such as Stuart Hall and Raymond Williams.

But this can be pressed still further. As I now want to show, many writers have moved sufficiently far from the terrain of historical materialism altogether to locate their projects within the horizon of a developing 'post-Marxism'.

In the Tracks of Post-Marxism

Not surprisingly this is a highly contested field and in Figure 4.2 I have tried to fix some of its shifting contours as they traverse human geography. Other disciplines and other discourses would require other diagrams. This is very much a map of the moment and

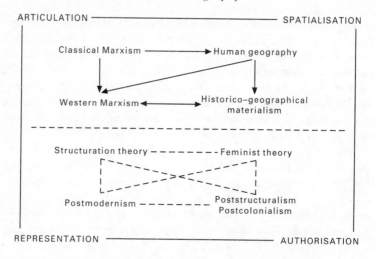

FIGURE 4.2   *Marxism, Post-Marxism and Human Geography*

I would be surprised if its configurations remained stable for very long or if other (and better) maps of the same terrain could not be produced. On it I distinguish two streams, each of which is in some sense a critical response to historical materialism – which is why I insist on its seminal importance: unequalled, I suspect, by any other discourse in the history of postwar geography – and each of which also maintains a tense relation to the other. It is this 'agonistic' grid, with its matrix of critical responses and counterarguments, that converts the map into something more than a convenient classi-fication by capturing the politico–intellectual dynamics that surge through and shape its continuing transformation.

Before I set off with this rough map as my guide I want to place some confidence limits around my journey. First, I do not mean to imply that there is any simple progression as one moves from the top of the diagram to the bottom. Marxism is by no means spinning its wheels, though events in Eastern Europe and the So-viet Union plainly shattered its more rigid orthodoxies, and in the West historical materialism continues to develop, critically and for the most part constructively, in response to discourses that are in their turn often responding to its formulations. Secondly, these later moves have more in common than a critical relation to Marxism: the discourses placed below the fold on the diagram conceive of theory in a radically different way from those that appear above the fold. In general, the various post-Marxist discourses are much less 'architectonic' in their sensibilities, which is to say that they are much more cautious about advancing generalisations that claim universality or completeness. This does not mean that they mark a return to radical empiricism, still less that they have succumbed to theoretical paralysis: only that they are much more suspicious of the return of Grand Theory and that they seek to undo its closures and subvert its imperialisms. Thirdly, I regard the quadrants that frame the diagram as questions that ought to frame any critical social theory and that should therefore also orientate the construction of any critical human geography.

Discursive Spaces

On one side of Figure 4.2 are those for whom political economy offered an analysis that was too structural − too concerned with the logic of capital − and who sought to open a wider conceptual space for human agency. To be sure, this was not a new problem. The political project of historical materialism in both its classical and its modern Western forms had long been skewered by what Anderson (1983, p. 34) called a 'permanent oscillation' between two principles of explanation: the structural logic of the mode of production and the conscious and collective agency of human subjects. Marx knew that people make history, of course, but he also recognised that they do not do so just as they please nor in circumstances of their own choosing. Towards the end of the 1970s one group of writers, working out the implications of this deceptively simple formulation, moved beyond Marx's original theses − though his writings remained indispensable to many of their arguments − to fashion what Giddens, its principal author, termed a 'post-Marxist' theory of structuration that would be capable of integrating the variable intersections between 'agency' and 'structure' within the same conceptual schema. How far this particular project has really moved from historical materialism is still a matter of debate. Not only has Giddens reaffirmed many of Marx's central characterisations of capitalism (including, on occasion, the labour theory of value), but some critics insist that many of his leading propositions, which are supposed to strike out in radically different directions, were in fact anticipated in various ways by Marx and the development of other traditions of Western Marxism (Wright,

1989; Gregory, 1990). Giddens is unrepentant – his reformulation of social theory is not only a critique of historical materialism, he declares, but also a 'deconstruction' of historical materialism – and yet there is no doubt that many of those who have been associated with his ideas, in human geography at any rate, have retained a much closer filiation with Western Marxism than Giddens allows himself.

On the other side – and in some measure distanced from structuration theory – are those for whom political economy is a thoroughly masculinist discourse. The relations between feminism and historical materialism are complex, and I have no wish to minimise the connections between them. Many of the attempts to construct a feminist geography were (and are) indebted to an avowedly socialist feminism. But the development of such a geography has none the less had to confront the central objection that historical materialism is, by its very nature, so preoccupied with questions of class that modalities of gender and sexuality are marginalised. This strategy of displacement is not confined to historical materialism, however, and structuration theory is by no means immune. Giddens has proposed a typology of societies that is intended to clarify some of the distinctive features of modernity: and yet this turns on a distinction between 'class-divided' and 'class' societies, which plainly confirms the centrality of class and fails to accord gender the same constitutive importance within modernity. Some feminist critics would object to Giddens's very style of theorising. In their view its temper replicates a masculinist mode of knowing which – like that of much mainstream political economy – is inclined to be abstract, authoritarian and univocal.

For all the tensions between structuration theory and feminist theory, however, they both display the same double movement that characterised the engagement between historical materialism and human geography. In each case social theory was originally projected into human geography as a way of resolving an 'internal' series of dilemmas or absences (which were none the less shared by the other humanities and social sciences); then, as a direct consequence of this conceptual mapping, the a-spatiality of social theory was itself called into question. In every case it is this return movement that has widened the discourse of geography still further and, as I now want to show, impelled the continuing transdisciplinary exploration of deep space.

In its early versions (for example Giddens, 1979) structuration theory was incorporated into human geography as a way of overcoming the profound dualism between structure and agency that skewered the analysis of space and place. There were parallel projects of 'articulation' in other disciplines that had foundered on similar problems, perhaps most noticeably in social history, but Giddens's work was distinguished from most of them by its philosophical and theoretical rigour. I am not sure that it can be described as a 'Grand Theory' – at least not in the usual sense of that term. In my view structuration theory is better seen as a developing research programme in which theoretical claims and empirical materials move in an advancing spiral or interrogation and reformulation: a way of thinking about things that modifies the imperial claims of 'Theory with a capital T'. Nevertheless the theoretical sensibilities of Giddens's project undoubtedly found a particularly receptive audience in a discipline that had been so closely attentive to the theoretical imperatives of spatial science and historico–geographical materialism. I do not think this receptivity was a matter of seeking academic credentials or following intellectual fashion. To take only the most obvious example, whatever the similarities between structuration theory and E. P. Thompson's socialist–humanist history – and these are not inconsiderable – Thompson's bitter polemic against the *poverty* of theory stood in the sharpest contrast to Giddens's insistence on the *power* of theory (cf. Thompson, 1978; Giddens, 1987).

There are other differences between them too, and one of the most important turns on Giddens's greater sensitivity to spatiality. In its later versions (for example Giddens, 1981, 1985) structuration theory began to register the claim that people make not only histories but also geographies: that time–space relations are not incidental to the constitution of societies and the conduct of social life. The interpenetrations of structure and agency could only be grasped, so Giddens seemed to say, by explicating the ways in which time and space are 'bound into' the conduct of social life. Giddens develops this claim by making a simple analytical distinction that has far-reaching implications (Figure 4.3). He argues that much of social life is cast within systems of face-to-face interaction that are, in an important sense, embedded in *place*. In the course of their day-to-day lives people move more or less routinely from one locale to another, tracing out paths in time and space, and drawing upon elements of those different settings in the conduct of their affairs. This complex weaving of the fabric of everyday life can be captured – graphically if not theoretically – in the sequences of time–space routinisation displayed in Hägerstrand's time–geographies. But

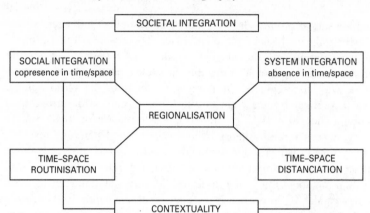

F<small>IGURE</small> 4.3   *Time–Space Relations and Structuration Theory*

one of the most characteristic consequences of modernity, so Giddens argues, is the progressive disembedding of spheres of social life from the immediacies of the here and now. This does not mean that social life is no longer anchored in place – it still, quite literally, 'takes place' – but those mooring lines become 'stretched' across variable spans of time and space. This process of time–space distanciation constitutes systems of mediated (that is, indirect) interaction that dissolve and recombine local networks of interpersonal relations across an increasingly global space. Giddens pays particular attention to the development of successive systems of communication, including writing, printing, telecommunications and electronic media, and to the development of successive systems of exchange, including money and networks of credit transfer. The modern world is shaped by the intimacy of the intersections between the two: most obviously through the ways in which electronic networks enable financial markets across the continents to implode in dizzying constellations of buying and selling (see Gregory, 1989).

Giddens insists on the importance of time–space distanciation because it has such radical implications for conventional conceptions of 'society' and for ordinary constructions of 'place'. Society can no longer be conceived as a totality with clear-cut boundaries, so he claims, since there is no reason to suppose that these webs of interaction will cohere into stable geometric configurations. If, as Mann (1986, p. 4) urges, 'societies are much messier than our theories

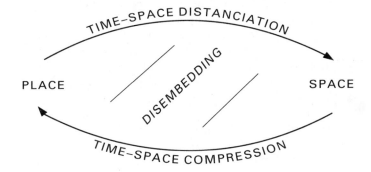

FIGURE 4.4 *Time–Space Distanciation and Time–Space Compression*

of them', then – as he also acknowledges – this is in large measure a direct consequence of their spatialities. By extension, one might argue that all the time human geography remained committed to a spatial science predicated on abstract, geometric order – on pattern – it was constitutively unable to grasp these unstable and emergent configurations of modernity. The reverse side of these vast global transformations is what Harvey (1989) calls 'time–space compression.' This connotes a chronic and deeply unsettling change in our everyday experience of time and space, in the course of which, so Giddens (1990, p. 19) claims, place becomes 'phantasmagoric': places are 'thoroughly penetrated by and shaped in terms of influences quite distant from them' (Figure 4.4). But what Giddens largely ignores – and what has provoked some of Harvey's most energetic writing in recent years – is that these challenges to deeply sedimented ideas of society and place have issued in a profound crisis of representation. This turns on the possibility of comprehending and somehow re-presenting these intricate, multiple and compound geographies that mix 'presence' and 'absence' in such volatile ways. Harvey's (1989) response is to reaffirm the importance of Marx's work, but a number of other writers have moved beyond the horizons of both historical materialism and structuration theory to explore the possibilities of postmodernism.

Feminist geography turns on a crisis of representation too. Although this can hardly be explained by processes of time–space compression, it has important implications for the spatiality of social life. Feminist geography was initially concerned with challenging the orthodoxies of what one might well call a half-human geography, one which virtually ignored the other half of humankind, through the construction of a 'geography of women' that drew attention to the specificity of women's experience of place and the contours of their activity spaces. So much of human geography, like the other humanities and social sciences, assumed that the masculine world was the normal world – indeed, the *only* world – not only by its sexist language but by its very themes, propositions and (even) philosophies. Much of the early work in feminist geography emerged in close conjunction with historico–geographical materialism, and this proximity was indexed by a focus on geographies of waged and non-waged work. These modalities of economic exploitation are immensely important, of course, but so too are a series of other questions including (for example) male violence towards women, which have their own spatialities but which cannot be derived directly from historical materialism. Although this early projection of feminism into geography challenged the vocabularies, the empirical bases and, on occasion, even the logics of 'malestream' geography, it seems to have had little direct impact upon feminist theory itself. Part of the reason for this was perhaps the comparative simplicity of early feminist geography. If these first studies took little explicit notice of more complex debates within other areas of feminism, however, I suspect that the strategy was a deliberate one: so many thematic and theoretical innovations within human geography had had their origins in the conceptual stratosphere that the introduction of ideas at a much more immediate and accessible level said much about the very different political and intellectual project advanced by feminism. Feminist geography was conceived from the very beginning as a discourse *about* exclusion and not as a discourse *of* exclusion.[9]

None of this denies the sophistication of feminism more generally, and subsequent developments have seen questions of spatiality placed at the heart of a feminist theory that has come to articulate a distinctive 'politics of location'. This is a rich and vital field, and I worry about trespassing on it. But when bell hooks (1990, pp. 145–9) chooses 'the margin as a space of radical openness'; when she writes about the effort 'to change the way I speak and write, to incorporate in the manner of telling a sense of place, of not just who I am in the present but where I am coming from'; when she urges the effort 'to create space where there is unlimited access to the pleasure and power of knowing': when she says all these things she means her spatial metaphors to be understood in the most insistently material of senses. She wants to open a 'space of resistance' for the production of a counterdiscourse *'that is found not just in words but in habits of being and the way one lives'* (my emphasis). This project is a much more politicised one than structuration theory and for this reason raises much more urgent questions about authority and authorisation.

Multiple Voices

The engagements with historical materialism, structuration theory and feminist theory have, in different ways and to varying degrees, challenged the conventional ways of staging the world-as-exhibition. They have raised serious questions about the vantage points adopted by human geography and the other humanities and social sciences and, indeed, subverted the optics of representation upon which those discourses have traditionally relied. Many writers are now much more sceptical about the ways in which the characteristic impulses of human geography and social theory act, as Thrift (1985) puts it, 'to complete the incomplete, to structure the partially structured [and] to order the only partly ordered.' In Figure 4.2 I have distinguished two responses to this: on the one side, postmodernism, and on the other side, poststructuralism and postcolonialism.

Postmodernism has interested a number of writers who have argued that its sensitivity to difference and its interest in spatiality provide the opportunity to reconstruct human geography in ways that recuperate some of its traditional concerns, which were virtually erased by spatial science, and to fashion them into a new politico–intellectual project. Many of these discussions have taken architecture as their paradigmatic model of postmodernism, and it is not difficult to understand its attractions for those who are drawn to the visibilities of the cultural landscape or to the materialities of investment and intervention in the built environment (Dear, 1986; Ley, 1987). But whether architecture can properly service all the demands that are placed upon it is problematic. Insofar as postmodernism is supposed to be about resisting any attempt at the domestication of difference through the inscription of a master code or metanarrative, it is difficult to see how any one discourse can be emblematic of all the others. My particular fear, however, is that the attempt to use architecture as a figure for postmodernism invites a crude cartoon of modernism.

We are often told that postmodernism repudiates the universal geometries of Le Corbusier and other modernist architects, for example, and replaces them with a new sensitivity to difference: to the specificities of place. My point is not so much that other versions of postmodern architecture have taken the corporate brutalities of that austere high modernism even further – which they plainly have – but that *other modernisms* in *other spheres of social life* have made much more radical interventions than this account allows. Modernism is a portmanteau term that has to carry a lot of baggage, I realise, but Lunn (1985) suggests that it can be unpacked into the following general characterisations.

1. A challenge to the conventions of realism and naturalism, which represented art as a transparent reflection or 'mirror' of the real: 'Modern artists, writers and composers often draw attention to the media or materials with which they are working' and their work 'often wilfully reveals its own reality as a construction or artifice' (p. 34).
2. A heightened awareness of simultaneity and juxtaposition: 'In much modernist art, narrative or temporal structure is weakened, or even disappears, in favour of an aesthetic ordering based on synchronicity' in which 'things do not so much fall apart as fall together' (p. 35).
3. An interest in paradox, ambiguity and uncertainty: 'Modernists view reality as necessarily constructed from relative perspectives, while they seek to exploit the aesthetic and ethical richness of ambiguous images, sounds and authorial points of view' (p. 36).
4. A rejection of the integrated human subject and the centred human body (p. 37).

These concerns clearly anticipate the present agenda of postmodernism, most particularly in their challenge to the taken-for-granted and in their willingness to experiment with other, no less 'truthful', representations of the world. This is not to say that modernism was without its problems; it too was scarred by sexism, and it was complicit in various racisms and colonialisms. But in confronting and understanding these entanglements – rather than simply sweeping them aside and assuming them to have been superceded – it may be possible to fashion a clearer understanding of the persistence of these same dilemmas in postmodernism. These are plainly political questions, and if they are not attended to then I fear the interest in the crisis of representation will tremble on the edge of an aestheticism. It is of course important to think about formal questions of composition and textual strategy, and these are not secondary matters at all. For the most part, it seems to me, human geography has been astonishingly conservative in its representations and until recently has shown remarkably little interest in the assumptions built into its cartographies, illustrations and narratives. This is changing, but these issues evidently cannot be broached in scholastic seclusion (an odd notion these days in any case) because they have the most practical, insistently material of consequences (see Harley, 1988; 1989).

One of the most significant contributions of postmodernism is supposed to be its attention to 'multiple voices', to the dangers of universalising a particular point of view, but in many cases this remains little more than a promissory note. Many so-called experimental ethnographies, which have attracted so much attention in human geography, nonetheless continue to marginalise women's voices, for example, and the relations between feminism and postmodernism are far from unequivocal (Nicholson, 1990). But poststructuralism and postcolonialism raise the same question in a larger and still more troubling arena. Poststructuralism is an awkward term, invented by American commentators to characterise a particular style of French intellectual work. One of its most characteristic concerns is a distinctly non-humanist conception of the human subject, the so-called 'decentring of the subject', which pays particular attention to the ways in which people occupy different, overlapping and sometimes contradictory subject-positions. These compound inscriptions of class, gender and race ought to be of great concern to any human geography, and make most of its assumptions about identity, consciousness and agency acutely problematic (see Deutsche, 1991). Postcolonialism is an even more difficult term, not least because it is far from clear that colonialism has been relegated to a distant past. What is more, the history of modern human geography is so closely bound up with the history of colonialism that these complicities have introduced a series of unacknowledged and unexamined assumptions into the very heart of the Anglo–American discipline that are profoundly insensitive to the meanings, values and practices of other cultures. Surprisingly Said's (1978) critique of Orientalism had little immediate impact on human geography, but the development of a more discriminating postcolonial critique – one which recognises that what Said described as a monolithic Orientalism was in fact fractured, heterogeneous and complex, made up of different constellations of power and knowledge in different sites – has made it impossible to ignore the privileges tacitly assumed by many British and North American writers. Even some of the seemingly most radical of writers have assumed a vantage point – and a voice – that tacitly adopts the positions and assumptions of a Western intellectual culture or which openly privileges 'the West' as a model and mirror for other peoples and other societies. Western Marxism, which once seemed so liberating in its break from the classical Marxian canon, is now seen by many commentators on the left as a distinctly Western discourse that suffers from the imperialisms and closures of its own adjective (Young, 1990). Structuration theory is preoccupied with constructions of modernity in which the capacities of people outside the West to think and act in different ways is virtually ignored. And early feminisms are seen as 'essentialist', collapsing the different situations, experiences and concerns of different women into a single model of 'woman' invariably drawn around the figure of the white, middle-class, heterosexual writer (Spivak, 1988). The very anger with which these various objections are often stated makes it clear that they address not simply (or even primarily) representation but also, and more urgently, *authorisation*. By what right and on whose authority does one claim to speak for those 'others', to call them into presence and to display them in the world-as-exhibition? On whose terms is a space created in which they are allowed to speak? From this perspective, representation in both its political and its textual senses is all too often turned into the art of incorporation and subsumption.

I have no immediate answers to these questions, but I do not doubt their seriousness. They impact upon some of the most taken-for-granted (and, as a result, rarely examined) practices of geographical inquiry. But in decentring our familiar assumptions, they must surely not condemn us to our own eccentric worlds. The present challenge for human geography is, I think, to find ways of comprehending those other worlds – including our relations with them and our responsibilities towards them – without at the same time being invasive, colonising and violent.

Noah's Ark

I hope the meaning of the passage from Julian Barnes's wickedly funny *History of the world in 10½ chapters* is now clear. While I think the dialogue between social theory and human geography has been immensely productive, I do not think social theory is an intellectual Noah's Ark that can save human geography from the floodwaters. Let me suggest three reasons, which flow from the arguments set out in this essay. In the first place the hull of social theory is so riddled with woodworm that major reconstruction is necessary to keep the vessel afloat. Social theory does not come ready made and, like any other discourse, it smuggles in its own assumptions and blind-spots. It is always partial, but those various partialities – which are embedded in our own human geographies – need to be called to account. In the second place, any new ark ought not to made entirely of gopher wood: it is the height of madness to assume that any single set of materials can serve all purposes equally well. Many critics now object to 'totalising theory', often in oddly totalitarian terms, but my concern is not so much that one ought to dispense with metanarratives (plural), but rather that one must attend carefully to what it is they put in place and, equally, what it is they exclude. Since no single theoretical system is capable of providing a complete and satisfactory set of answers, we need to find ways of living – critically and creatively – with theoretical dissonance. And in the third place, that ark must not be beached on top of a mountain. Social theory is not simply an intellectual workout, an exercise in conceptual gymnastics: if it fails to address significant political questions, to engage with the concerns of ordinary men and women – in all their variousness – and to enlarge our 'imaginative geographies', then the woodworm will surely do its work.

Notes

1. The metaphor brings with it other baggage, of course, and the language of exploration, discovery and, indeed, 'travel' raises more awkward questions than I can address here.
2. The term 'spatial science' comes from Hartshorne (1959, p. 157), who not only described geography as a spatial science but identified two others: significantly for the argument that I develop here these were astronomy and geophysics. I make this point to unsettle those who have portrayed Hartshorne as the architect of a geography wholly antithetical to spatial science; there were differences between his project and the New Geography that emerged in the 1960s but there were also powerful continuities.
3. The central sections of this essay anticipate and draw upon some of the arguments I have since set out in *Geographical Imaginations* (Oxford: Basil Blackwell), and an elaboration of those ideas will be found in that book.

4. I am aware that Habermas's later writings mark a series of significant departures from his previous discussion of knowledge-constitutive interests; but he has not altogether abandoned those early concerns, and in any case many of his discussions of science and technology as ideology are separable from those theoretical entanglements and continue to have a considerable purchase on the present.
5. Although Weber drew attention to the highly constricted nature of this conception of rationality, he did not intend this as a criticism of marginalist economics: see Clarke (1982).
6. It should not be forgotten that geography was also entered on the other side of the ledger: that its increasingly technocratic character was complicit in the instrumentalities that many radical movements were contesting; that it was shot through with assumptions about class, ethnicity and gender that all but paralysed the search for social justice; and that it was implicated in the planning and execution of US strategy in Vietnam, not least in the waging of ecological warfare against the North Vietnamese. *Antipode: a journal of radical geography*, which began publishing in August 1969, was at the forefront of a critical response to these developments within the Anglophone discipline.
7. I am thinking particularly of Althusser and Poulantzas: see Benton (1984).
8. I am not starry-eyed about this. Benhabib (1986) argues that critical social theory ought to involve both an explanatory–diagnostic and an anticipatory–utopian moment, but there is no doubt that critical human geography has shown more of an interest in the first than in the second. It is particularly sobering to realise how rapidly discussion of Harvey's *Social justice and the city* moved away from the first two words of the title and fastened on the last two.
9. That said, I recognise that many feminist writers insist that men cannot be feminists and I respect their objections to attempts to coopt their work into some supposedly more general (which is to say decidedly more masculine) framework. Moore (1988) has described this as a kind of 'gender tourism' in which 'male theorists are able to take package trips into the world of femininity' secure in the knowledge that they have return tickets to the world of masculinity. For a preliminary attempt to explore some landscapes of masculinity see Jackson (1991).

References

Anderson, P. (1983) *In the Tracks of Historical Materialism* (London: Verso).
Baynes, K., J. Bohman and T. McCarthy (eds) (1987) *After Philosophy: End or Transformation?* (Cambridge, Mass: MIT Press).
Benhabib, S. (1986) *Critique, Norm and Utopia: a study of the foundations of critical theory* (New York: Columbia University Press).
Benton, T. (1984) *The Rise and Fall of Structural Marxism: Althusser and his influence* (London: Macmillan).
Castells, M. (1983) *The City and the Grassroots: a cross-cultural theory of urban social movements* (London: Edward Arnold).

Clarke, S. (1982) 'From marginalism to modern sociology', in his *Marx, marginalism and modern sociology* (London: Macmillan), pp. 186–242.

Clifford, J. (1986) 'Partial truths', in James Clifford and George Marcus (eds), *Writing Culture: the poetics and politics of ethnography* (Berkeley: University of California Press), pp. 1–26.

Dear, M. (1986) 'Postmodernism and planning', *Environment and Planning D: Society and Space*, vol. 4, pp. 367–84.

Deutsche, R. (1991) 'Boys town', *Environment and Planning D: Society and Space*, vol. 9, pp. 5–30.

Eckersley, R. (1990) 'Habermas and green political thought', *Theory and Society*, vol. 19, pp. 739–76.

Foucault, M. (1979) *Discipline and Punish: birth of the prison* (London: Peregrine Books).

Foucault, M. (1980) *Power/Knowledge: selected interviews and other writings* (Brighton: Harvester Press).

Giddens, A. (1979) *Central Problems in Social Theory: action, structure and contradiction in social analysis* (London: Macmillan).

Giddens, A. (1981) *A Contemporary Critique of Historical Materialism*, Vol. 1, *Power, property and the state* (London: Macmillan).

Giddens, A. (1985) *A Contemporary Critique of Historical Materialism*, Vol. 2, *The nation-state and violence* (Cambridge: Polity Press).

Giddens, A. (1987) 'Out of the orrery: E. P. Thompson on consciousness and history', in his *Social Theory and Modern Sociology* (Cambridge: Polity Press), pp. 202–24.

Giddens, A. (1990) *The Consequences of Modernity* (Stanford: Stanford University Press).

Gregory, D. (1989) 'The crisis of modernity: human geography and critical social theory', in R. Peet and N. Thrift (eds), *New Models in Geography*, Vol. 2 (London: Unwin Hyman), pp. 348–85.

Gregory, D. (1990) '"Grand maps of history": structuration theory and social change', in J. Clark, C. Modgil and S. Modgil (eds) *Anthony Giddens: consensus and controversy* (Brighton: Falmer Press), pp. 217–33.

Gregory, D. (forthcoming) *Geographical Imaginations* (Oxford: Blackwell Publishers).

Habermas, J. (1971) *Toward a Rational Society* (London: Heinemann).

Habermas, J. (1978) *Knowledge and Human Interests* 2nd edn (London: Heinemann).

Habermas, J. (1987) *The Theory of Communicative Action*, Vol. II, *The critique of functionalist reason* (Cambridge: Polity Press).

Haggett, P. (1965) *Locational Analysis in Human Geography* (London: Edward Arnold).

Haggett, P. (1990) *The Geographer's Art* (Oxford: Blackwell Publishers).

Haraway, D. (1991) *Simians, Cyborgs and Women: the reinvention of nature* (New York: Routledge).

Harley, J. B. (1988) 'Maps, knowledge and power', in D. Cosgrove and S. Daniels (eds), *The Iconography of Landscape* (Cambridge University Press), pp. 277–312.

Harley, J. B. (1989) 'Deconstructing the map', *Cartographica*, vol. 26, pp. 1–20.

Hartshorne, R. (1959) *Perspective on the Nature of Geography* (Washington:

Association of American Geographers).

Harvey, D. (1973) *Social Justice and the City* (London: Edward Arnold).

Harvey, D. (1982) *The Limits to Capital* (Oxford: Basil Blackwell).

Harvey, D. (1989) *The Condition of Postmodernity: an enquiry into the origins of cultural change* (Oxford: Blackwell Publishers).

Heisenberg, W. (1972) *Physics and Beyond: encounters and conversations* (New York: Harper and Row).

hooks, b. (1990) Yearning: race, gender and cultural politics (Toronto: between the lines).

Jackson, P. (1989) *Maps of Meaning: an introduction to cultural geography* (London: Unwin Hyman).

Jackson, P. (1991) 'The cultural politics of masculinity', *Transactions of the Institute of British Geographers*, vol. 16, pp. 199–213.

Jameson, F. (1990) *Postmodernism or the Cultural Logic of Late Capitalism* (Durham: Duke University Press).

Ley, D. (1987) 'Styles of the times: liberal and neoconservative landscapes in inner Vancouver, 1968–1986', *Journal of Historical Geography*, vol. 13, pp. 40–56.

Lunn, E. (1985) *Marxism and Modernism: Lukàcs, Brecht, Benjamin, Adorno* (London: Verso).

Mann, M. (1986) *The Sources of Social Power*, Vol. 1, *From the beginning to C. 1760* (Cambridge University Press).

Massey, D. (1984) *Spatial Divisions of Labour: social structures and the geography of production* (London: Macmillan).

Merchant, C. (1990) 'The realm of social relations: production, reproduction and gender in environmental transformations', in B. L. Turner II, W. C. Clark, R. W. Kates, J. F. Richards, J. T. Mathews, W. B. Meyer (eds), *The Earth as Transformed by Human Action* (Cambridge University Press), pp. 673–84.

Mills, C. Wright (1959) *The Sociological Imagination* (New York: Oxford University Press).

Mirowski, P. (1988) 'Physics and the "Marginalist Revolution"', in his *Against Mechanism* (Totowa, NJ: Rowman and Littlefield), pp. 11–30.

Mirowski, P. (1989) 'The ironies of physics envy', in his *More Heat than Light: economics as social physics, physics as nature's economics* (Cambridge University Press), pp. 354–95.

Mitchell, T. (1988) *Colonising Egypt* (Cambridge University Press).

Mitchell, T. (1989) 'The world-as-exhibition', *Comparative Studies in Society and History*, vol. 31, pp. 217–36.

Moore, S. (1988) 'Getting a bit of the other: the pimps of postmodernism', in R. Chapman and J. Rutherford (eds), *Male order* (London: Lawrence and Wishart), pp. 165–92.

Nicholson, L. (ed.) (1990) *Feminism/Postmodernism* (New York: Routledge).

Poster, M. (1990) *The Mode of Information: poststructuralism and social context* (Cambridge: Polity Press).

Rouse, J. (1987) *Knowledge and Power: toward a political philosophy of science* (Ithaca: Cornell University Press).

Said, E. (1978) *Orientalism* (London: Routledge & Kegan Paul).

Sheppard, E. and T. Barnes (1990) *The Capitalist Space-Economy: geographi-*

cal analysis after Ricardo, Marx and Sraffa (London: Unwin Hyman).

Smith, N. (1990) *Uneven Development: nature, capital and the production of space*, 2nd edn (Oxford: Blackwell Publishers).

Soja, E. (1989) *Postmodern Geographies: the reassertion of space in critical social theory* (London: Verso).

Spivak, G. C. (1988) *In Other Worlds: essays in cultural politics* (New York: Routledge).

Thompson, E. P. (1978) *The Poverty of Theory and Other Essays* (London: Merlin).

Thrift, N. (1985) 'Bear and mouse or bear and tree? Anthony Giddens's reconstitution of social theory', *Sociology*, vol. 19, pp. 609–23.

Woolgar, S. (1988) *Science: the very idea* (London: Tavistock).

Wright, E. O. (1989) 'Models of historical trajectory: an assessment of Giddens's critique of Marxism', in D. Held and J. B. Thompson (eds), *Social Theory of Modern Societies: Anthony Giddens and his critics* (Cambridge University Press), pp. 77–102.

Young, R. (1990) *White Mythologies: Writing History and the West* (London: Routledge).

Part II

Perspectives in Human Geography

5

The Environmental Challenge

TIM BAYLISS-SMITH AND SUSAN OWENS

Introduction

The relationship between people and the natural environment has always been one of the central concerns of geography. From a somewhat disreputable past, tainted with the excesses of environmental determinism, we have arrived at a situation in which many geographers are centrally engaged in debates about environmental issues and policies. It is in the nature of these issues, however, that their analysis requires interdisciplinary treatment involving the natural and the social sciences as well as the humanities. We focus in this chapter on those areas in which human geographers, alongside other social scientists, have made important contributions to the debate.

'The environment' is a field with great breadth and diversity, and we hardly need to reiterate the way in which environmental issues have climbed to a prominent position on the political agenda, both nationally and internationally, during the past two decades. We can only touch in this chapter on some major themes, and we make no claim to be comprehensive. We therefore focus on five areas, each of which has been the subject of lively debate in recent years, with new empirical work and theoretical discussion to which geographers have made signficant contributions. We review first the social meaning of environment, itself a much disputed area, and the way in which different perspectives condition our perception of environmental problems. Closely linked to this is the analysis of environmentalism as a social movement, and we consider attempts to explain this phenomenon and to fit it into a coherent theoretical framework. We then turn to consider the question of causes of environmental problems, using famine as a case study to illustrate how simplistic and reductionist 'explanations' and prescriptions can be dangerous. Turning then to a different example – that of pollution in the West – we address the question, 'what determines the outcome of environmental conflict?' and discuss the implications of relevant empirical and theoretical work. Finally we consider the role of formal techniques, such as environmental assessment, in the decision-making process, and the evolving debate about their utility and limitations.

The Social Meaning of Environment

Einstein's definition of the environment as 'everything that isn't me' is appealing in its simplicity, but it evades the difficulty of understanding the social meaning of environment, and of disentangling the influence of different interpretations on the perception and definition of environmental problems.

Although 'environment' is a multidimensional concept, we can distinguish interpretations that are broadly anthropocentric from those with a bioethical basis. In the former the environment is seen as provider for human society of life support, resources, healthy surroundings and aesthetic satisfaction; it encompasses concern about survival, resource depletion, health and amenity (Goodin, 1976, discussed by Blowers, 1985). This philosophy is often associated with the view that environmental problems can be solved by 'resource management', the judicious use of natural resources so that they provide maximum benefit for humankind.

The neoclassical economic analysis of environmental problems also tends to see the environment in terms of utility. Environmental goods such as clean air and clean water are not exchanged in markets, and pollution is a 'negative externality'– a cost imposed on others without consent or compensation. Environmental problems, according to this perspective, occur because the conditions under which the unregulated market allocates resources efficiently are violated by the existence of common property resources, such as the atmosphere, and by externalities such as pollution (see, for example, Beckerman, 1989; Common, 1988; Pearce *et al.*, 1989). Solutions can then be seen in terms of correcting market failure by, for example, pricing previously 'free' environmental goods or taxing pollution. To do this implies that the environment has utility, though many economists accept that as well as having use value, the environment also has 'existence value' (Pearce, 1989).

It is the concept of 'existence value' that is absent from the more purely anthropocentric perspectives on the environment. The belief that the non-human world has interests and moral significance quite independent of its social utility forms a distinct strand of environmental philosophy. It is impossible to do justice here to what has developed into a complex debate (for further discussion, see Johnson, 1991; Paehlke, 1989; O'Riordan, 1981; Sprigge, 1991), but it is important to recognise the influence of these two fundamental perspectives – the anthropocentric and the bioethical – on the modern environmental movement. We return to this point below.

Some authors have been deeply critical of what they see as environmentalists' preoccupation with 'nature'. Pepper (1987, p. 76) argues that pressure groups campaign 'about what they imagine to be "nature" – i.e. whales, seals, other wildlife, the tropical rain forest', while showing scant concern about the environments of those living, for example, on inner-city housing estates (let alone in desperate conditions in Africa, Asia or Latin America). In similar vein, Weston (1986, p. 2) insists that 'the environment is much more than "nature"; it is the social, political, economic and physical world in which we live'.

However, while neglect of human conditions may be a feature of some bioethical and aesthetic/amenity strands in the social meaning of environment, there is little evidence to support the view that the environmental movement has been solely concerned with nature. The survival, resource-depletion and public-health elements of environment have been at least as important. In the late 1960s and early 1970s, for example, the major preoccupation of environmentalists was a neo-Malthusian concern about the depletion of non-renewable resources and the impossibility (as they saw it) of continued growth in a finite world. Their concern was for survival or at least, as critics were swift to point out, for survival of the more affluent sections of humanity. As concern has shifted towards the need for sustainable development, it retains a strongly utilitarian dimension. Furthermore, many environmental campaigns have centred around such issues as energy, pollution and transport, often with a strong public-health component (the campaign to remove lead from petrol is a classic example); and mounting concern about major problems in the Third World, such as deforestation and erosion, is directed not only at impacts on 'nature', but at the survival, both cultural and economic, of indigenous peoples.

Clearly the meaning of environment has important philosophical and political dimensions. We can gain further insight into these by considering the origins and nature of the modern environmental movement.

Environmentalism

Environmentalism, as a social movement, has proved at least as rich a source of fascination to social scientists as environmental problems per se. Geographers, alongside sociologists, social psychologists and political scientists, have been prominent in this debate and have made important contributions to our understanding of the origins, evolution and ideologies of the modern environmental movement.

Although the modern movement is widely agreed to have its origins in the 1960s, the philosophical and ideological roots of environmentalism have a much longer history. David Pepper (1984), in a comprehensive synthesis, traces diverse roots in classical science, in nineteenth-century conservationism and romanticism, in the writings of Malthus and Darwin and in a range of political ideologies. Lowe and Goyder (1983) also demonstrate that the movement has a long history, but they place particular emphasis on its roots in the late Victorian period when:

> there was a reversal of the rationalist, progressivist outlook deriving from the 'Enlightenment' which, with its confidence in the perfectibility of all things, had looked always to the improvement of nature and society through the exercise of human reason and ingenuity (Lowe and Goyder, 1983, p. 19).

These authors argue that environmental concern was an integral part of the late Victorian intellectual reaction to many of the tenets of economic liberalism. Groups led by social philosophers such as John Ruskin and William Morris gave expression to doubts about industrialism and urbanism, and vigorously opposed destruction of the cultural heritage and the natural world, which 'stood for continuity, stability and tradition, against the restless and rootless stirrings of industrial capitalism' (ibid., p. 20).

Lowe and Goyder identify two further 'eras of environmentalism' that stand out as particularly active periods in the evolution of the movement. One was in the middle interwar years, when the social base widened and many new pressure groups were formed, and the third – essentially the emergence of modern environmentalism – was apparent in the 1960s and early 1970s. We might now add a fourth, associated with the resurgence of concern about all things 'green' identifiable from the mid-1980s onwards. The essential point, however, is one of continuity of many ideas over a period of a century or more, though specific issues and the political expression of concern have varied both in time and space.

It is hardly surprising that a movement with a long history and diverse roots should be eclectic in the extreme, or that it should tend to defy both classification and simple explanation. In Lowe and Goyder's study of environmental groups in politics the movement is taken as 'an episode of collective behaviour, whose formal manifestations are the separate environmental groups' (ibid., p. 1), though they recognise that groups are only one indicator of a wider social movement and include in their definition a much broader, sympathetic 'attentive public'. Research has tended to focus (as in Lowe and Goyder's work) on Western environmentalism, but there is also increasing interest in environmental movements in the Third World and in what used to be the Eastern bloc (Adams, 1990; Durning, 1990; Pryde, 1991; Urfi, 1987; Waller, 1989). Many underlying themes are similar, however.

Most studies confirm that the environmental movement embraces a wide range of interests and objectives, but the ecocentrist/ technocentrist divide formalised by O'Riordan (1981) has nonetheless provided an enduring analytical framework. Ecocentrism is associated with a non-utilitarian view of the natural world, with bioethics, antimaterialism, rejection of notion of 'objective' science and little faith in the 'technical fix'. In contrast, technocentrists see increased material wealth as universally desirable, and achievable with sound resource management; theirs is a world in which 'value-free' science and technology ensure almost infinite potential to use natural resources in the service of humankind. Though much complexity is inevitably lost when a wide spectrum of values and beliefs is reduced to a simple dichotomy, it remains the case that 'the two modes are eminently recognisable in almost any public debate about environmental issues' (Pepper, 1984, p. 30). This is so in spite of the way in which the concept of sustainable development has tended to blur some of the divisions, at least in relation to previously polarised positions on economic growth and the environment.

One of the most interesting aspects of environmentalism 'is the challenge it has posed to existing political structures, orientated as they are to conventional conflicts between economic classes and the functional accommodation of producer interests' (Lowe and Rudig, 1986, p. 529). The movement as a whole cannot be identified with any single political ideology, nor is there any simple alignment of the ecocentrist/technocentrist dimension with the traditional left–right divide. Environmentalists have often claimed that green issues somehow transcend other political ideologies (see, for example, Porritt, 1984; Paehlke, 1989), ecocentrists because they claim to represent a wholly new paradigm, and technocentrists because they tend to regard environmental problems as politically neutral. The latter assertion can be readily dismissed, but the view that ecocentrism constitutes a 'new paradigm' has received a considerable amount of attention in the literature.

David Pepper (1984) points to the paradox of an ecocentrist movement that, as a proponent of radical social change, is essentially progressive and often seen as left of centre, while in other respects can be accused of being élitist and reactionary, pursuing essentially class-based interests in the preservation of the status quo. Ecocentrism has many roots and values in common with anarcho-communism and socialism: there is a striking similarity in the writings of, for example, Peter Kropotkin, Robert Owen and William Morris with those of modern ecocentrists. On the other hand the neo-Malthusian emphasis of some sections of the environmental movement in the 1970s on zero population and economic growth, with scant regard for the disastrous implications of such policies for the poor, led to bitter accusations of 'ecofascism' and, for a time at least, deep suspicion of environmentalism on the part of the underprivileged, at both the global and national scales. The vision of a decentralised society that has permeated so much ecocentrist literature (typified by the 'Blueprint for Survival' of Goldsmith *et al.*, 1972) can also be viewed either as progressive (in the anarcho-socialist tradition) or deeply conservative in its (sometimes implicit) assumptions about social structures and gender-specific roles.

During the 1980s the simplistic notion of zero growth was subject to much critical scrutiny and to a large extent superceded by the concept of 'sustainable development'. This first appeared in the World Conservation Strategy (IUCN and WWF, 1980) but is more usually associated with the report of the World Commission on Environment and Development (WCED), the Bruntland Report, published in 1987. Both, in contrast with earlier work, had a strong

Third-World dimension. Brundtland captures the essence of sustainability as follows: [handwritten annotation]

Environment and development are not separate challenges; they are inexorably linked. Development cannot subsist upon a deteriorating environmental resource base; the environment cannot be protected when growth leaves out of account the costs of environmental destruction (WCED, 1987, p. 37).

What was needed, the report argued, was economic development that was sustainable in terms of its impact on the resources of the biosphere; this does not imply zero growth, but it does recognise limits – possibly extendable – imposed by the need to respect the integrity of biogeochemical cycles.

Although in practice sustainability is proving difficult to define (let alone to achieve), the concept has been instrumental in changing the perception of 'environment' from that of a luxury affordable only by the rich to that of a necessity, both for survival and for further economic development. This change has made it more difficult for critics to sustain the argument that environmentalism is only about maintaining the privileges of the better off (though new controls must be clearly justified if they are not to be seen as economic protectionism in disguise). This is one instance where it is crucial to make a distinction between different meanings of 'environment': in the sense of survival, health and destruction of renewable resources, it is typically the poor that suffer most from environmental degradation and have potentially the most to gain from improvement (this point emerges clearly from our consideration of famine below). When 'environment' means amenity, aesthetics and bioethics, the argument becomes more complex.

While it is impossible to define environmentalism in terms of any single set of political values, it does not follow, as has sometimes been implied, that it transcends well-established political divisions. It clearly does not. The current state of this particular debate was probably best summed up by Scott (1990, p. 100) in his recent work on ideology and new social movements:

Rather than view ecological ideology as coherent and unambiguous, as its critics and some of its supporters have tended to do, it may be better to view it as disparate and eclectic in some respects. First, it has taken elements from existing ideologies . . .

and given them an ecological slant. Second, these pre-existing ideological cleavages differentiate varieties of ecological ideology.

We might expect some light to be shed upon environmental ideologies by a careful analysis of the factors behind the rise of modern environmentalism. Attempts to explain this phenomenon have attracted a great deal of attention from social scientists. In addition to a considerable body of essentially atheoretical survey research (attempting to measure, for example, the degree and stability of environmental concern, and to correlate environmental beliefs with demographic characteristics), we have seen the development of basic theoretical perspectives as well as specific case studies of environmental pressure groups and conflicts.

One of the most influential concepts has been Ronald Inglehart's thesis of 'postmaterialist value change' – the shift from predominance of economic and basic security values towards 'higher-order' needs for love, esteem and status, and for intellectual and aesthetic satisfaction (Maslow, 1970). Inglehart (1971, 1977, 1981) argued that such a shift in values could be identified in Western society during the postwar period of relative prosperity and security and, though not initially addressing environmental issues, he suggested in later work that postmaterialists 'furnish the ideologues and core support for the environmental, zero-growth and anti-nuclear movements' (Inglehart, 1982, quoted in Lowe and Rudig, 1986, p. 516).

Related to the concept of 'postmaterialist value change' is the hypothesis, mentioned above, that ecocentrism represents a new paradigm, involving a challenge to the core values and beliefs of industrial capitalism. This thesis is most coherently expressed in the work of sociologists Stephen Cotgrove and Andrew Duff (1980, 1981), who explored the attitudes of radical environmentalists, industrialists and trades unionists. They found that ecocentrism was characterised by a complex 'world view', not restricted to environmental issues. Elements of this world view (on collectivism and workplace relations, for example) were shared with trades unionists but there was a divergence on issues of growth and material prosperity. Significantly Cotgrove and Duff also found that it was not simply the 'middle class' who espoused ecocentrist ideals, but a specific element of the middle class mainly employed in the service sector. This observation led them to offer one possible explanation for environmentalism as 'an expression of the interests of those whose class position in the non-productive sector locates them at the periphery of the institutions and processes of industrial capitalist societies (Cotgrove and Duff, 1980, p. 341). Others have also based explanations for environmentalism on the concept of a 'new class' that seeks to establish itself as a political élite and has an objective self-interest in the maintenance and extension of the welfare and regulatory states. Lowe and Rudig (1986) provide an excellent review of this work. It might be fruitful to extend this line of argument to analysis of the links between environmentalism and radical intellectual movements in different cultural contexts: a notable feature of environmental movements in the former socialist states, for example, has been their close interconnection with ethnic nationalism (Amonashrilli, 1990; Smith, 1991).

The theory of postmaterial value change does not provide an entirely satisfactory basis for environmental sociology. It has been criticised on a number of grounds (Lowe and Rudig, 1986), but two points are particularly important. First, such 'explanations' for environmentalism effectively divorce the movement from real environmental problems. As Lowe and Rudig (1986, p. 518) put it:

> The environment is seen as just one among many 'post-materialist' issues which suddenly emerged to prominence, unrelated to any change in the environment, through a shift in values among people who had nothing else to worry about.

A second problem is that value change explanations, based upon Maslow's (1970) 'hierarchy of human needs', assume that environmental quality is a luxury, the concern only of people with 'nothing else to worry about'. For many crucial aspects of environmental concern, such an assumption simply cannot be justified. Nowhere is this better illustrated than in the complex set of human–environment interactions leading to hunger and famine. Such problems have formed an important constituent part of environmentalism. Acknowledging, then, that our understanding of the movement as a whole is still incomplete (and may require the benefit of hindsight before it is more fully developed), we move on to consider this particular environmental issue in some detail, illustrating the complexity of underlying factors and the danger of simplistic 'solutions'.

Hunger and Hazards as Environmental Issues

Despite the opportunity offered by modern travel, few people in the West have first-hand experience of the Third World – perhaps not many more than in colonial times. Nevertheless the problems of the Third World have entered into popular consciousness in a quite striking way. There is also a strong awareness of the inter-dependent character of environmental problems and their regional if not global character, and this new world-view is perhaps the most fundamental change in our late twentieth-century culture. As MacLuhan (1967, p. 62) remarked 25 years ago, 'we now live in a global village, a simultaneous happening':

> In an electric information environment minority groups can no longer be contained – ignored. Too many people know too much about each other. Our new environment compels commitment and participation (McLuhan 1967, p. 44).

Although conceived of in terms of information flow, this 'global village' metaphor is equally valid for the hydrological cycle, the ozone layer and the diffusion of carbon dioxide.

How are the environmental problems of the Third World now being defined, and how are they being explained? We concentrate here on the related issues of hunger and hazards. In the past decade some excellent geographical analyses have emerged from areas such as the Sahel, Bangladesh and New Guinea, on the origins of vulnerability to hazards, on indigenous technical knowledge and other coping mechanisms, and how this protection is eroded or enhanced by development policies (Watts, 1983a; Hewitt, 1983; Stoddart and Pethick, 1984; Richards, 1985; Blaikie and Brookfield, 1987; Corbridge, 1988; Adams, 1985, 1990). In this work food is generally regarded as the most fundamental of the resources that people derive from their environment. As such, the extent to which a population has an assured and adequate food supply represents a key measure of the adequacy of that population's ecological relationships, at least in the short term. In this sense famine fits clearly into the utilitarian category of environmental concern.

If we adopt this perspective then a famine or natural disaster that affects a population becomes a symptom of the loss of control experienced by that population over the environmental and socioeconomic processes governing its life-support system. In the West most people would now agree that this 'loss of control' is not merely the tragic fate of millions of Third-World peasants, but is something we are all beginning to experience in our interdependent, greenhouse world, and certainly something for which we all share responsibility. We are all castaways in the same lifeboat, or to use another metaphor that has often appeared in the environmental literature, we are all astronauts on Spaceship Earth and have a common interest in its life-support system.

A world-view that emphasises linkages at different spatial and temporal scales was once exclusive to geographers in their academic isolation. To an astonishing degree it has become the world-view that is generally shared among most literate people in the Western world. However, this rising tide of concern for human–environment relationships does not necessarily mean that our understanding of the world is thereby improved, and this is well illustrated by the many and varying perceptions of 'the world food problem'.

The statistics on nutritional status have always been imperfect, but the overall picture is very clear: despite major advances in technology and a Green Revolution in tropical agriculture, the world food problem is not really diminishing. A growing number of people are suffering from a deficient food intake, but at the same time they are found in a smaller number of countries in the world, and represent a shrinking proportion of the total world population (Grigg, 1985). So although deficient food intake remains a worldwide problem, to a greater extent than in the 1950s its direct effects are confined to certain social groups living in certain geographical regions. It is among the rural poor of sub-Saharan Africa and South and East Asia that we find today the principal victims of food deficit (FAO, 1987). Moreover, within these regions those at risk are found par- *environment vulnerability* ticularly in communities living in environments that are subject to seasonal droughts, floods, hurricanes and storm surges. Those who suffer from poverty and malnutrition tend, therefore, to be the same people who are vulnerable to the effects of natural hazards.

The fact that the main victims of malnutrition, famine and natural hazards are now confined to marginal rural environments and to marginalised groups of people within these environments affects our perception of their problems, and encourages myths and misconceptions. The places where vulnerable people live are little frequented by the successful, the prosperous and the powerful, while the poor, who must make a living in such areas, have little voice or representation. There is 'dry-season bias' and there is 'tarmac bias', since outsiders seldom travel away from roads or in difficult seasons of the year (Chambers, Longhurst and Pacey, 1981). As a result, although worldwide concern can be stimulated by television images of famine, drought or flood, the underlying causes of each crisis are usually not widely understood.

Every time there is a food crisis that briefly focuses the world's attention on what are otherwise forgotten peoples and remote places, the media provides instant analysis. They tend to answer the question 'why?' in one of the following ways:

- Famines result from environmental degradation or from perturbations in climate, latterly both interpreted as symptoms of the greenhouse effect.
- Famines are a symptom of a Malthusian crisis, and result from population growth exceeding the limits of subsistence resources.
- Famines are caused by the decline in traditional ecological practices, which used to allow people in non-Western societies to live in harmony with their environment. = Symptom of de-contextual. gist a people of sin in the South
- Famines are caused by those who manage or mismanage the economic system, for example by the inefficiency or corruption of national governments, or the self-interest of those who manipulate international terms of trade, bank loans and aid programmes.
- Famines are the result of isolation, ignorance and conservatism, which means that peasants operate in a situation of bounded rationality, and hence make bad decisions.

While these models are more sophisticated than primitive ideas that would blame the hungry for their own misfortune, none provides by itself an adequate explanation for most cases of deficiency in food supply. But if any one of the five models is isolated, supported, and given status as an 'explanation', then it quickly can be made to seem convincing. Each theory can be 'tested' through a careful selection of evidence, and each also has the power to convince through its own internal logic. It is in this way that explanatory models can achieve the status of ideology, with a far-reaching influence on public attitudes and policies. The process has been well demonstrated by David Harvey (1974) in his comparison of the Malthusian and Marxist models of population and resources. These alternative views were crucial elements of the polarised environmental debate that followed a series of neo-Malthusian publications in the early 1970s – particularly Dennis Meadows *et al.'s* (1972)

Limits to Growth and the writings of Paul Ehrlich (for example, 1970), who saw population growth as the root of all environmental problems. We now consider briefly the plausibility of each of the above five models in turn.

A More Hostile Natural Environment?

This model tends to regard human beings as helpless victims of their capacity to pollute and disrupt their planetary habitat. Linked to the idea that environmental problems somehow transcend political and economic systems, this view has become prevalent during the past two decades (and is perhaps more prominent in public perception than either Malthus or Marx). Until the 1970s disasters such as the Sahelian drought of 1972–4 and the succession of tropical cyclones that devastated Bangladesh at the time of its independence were regarded as random events. Attempts to demonstrate that droughts or hurricanes were becoming more frequent failed to convince, for lack of long-term data and because of clear evidence in history of geophysical events of equal or greater magnitude (Lamb, 1977). The human impact of droughts and storms may not have been as devastating in the past, but that was not because nature itself was less hostile then than now.

Events since the 1970s must cause us to revise this assessment. The scientific consensus is now that global warming (whatever its cause) has indeed been occurring, particularly from the 1880s to the 1940s and since the late 1960s. Not all regions have experienced the erratic but gradual rise in temperature (not, for example, the US), but as a general consequence we must now take seriously a predicted future of greater climatic extremes, causing droughts, floods and greater storminess.

In its fascination with this new scientific consensus there is a danger that popular opinion will begin to ascribe all problems, including malnutrition and famine, to the 'greenhouse effect'. A large body of research shows that, on the contrary, natural events only become hazardous when human beings locate themselves in vulnerable places and depend for their livelihoods on vulnerable resources (Sen, 1981; Watts, 1983b; Swift, 1989). Climate itself is not hazardous, but people may create for themselves hazardous circumstances through an inadequate adaptation. Since at least the 1960s geographers have been prominent in this area of work (White, 1974; Burton, Kates and White, 1978), and it is clear that the need for a better understanding of both physical and human dimensions of hazard occurrence is not going to diminish.

An Overpopulated World?   Malthus vs. Rome & Club
                                        2' the other
                                        2. theory

The second myth about famine is the biological fallacy of Malthus, which regained ground in revised form during the 1970s. As a result the spectre of overpopulation is often linked in the popular mind with environmental problems such as the greenhouse effect, even though such phenomena are much more the result of *how* we use the planet than of *how many* of us use it. Even so, the connection that Malthus made between a slowly expanding food supply and a rapidly growing demand because of population growth retains its power to convince.

Population growth is undoubtedly part of the problem of undernutrition (FAO, 1987). It is equally certain that it is never the complete explanation, and indeed restraining population is not necessarily an important part of any solution. But the real problem with the Malthusian model is that it offers a simplified and abstract view of the real world, and so produces a distorted diagnosis of poverty or hunger and an equally distorted prognosis of what to do about it (Harvey, 1974). The true role of population growth is only revealed by a microscale analysis of why agricultural land is degraded or is unavailable to those in need, or why certain households do not achieve a food supply that is adequate or secure. Such an analysis will reveal the importance of factors such as land tenure, overgrazing, economic dependency or marginalised social status, which will not emerge from regional models of population demand and aggregate food supply.

A Lost World of Traditional Wisdom?

For thousands of years being able to cope with uncertainty in food supply has been vitally important for agrarian people living in fluctuating environments. It is therefore not surprising that in the most deprived regions of the Third World we find societies that have developed a sophisticated range of responses or coping mechanisms (Chambers, 1983). These include social and economic measures for counteracting droughts, floods and storms, as well as other unpredictable intermittent events such as births, deaths and marriages (De Garine and Harrison, 1988). Strategies to counter uncertainty include environmental management practices, social adjustments, for example the reciprocal exchange of food or labour, and biological adaptations such as changes in activity levels (Longhurst, 1986; Rahmato, 1987; Corbett, 1988).

A crisis that goes beyond the normal extremes of seasonality or market fluctuation will require more extreme measures to prevent famine. In Hausaland, northern Nigeria, for example, these crisis measures include salvage operations on the farm, the sale or mortgage of assets, and migration, sometimes with animals (Watts, 1983a, 1988). Relief measures and patron assistance are also important. In recent years the tendency has been for some of these responses to be thwarted, while others have become necessary even in the face of normal seasonality. In Hausaland as elsewhere there is plenty of evidence that the effectiveness of the traditional coping strategies is being eroded, and they are no longer sufficient to prevent periodic hunger and destitution.

If they are no longer viable today, how effective were these adaptations in the past? We must confront this question before considering the revival of traditional practices as a plausible strategy for coping with the ruder shocks of the twenty-first century. The vision of a past 'golden age' of successful adaptation contains a grain of truth, but if accepted uncritically (as in some of the ecocentrist literature) it becomes yet another dangerous myth. While it is true that in many areas the rate of degradation and the scale of destitution has greatly accelerated in modern times, there is also plenty of evidence that the various circumstances that give rise to degradation and hunger have occurred again and again in human history.

Even in the Stone Age there were environmental crises. In Papua New Guinea the highlanders were once regarded as a 'newly-emerged' people lacking the technology or the cultural values that elsewhere result in resources being degraded and food supplies becoming insecure. However recent work by geomorphologists and archaeologists points to the great antiquity of agricultural impacts in New Guinea that led to a widespread conversion of forests to grassland 4000 years ago. Long before people in the classical world of the Greeks and Romans were having to confront problems of soil erosion, deforestation and population pressure, New Guinea highlanders had also created for themselves problems on an equivalent scale (Blaikie and Brookfield, 1987; Bayliss-Smith and Golson, 1992). In the New Guinea case, wetland drainage, terracing and sustainable agroforestry practices were all adaptive responses to problems that undoubtedly included seasonal hunger, while malnutrition was widespread at the time of European contact in the 1930s (Dennett and Connell, 1988; Bayliss-Smith, 1991).

We should therefore resist what Robert Chambers (1983, p. 85) calls the temptation 'to revive the Noble Savage . . . as the Rational Peasant whose actions are perfectly judged exercises in optimisation that even well-informed computers can only struggle to simulate'. It is obvious that plenty of these well-informed and rational decision-makers must always exist in rural society, but it is equally apparent that in recent decades these people have been powerless to prevent famine and disaster vulnerability. What has gone wrong?

An Exploitative Political Economy?

It is ironic that the 1980s, a period of collapse for official Marxist ideology, should also have seen the tacit acceptance of the underlying Marxist arguments as they relate to hunger and hazards. Poverty, vulnerability, powerlessness and their nutritional consequences are now widely accepted as symptoms of 'underdevelopment', or some other euphemism for the same phenomenon. Underdevelopment itself is widely interpreted as a symptom of a process whereby surplus value and surplus product are extracted from people under conditions of unequal exchange. The Brandt Report, the Brundtland Commission and even the World Bank (using different language) all accept this basic thesis. Overdevelopment and the resulting environmental crisis is the other side of the coin, but the coin is now recognised as having two sides.

What still divides those who analyse these problems is not the reality of the processes of political economy, but the degree of primacy to accord to them. What perplexes governments and international agencies is that global capitalism seems to generate prosperity for increasing numbers but simultaneously impoverishes a significant proportion, whose circumstances thereby become more marginalised. There is also a belated recognition that women everywhere are likely to be an exploited group within a capitalist system that undervalues (in fact, ignores) domestic work and childrearing. And recently, too, an awareness of the environmental impacts of all forms of 'development' has distracted policy makers from these basic questions of social justice (Adams, 1990).

An analysis of the political economy that marginalises the weak and so enhances their vulnerability must be part of any attempt to explain why certain people experience hunger and catastrophe, whereas others are relatively protected (Sen, 1981; Chambers, 1989; Swift, 1989). However, when 'underdevelopment' is regarded as the whole truth then it degenerates into economic determinism and becomes as misleading as the Doomsday, Malthusian and Rational Peasant models.

The Bounded Rationality of the Vulnerable?

In a pure market economy there is no such thing as a lucky capital-ist. There are good entrepreneurs and bad entrepreneurs, and the bad ones go out of business because of suboptimal decisions made in a situation of imperfect knowledge. When translated to peasant society, this model implies that poor farmers are those who oper-ate inefficiently because of ignorance, isolation and conservatism. The Green Revolution of the 1970s involved the adoption of high-yielding varieties of rice and maize and a new high-input technology, and was visualised by many in the West as a great leap forward that would extend limits to growth and enable peasants to escape from the bounded rationality of their traditional farming practices. In fact the Green Revolution has been adopted in a very partial way, and with very mixed results (Bayliss-Smith and Wanmali, 1984). In contrast, where we see successful 'revolutions' in agriculture they usually emerge out of existing indigenous technical knowl-edge, whereas transplanted knowledge and technology is seldom so successful (Richards, 1985).

In health and nutrition too, research shows that most of what people want to do is correct and sensible, in other words rational, but much of the time people are unable to act on their knowledge (Pacey and Payne, 1985). It is not their rationality that is bounded, but rather their freedom from constraints. This simple truth has many important policy implications. For example, if we were to believe that ordi-nary peasants make bad environmental decisions because they are rationally bounded, then there would be a clear need for the estab-lishment of a centralised corps of management that is not so bounded. In fact this top-down managerial approach which ignores or even despises local knowledge is inefficient, and indeed may even cre-ate its own disaster. As Sen (1981) has demonstrated, the history of many famines is a history of centralised mismanagement in the face of a depleted but still adequate food availability.

As we have seen, some of the disagreement over the causes of famine and disaster-vulnerability reflects genuine differences in ideology and interpretation. In addition some differences stem from the great range of geographical scales that need to be considered. The seasonal food deficit that is being experienced in a particular household has a proximate cause that probably relates to recent events of local origin. It also has an ultimate cause that relates to long-term processes of population growth, environmental degradation and/or marginal status within an emerging regional, national and international political economy. In other words there is a nested hierarchy of scales, extending from the person in his or her household within a particular community or locality, up to the regional and larger geopolitical units in which the micro-reality is located.

Geographers traditionally operated at the scale of the region, but they have been forced to move to different scales in the search for a better explanation. In relation to food scarcity, many social scientists now identify the household as the most satisfactory scale for analysis (Dugdale and Payne, 1987; Corbett, 1988). However those who formulate policy must generalise at a larger spatial scale, even though no one can be confident that improvements in social justice at the macroscale will necessarily trickle down to particular communities or individuals in need. On the other hand, policies directed at particular communities will fail unless they take heed of wider geopolitical realities, for example market prices, civil wars dependence on the infrastructure provided by central government, such as roads. What is needed, and what geographers should seek to provide, is an integrated analysis that acknowledges this nested hierarchy of spatial scales, as well as recognising the historical and cultural dimension of every pattern of resource use.

In summary, understanding malnutrition and famine will usually require us to integrate elements from each of the five models considered, and other kinds of explanation. The new challenge for geography is to confront the full complexity of human–environment relationships: it will be unable to contribute much to explanation if it adopts a reductionist approach in its attempt to make sense of an increasingly hazardous real world.

The need to avoid reductionist explanations, to take account of both the specific and the general and to consider the role of individual agents as well as underlying structural factors, has in fact become an increasingly important theme across the whole environmental field. It applies as much to environmental conflict in the West as to problems of ecological degradation and hunger in the Third World. In our next section we see how this theme has been developed in a Western context, and in particular in relation to a specific conflict over pollution in the UK.

Environmental Conflict: what Determines the Outcome?

In the preceding section we considered the nature and causes of a major environmental problem: there are many other examples of this broadly 'problem-centred' approach. But case studies of specific environmental conflicts have also formed an important part of the tradition of analysis of environmental issues and policies, especially in Western countries. Some classic studies in the 1970s, concerning, for example, bitter conflicts over power lines, reservoirs and roads (Gregory, 1971; Kimber and Richardson, 1974; Smith, 1975), made an important contribution to the literature. Case studies have tended, however, to be descriptive and atheoretical, often failing to locate issues and events within a broader conceptual framework or to use the findings for the advancement of theory. An important exception to this generalisation has been the work of Andrew Blowers, particularly his classic study of conflict over brickworks pollution in Bedfordshire (Blowers, 1984, 1985).

Blowers identifies certain key questions that are fundamental to any analysis of environmental conflict:

– Why are there environmental conflicts?
– What issues and interests are involved?
– What are the sources of power and how are they deployed?
– What are the social and geographical implications and consequences of such conflicts?
– What are the most satisfactory explanations of the outcome?

In addressing these questions (which are not unlike those we might ask about broader problems such as famine) we may adopt a number of different theoretical perspectives. Many studies of environmental conflict have implicitly assumed a pluralist system with emphasis on the role of, and competition between, individual agents. Pluralism is characterised by participation, an open decision-making process, a responsive political system and (in some models) a neutral state. Actors influence events, power is not concentrated and the outcome of conflict will be determined by the balance of interests in any particular circumstances. An alternative, structuralist perspec-

structuralist [handwritten annotation] tive sees outcomes determined not by the actions of individual agents, *approach* [handwritten annotation] but by more fundamental aspects of social change such as class relations and economic restructuring. Broadly, the modern state will *more look* [handwritten annotation] act to create conditions favourable to capital accumulation, though *at the* [handwritten annotation] the outcome of specific conflicts may not be constrained in this *background* [handwritten annotation] way. Pepper (1984) and Sandbach (1980) provide good examples of the structuralist perspective in their respective analyses of environmentalism and environmental conflict.

Corporatism is an additional perspective combining aspects of both agency-based and structuralist explanations (Blowers, 1985). It recognises that certain interests have privileged access to decision makers and that state agencies may cooperate with them. It also incorporates the important concept of 'non-decision making', a term first used by Crenson (1971) in his study of pollution politics in North-American cities, to describe the way in which certain groups have the power to prevent the emergence of issues on the political agenda and the inability or unwillingness of those adversely affected to make a successful challenge.

Blowers acknowledges that case studies are idiosyncratic, but argues that they illustrate the processes at work in society and can illuminate the relationship between structures and agencies. His study of the London Brick controversy is illustrative of many similar conflicts. It also benefits from the special insights of participant observation, since he was a member of Bedfordshire County Council throughout the period concerned. To understand his arguments it is necessary to have an overview of the course of the conflict itself.

In 1979 the London Brick Company proposed two new plants in a traditional area of brickmaking in Bedfordshire. These plans met with considerable resistance, orchestrated by a group chaired by the Marquis of Tavistock and including environmentalists, local politicians and business and farming interests. Pollution was the key issue in the controversy, encompassing both health and amenity aspects of environmental concern. London Brick maintained that the controls demanded by their opponents were neither technically nor economically feasible and in this were supported by the government's central air pollution inspectorate. Nevertheless Bedfordshire County Council attempted to apply a pollution control condition to planning permission for the first phase of the new works. Soon afterwards London Brick announced its intention to shift priority to investment in Cambridgeshire, where it had recently received consent for new works without a pollution condition. Then, as recession deepened, it selected the second largest works in Bedfordshire for closure, with the loss of 1100 jobs, but also let it be known that if an acceptable permission could be obtained in Bedfordshire it would regain priority for investment. Employment, not pollution, now became the major issue and the company and the trade unions formed a powerful alliance of interests. Permission for a new works in Bedfordshire was ultimately granted without any pollution condition on the first phase.

Blowers finds support for the structuralist interpretation of this outcome on a number of points. First, considering the longer term (including the subsequent fortunes of brickmaking in Bedfordshire), he argues that changing economic factors could be seen to be of singular importance: though the conflict in Bedfordshire was intense and protracted, it impinged little on the overall strategy of the company. Second, the conflict demonstrates the advantages conferred by the relative mobility of capital. Third, the company received support from the state, implicitly throughout the conflict and explicitly from the then Alkali Inspectorate. He concludes that:

> The structuralist case seems both persuasive and plausible offering an explanation which stresses the wider economic context, the relative power of capital over labour and more local interests, and the limits of political change open to the state in a capitalist economy (Blowers, 1985, p. 22).

On the other hand Blowers acknowledges the existence of a plurality of interests, each of which exerted some influence on the course of the conflict and on its specific outcomes. Thus:

> In several respects – the competition among interests, their ability to penetrate the decision-making process, the visibility and openness of decision-making – this case demonstrates the role of agencies in a pluralist political system (ibid., p. 23).

However this explanation is inadequate for a number of reasons, most crucially because it fails to analyse the interests represented by the participants and consequently the sources of power they were able to command. London Brick was ultimately more powerful than the opposition because of its privileged access to government officials and decision makers and its considerable regional and national influence. These structural advantages are, however, 'mitigated by the variety of economic and political circumstances that enable agencies to affect the precise outcomes reached at different times and in different places' (ibid., p. 24). Structural and agency-based perspectives are not mutually exclusive in attempting to explain the outcome of environmental conflict.

Science, Policy and Public Participation: Assessing Environmental Impacts

Our final important area of debate also relates to the question, 'what determines the outcome of environmental conflict?' It is the debate over the role in the policy process of more or less formalised procedures and techniques such as environmental assessment (EA) and risk assessment. We are concerned less with the techniques themselves than with conflicting views about their neutrality and their ultimate influence on the outcome of events. Geographers have been at the forefront of the development of such techniques; pioneering work on environmental impact assessment in the UK, for example, was carried out in the Department of Geography at the University of Aberdeen during the 1970s (stimulated in part by the pressures arising from the development of North Sea oil and gas resources). We focus here on EA, though the debate is relevant to a broader concept of assessment and public participation that would also incorporate, for example, various forms of public hearing and consultation.

The concept of EA – the prior identification of the environmental effects of developments – originated in the US in the 1960s and was embodied in the 1969 *National Environmental Policy Act*. This required that all federal agencies produce environmental impact statements for major projects, detailing their anticipated environmental effects and, where appropriate, measures that would be taken to ameliorate them. Many countries now have some form of environmental impact legislation. The European Community's Environmental Assessment Directive became law in all member states in 1988, with the aim of anticipating and mitigating the negative environmental effects of new development and, of course, of ensuring that similar measures are applied in all member states to avoid unfair competition and 'environmental dumping'. Even in the Third World EA is becoming more prominent, as governments and aid agencies attempt to reduce the environmental damage all too often associated with 'development'. International organisations such as the World Bank have come to require environmental assessment of projects as a condition for funding.

EA grew partly out of dissatisfaction with cost benefit analysis (CBA). CBA requires that all the costs and benefits expected to flow from particular decisions be reduced to a common metric, and money has proved the most convenient measuring rod. Such a transformation is particularly difficult, however, for many environmental intangibles and early attempts to incorporate them into CBA, most infamously in the attempt of the Roskill Commission to evaluate alternative sites for London's third airport, were severely criticised (see, for example, Adams, 1970; Buchanan, 1981; Self, 1970).

EA does not require that all impacts be measured in monetary terms. New trunk roads in Britain, for example, are assessed using a combination of CBA and EA. The former places monetary values on such variables as time saving, reduction in accidents and savings in vehicle-operating costs. The latter assesses, in non-monetary terms, such effects as noise, visual impact and ecological damage. To some extent this simply defers the problem of comparing tangible and intangible costs and benefits, and critics believe that environmental costs are subsequently afforded very low priority when decisions about new roads are made. Some economists argue that the monetary valuation of environmental goods, though difficult, would give the environment a higher profile in the decision-making process (for example, Common, 1988; Pearce, 1989). Others maintain that attempting to put a price on intangibles through techniques that measure people's 'willingness to pay' are methodologically and conceptually flawed (see, for example, Sagoff, 1988). This issue developed into a lively debate in the 1980s.

Though it can be a broader, more qualitative assessment, EA shares *environmental utilitarian* with CBA the utilitarian notion of balancing costs and benefits, with its roots in the neoclassical economic concept of allocative efficiency: the new allocation of resources resulting from any policy decision is considered to be more 'efficient' if those who gain, gain enough to compensate those who lose, whether or not they actually do so. In other words it is the *net* benefits of decisions that count, hence the need in CBA to reduce diverse costs and benefits in time and space to a single figure representing 'net present value'. EA does not seek to do this, but conceptually it is part of the same process of weighing up the social costs and benefits of particular actions.

Broadly, we may consider the critique of techniques such as EA on two levels – that which focuses on the methodology and that which claims to identify fundamental flaws in principles or application.

Methodological issues will be dealt with fairly briefly here, though there is now a huge literature dealing with methodologies for environmental impact assessment, typically based on some form of impact matrix (Wathern, 1988, provides a good overview). Important questions include what should be the subject of EA (one of the issues that held up the EC directive for five years) and where the boundaries of an assessment should be drawn. How, for example, should analysts treat (or even identify) second- and third-order effects, which might be distant in time and space? The problem is illustrated by a question that arose at the Windscale inquiry into a nuclear-reprocessing facility in the UK – whether the impact of the plant extended to the effects of uranium mining on Aboriginal sacred sites in Australia.

Measurement of impacts is another important issue: often these will be in physical units and must give rise ultimately to the problem of comparing and combining incommensurables; and some impacts remain stubbornly difficult to quantify. Then there is the issue of how the information should be presented. The earlier environmental impact statements in the US became so enormous in an attempt to avoid challenge by environmental groups in the courts that the legislation had to be revised to restrict their scope. All of these questions have exercised the minds of researchers for at least two decades. Few would argue that they have been satisfactorily resolved, though many would agree that the formal requirement to consider the potential environmental effects of a defined range of projects (in the EC this includes power stations, trunk roads and major chemical works, for example) is a step in the right direction.

The higher-level critique has largely been concerned with two more fundamental aspects of techniques such as EA. First, it has entailed a rejection of the positivist notion that such techniques provide objective, 'value-free' information to inform the political process, and the idea (implied especially in some of the earlier literature) that the 'science' of EA and the 'politics' of decision making are neatly separate. Second, it has questioned the pluralist assumption that more information and more debate will lead to better policy decisions. Many authors have focused on the potential for powerful groups to manipulate formalised decision-making techniques in their own interests, and/or for the state to use them in the process of legitimation.

For some critics EA was suspect because it was 'basically defensive: . . . about preserves, about territorialism, about exclusion, non-access, non-use of resources' (Eversley, 1976, p. 131). Eversley saw EA as an élitist instrument that, far from being value-neutral, could be used by those in a privileged position to protect amenities and thereby deny the benefits of economic progress to those who did not already enjoy them. If EA delayed aid for a hydro-electric dam, or prevented the violation of a beautiful landscape by power lines, for example, this would increase the cost of electricity for the poor, but protect the amenities of only a few. In a Third-World context the few who enjoy such amenities (for example, through the conservation of wildlife) might not even be inhabitants of the country concerned. But environmental issues do not fit easily into this rather simplistic model of class conflict. Such criticisms imply that large-scale development and associated environmental degradation are invariably in the interests of the poor, and they also assume a degree of success for environmental opposition in preventing developments, which has simply not been the experience in practice. For other critics it has been the use of EA to *legitimise* developments that has been the main cause of concern.

Structuralists such as Francis Sandbach see the problem not in terms of middle-class activists using EA to block developments, but in terms of a corporatist alliance of capital and state using such techniques to 'convert political and normative issues . . . into bogus technical ones' (Sandbach, 1980, p. 104). The techniques would be used – rather like the system of public inquiries into major developments in the UK – to legitimise developments on the grounds that a thorough and objective investigation had taken place and environmental costs and risks had been weighed against the benefits of the project. In demanding better assessment procedures and more public participation, environmental groups had been 'duped into the dominant political ideology of pluralism whereas in fact the pressures to develop nuclear power, waste reprocessing . . . and a motorway network are closely related to the nature and demands of modern capitalism' (ibid., p. 125). Essentially similar criticisms might be applied to many prestigious aid projects in the Third World.

Unlike Eversley, Sandbach suggests that such developments are *not* in the interests of the mass of people. While environmental conflict may indeed sometimes involve the different ability of the lower and middle classes to mobilise resources, his emphasis is on conflict 'between the dominant capital classes and the rest of the community' (ibid., p. 133). Blowers might agree, though would probably favour a less rigidly structuralist interpretation.

Brian Wynne (1975) addresses more explicitly the question of the 'neutrality' of all forms of technology assessment, drawing on the long-standing philosophical perspective that argues that in science and social science the innocent collection of data is itself theory laden. Data collection, he argues, 'is selectively constrained and structured by the prior commitment to consensus around a particular idea of the goals, purpose and meaning of social life', and technology assessment is:

> an integral part of a much more broad-ranging attempt to secure social consensus around a corporate–industrial consumer society, in which the latter institutions control a much wider range of social activity than . . . hitherto (Wynne, 1975, p. 108).

Seen in this light, techniques such as EA are not at all neutral. Wynne, like Sandbach, sees them as part of a legitimation process, necessary to achieve a degree of consensus around corporate capitalist goals. This would explain the reluctance to extend the remit of EA from individual projects to the policies that underlie them (something for which the British public inquiry system has also been much criticised). 'When the light of examination reaches the door of corporate capitalist institutions and values', argues Wynne, 'the beam is hastily switched elsewhere' (ibid., p. 125).

The critique of these methods of assessment is a powerful one. It can itself be criticised for its emphasis on Western capitalism, though it might be argued that the need for legitimisation and consensus has been most acute in the Western democracies. In practice, however, the methods continue to be developed with scant attention to the more philosophical elements of the debate.

Another problem with the structuralist critique is that it appears to offer no scope for agents ever to modify the constraints within which they operate: developments will occur if they are in the interests of corporate capital and environmental groups who participate in assessment procedures and public inquiries are merely being duped into becoming part of the legitimation process. While many will recognise an element of truth in this, developments over the past few decades would also suggest that circumstances have not been immutable. Few could deny that environmental considerations have achieved a high, sometimes even dominant position on the political agenda, that legislation has tightened considerably and that attitudes towards the environment have changed beyond recognition. Perhaps the most interesting question for the 1990s is whether such developments really represent a paradigm shift – the beginnings of profound structural changes in the status quo – or whether they are merely another stage of adaptation and legitimation in late-twentieth-century capitalism.

Conclusion: Environmental Geography and the Social Sciences

In this chapter we have argued that an awareness of some form of environmental challenge is now widely shared. The environment that was for so long regarded in Western thought as a limitless frontier of commercial opportunity, or as a common property resource not needing special care, is being reassessed. This environment is now increasingly perceived to be fragile, neglected and hostile to the limitless expansion of human endeavour, and perhaps even to human life itself. The reasons for this perception are no longer in the realm of arcane knowledge: we all now recognise the functional linkages between the local environment and the biosphere, between North and South, and between rich and poor. The temptation to construct all-encompassing theories about the origins of the crisis has not been resisted, and we are bombarded in the media with so-called explanations.

In this situation the role of geography has become somewhat para-doxical. The subject has been displaced from its self-appointed position as the guardian of the interdisciplinary frontier between the natural and the social sciences. As the search for a more complete explanation for environmental problems has intensified, so scholars originating in other disciplines have found themselves converging on this crossroads. Meanwhile the new disciplines of environmental science and human ecology have emerged and have also established for themselves an interdisciplinary role. In all these cases the nature of research requires that individuals carve out for themselves a specialised niche, but more and more they are doing this within a strategy of collective endeavour that acknowledges explicitly the interdisciplinary linkages between social science and natural science aspects of the environmental problems. Geographers have the training to conceptualise these linkages with relative ease, although many have preferred instead to specialise within an ever-expanding field of knowledge.

In this context the environmental challenge represents a challenge to geography itself. We believe – and have tried to show through the various examples reviewed in this chapter – that we urgently need a holistic intellectual framework that will provide for us the means to uncover and to confront the interdisciplinary nature of environmental problems. We agree with David Stoddart's suggestion that:

> We need to claim the high ground back: to tackle the real problems: to take the broader view: to speak out across the subject boundaries on the great issues of the day (by which I do not mean the evanescent politics of Thatcher, Reagan and Gorbachev) (Stoddart, 1987a, p. 334).

Events in the five short years since Stoddart wrote these words give added point to his message: Thatcher, Reagan, Gorbachev have all been displaced, but meanwhile the world population has risen by 400 millions, a further half-million square kilometres of tropical forest has been cleared, a growing ozone hole has been discovered over the poles, and global warming has become a scientifically respectable paradigm. In this situation, as geographers we not only have an opportunity, we also have a responsibility to speak out on environmental issues, taking advantage of our training as generalists as well as making our contribution as specialists.

It has been fashionable within some sections of the discipline to talk about the morality (or lack of it) of recent geographical research, with criticism often targeted at the new geography of the 1960s and 1970s. As Stoddart has argued, from an environmental perspective this debate misses the point completely: 'the true obscenity . . . is advocacy of research on worthless trivia, while the great issues of the day are totally ignored' (Stoddart, 1987b, p. 293). But if we accept the environmental challenge as defining our research agenda for the foreseeable future, then it is vital that we examine carefully what it is we are trying to say, and how we should say it.

In this chapter we have considered some reasons for ideological, methodological and even factual disagreement in areas such as environmentalism, hazard response, the genesis of famine, and environmental assessment. Disentangling these conceptual issues is an intellectual challenge for all scholars in the environmental field. But what of geography itself? We would argue strongly that an important way forward for the subject is for it not to lose touch with its roots in regional geography. By examining the distinctiveness of places we can explore problems of people and environment within regions, and so help to bridge a gap between academic theory and real-world practice that in the environmental field can be enormous.

Geographers must therefore become literate theorists, but also must resist the temptation to reduce the real world to a set of homogenous abstractions. Seductive metaphors such as 'spaceship earth' and 'the global village' imply that the very existence of ecological interconnections and a global economy has somehow meant that everywhere has become the same. If geographers are to retain a distinctive and useful voice, then more than anyone they should be insisting that the proper analysis of environmental problems involves a respect for the basic facts of geographical diversity. The reductionist, ethnocentric or environment-free theories of social science need to be tested in 'a palpable, tangible real world peopled by the real men and women who have transformed it' (Stoddart, 1987a, p. 331). Yet even within the discipline of geography there are some who

> seem conspicuously ignorant of the fact that some parts of the Earth are hot, others cold; some wet, others dry; some high, others low; some forested, others desert; some empty of human beings, others desperately overcrowded and becoming more so; so that human societies throughout the world are divided by culture, language, religion, politics and *genres de vie* (Stoddart, 1987b, p. 293).

If we abandon the world-view of geography then we will be dealing with space and not place, with human agency rather than people, and with abstract categories and symbols rather than with specific situations. The harsh reality of pollution, hazard and hunger is specific in time and space. It is an insult to victims of environmental mismanagement for us to take refuge in what Stoddart calls 'a verbalized world where words too readily substitute for thought and action' (ibid.).

These, then, are the various dimensions of the environmental challenge. Firstly, worldwide, there is the daily struggle of people wishing to meet their modest but often unattainable objectives within an environment that is being divided, expropriated and degraded in ever more subtle ways. And, secondly, there is the challenge to those who seek to comprehend this process, to anticipate its various outcomes and to mitigate its worst effects. Geographical knowledge will be crucial in enriching this debate and in rescuing it from the cul-de-sac of reductionism, but that does not mean that geography as a discipline will necessarily be part of this project unless it can maintain its unified framework and its regional consciousness, and so avoid absorption by the social sciences at large.

References

Adams, J. (1970) 'Westminster: the Fourth London Airport?', *Area*, vol. 2, no. 2, pp. 1–9.

Adams, W. M. (1985) 'The downstream impacts of dam construction: a case study from Nigeria', *Transactions of the Institute of British Geographers*, NS, vol. 10, pp. 292–302.

Adams, W. M. (1990) *Green Development: Environment and Sustainability in the Third World* (London: Routledge and Kegan Paul).

Amonashrilli, P. (1990) 'Perestroika and the new pressure groups in Georgia: a successful ecological movement', *International Journal of Urban and Regional Research*, vol. 14, pp. 322–6.

Bayliss-Smith, T. P. (1991) 'Food security and agricultural sustainability in the New Guinea Highlands: vulnerable people, vulnerable places', *IDS Bulletin*, vol. 22, no. 3, pp. 5–11.

Bayliss-Smith, T. P. and J. Golson (1992) 'A Colocasian Revolution in the New Guinea Highlands? Insights from Phase 4 at Kuk', *Archaeology in Oceania*, vol. 17, pp. 1–21.

Bayliss-Smith, T. P. and S. Wanmali (eds) (1984) *Understanding Green Revolutions: Agrarian Change and Development Planning in South Asia* (Cambridge University Press).

Beckerman, W. (1989) *Pricing for Pollution* (London: Institute of Economic Affairs).

Blaikie, P. and H. C. Brookfield (1987) *Land Degradation and Society* (London and New York: Methuen).

Blowers, A. (1984) *Something in the Air: Corporate Power and the Environment* (London: Harper and Row).

Blowers, A. (1985) *Environment and Politics in a Capitalist Society* (Milton Keynes: Open University Press).

Buchanan, C. (1981) *The Stansted Controversy: No Way to the Airport* (London: Longman).

Burton, I., R. W. Kates and G. F. White (1978) *The Environment as Hazard* (New York: Oxford University Press).

Chambers, R. (1983) *Rural Development: Putting the Last First* (Harlow: Longman).

Chambers, R. (1989) 'Editorial introduction: vulnerability, coping and policy', *IDS Bulletin*, vol. 20, no. 2, pp. 1–7.

Chambers, R., R. Longhurst and A. Pacey (1981) *Seasonal Dimensions to Rural Poverty* (London: Frances Pinter).

Common, M. (1988) *Environmental and Resource Economics: An Introduction* (London and New York: Longman).

Corbett, J. (1988) 'Famine and household coping strategies', *World Development*, vol. 16, pp. 1099–112.

Corbridge, S. (1988) 'Marxism, post-Marxism and the geography of development', in R. Peet and N. Thrift (eds) *New Models in Geography* (London: Allen and Unwin), pp. 1–54.

Cotgrove, S. and A. Duff (1980) 'Environmentalism, middle class radicalism and politics', *Sociological Review*, vol. 28, pp. 333–51.

Cotgrove, S. and A. Duff (1981) 'Environmentalism, values and social change', *British Journal of Sociology*, vol. 32, pp. 92–110.

Crenson, M. A. (1971) *The Un-Politics of Air Pollution* (Baltimore: Johns Hopkins University Press).

De Garine, I. and G. A. Harrison (eds) (1988) *Coping with Uncertainty in Food Supply* (Oxford: Clarendon Press).

Dennett, G. and J. Connell (1988) 'Acculturation and health in the Highlands of Papua New Guinea', *Current Anthropology*, vol. 29, pp. 273–99.

Dugdale, A. E. and P. R. Payne (eds) (1987) 'A model of seasonal changes in energy balance', *Ecology of Food and Nutrition*, vol. 19, pp. 231–45.

Durning, A. B. (1990) 'Environmentalism South', *The Amicus Journal* (summer).

Ehrlich, P. (1970) *The Population Bomb* (New York: Ballantine).

Eversley, D. (1976) 'Some social and economic implications of environmental impact assessment', in T. O'Riordan and R. D. Hey (eds), *Environmental Impact Assessment* (London: Saxon House), pp. 126–41.

FAO (1987) *The Fifth World Food Survey* (Rome: Food and Agriculture Organisation).

Goldsmith, E. *et al.* (1972) 'Blueprint for survival', *The Ecologist*, vol. 2 (whole issue).

Goodin, R. E. (1976) *The Politics of Rational Man* (London: Wiley).

Gregory, R. (1971) *The Price of Amenity* (London: Macmillan).

Grigg, D. B. (1985) *The World Food Problem 1950–1980* (Oxford: Blackwell).

Harvey, D. (1974) 'Population, resources and the ideology of science', *Economic Geography*, vol. 50, pp. 256–77.

Hewitt, K. (ed.) (1983) *Interpretations of Calamity from the Viewpoint of Human Ecology* (Boston: Allen and Unwin).

Inglehart, R. (1971) 'The silent revolution in Europe: intergenerational change in post-industrial societies', *American Political Science Review*, vol. 75, pp. 991–1017.

Inglehart, R. (1977) *The Silent Revolution: Changing Values and Political Styles among Western Publics* (Princeton, NJ: Princeton University Press).

Inglehart, R. (1981) 'Postmaterialism in an environment of insecurity', *American Sociological Review*, vol. 85, pp. 880–900.

Inglehart, R. (1982) *Changing Values and the Rise of Environmentalism in Western Societies* (Berlin: International Institute for Environment and Society, Science Centre).

IUCN and World Wildlife Fund (1980) *World Conservation Strategy* (Gland, Switzerland: International Union for the Conservation of Nature).

Johnson, L. E. (1991) *A Moral, Deep World: An Essay on Moral Significance and Environmental Ethics* (Cambridge University Press).

Kimber, R. and J. J. Richardson (eds) (1974) *Campaigning for the Environment* (London: Routledge and Kegan Paul).

Lamb, H. H. (1977) *Climate Past, Present and Future*, vol. 2 (London: Methuen).

Longhurst, R. (1986) 'Household food strategies in response to seasonality and famine', *IDS Bulletin*, vol. 17, no. 3, pp. 27–35.

Lowe, P. and J. Goyder (1983) *Environmental Groups in Politics* (London: Allen and Unwin).

Lowe, P. and W. Rudig (1986) 'Political Ecology and the Social Sciences – the state of the art', *British Journal of Sociology*, vol. 16, pp. 513–50.

MacLuhan, L. M. (1967) *The Medium is the Message* (New York: Random House).

Maslow, A. H. (1970) *Motivation and Personality* (New York: Harper and Row).

Meadows, D. *et al.* (1972) *The Limits to Growth* (New York: University Books).

O'Riordan, T. (1981) *Environmentalism*, 2nd edn (London: Pion Press).

Pacey, A. and P. Payne (eds) (1985) *Agricultural Development and Nutrition* (London: Hutchinson).

Paehlke, R. C. (1989) *Environmentalism and the Future of Progressive Politics* (New Haven and London: Yale University Press).

Pearce, D. W., A. Markandya and E. Barbier (1989) *Blueprint for a Green Economy* (London: Earthscan).

Pepper, D. (1984) *The Roots of Modern Environmentalism* (London: Croom Helm).

Pepper, D. (1987) 'Environmental politics: who are the real radicals?', *Area*, vol. 19, no. 1, pp. 75–7.

Porritt, J. (1984) *Seeing Green: the Politics of Ecology Explained* (Oxford: Blackwell).

Pryde, P. (1991) *Environmental Management in the Soviet Union* (Cambridge University Press).

Rahmato, D. (1987) 'Peasant survival strategies', in A. Penrose (ed.), *Beyond the Famine: an Examination of the Issues behind Famine in Ethiopia* (Geneva: International Institute for Relief and Development, Food for the Hungry International).

Richards, P. (1985) *Indigenous Agricultural Revolution: Ecology and Food Production in West Africa* (London: Hutchinson).

Sagoff, M. (1988) *The Economy of the Earth* (Cambridge University Press).

Sandbach, F. (1980) *Environment, Ideology and Policy* (Oxford: Blackwell).

Scott, A. (1990) *Ideology and the New Social Movements* (London: Unwin Hyman).

Self, P. (1970) 'Nonsense on stilts: the futility of Roskill', *Political Quarterly*, vol. 41, pp. 249–60.

Sen, A. (1981) *Poverty and Famines. An Essay on Entitlement and Deprivation* (Oxford: Clarendon Press).

Smith, G. E. (1991) 'The state, the nationalities question and the Soviet Republics', in C. Merridale and C. Ward (eds), *Perestroika: The Historical Perspective* (London: Edward Arnold), pp. 202–16.

Smith, P. (ed.) (1975) *The Politics of Physical Resources* (Harmondsworth: Penguin).

Sprigge, T. L. S. (1991) 'Some recent positions in environmental ethics examined', *Inquiry*, vol. 34, pp. 107–28.

Stoddart, D. R. (1987a) 'To claim the high ground: geography for the end of the century', *Transactions of the Institute of British Geography*, NS, vol. 12, pp. 327–36.

Stoddart, D. R. (1987b) 'A verbalized world of polysyllabic gobbledygook', *Journal of Biogeography*, vol. 14, pp. 292–4.

Stoddart, D. R. and J. S. Pethick (1984) 'Environmental hazard and coastal reclamation: problems and prospects in Bangladesh', in T. P. Bayliss-Smith and S. Wanmali (eds), *Understanding Green Revolutions* (Cambridge University Press), pp. 339–61.

Swift, J. (1989) 'Why are rural people vulnerable to famine?', *IDS Bulletin*, vol. 20, no. 2, pp. 8–15.

Urfi, A. J. (1987) 'India wakes up to the environment', *New Scientist* 28 May, p. 64.

Waller, M. (1989) 'The ecology issue in Eastern Europe: protest and movements', *Journal of Communist Studies*, vol. 5, pp. 303–28.

Wathern, P. (ed.) (1988) *Environmental Impact Assessment: Theory and Practice* (London: Unwin Hyman).

Watts, M. (1983a) *Silent Violence: Food, Famine and Peasantry in Northern Nigeria* (Berkeley: University of California Press).

Watts, M. (1983b) 'On the poverty of theory: natural hazards research in context', in K. Hewitt (ed.), *Interpretations of Calamity* (Boston: Allen and Unwin), pp. 231–62.

Watts, M. (1988) 'Coping with the market: uncertainty and food security among Hausa peasants', in I. de Garine and G. A. Harrison (eds), *Coping with Uncertainty in Food Supply* (Oxford: Clarendon Press), pp. 260–89.

Weston, J. (1986) *Red and Green: The New Politics of the Environment* (London: Pluto Press).

White, G. F. (ed.) (1974) *Natural Hazards: Local, National, Global* (New York: Oxford University Press).

World Commission on Environment and Development (WCED) (1987) *Our Common Future* (Oxford University Press).

Wynne, B. (1975) 'The rhetoric of consensus politics: a critical review of technology assessment', *Research Policy*, vol. 4, pp. 108–58.

6

The Transformation of Cultural Geography

LINDA McDOWELL

Introduction

Cultural geography is one of the most exciting areas of geographical work at the moment. Ranging from analyses of everyday objects, views of nature in art or film to studies of the meaning of landscapes and the social construction of place-based identities, it covers numerous issues. Its focus includes the investigation of material culture, social practices and symbolic meanings, approached from a number of theoretical perspectives. I shall attempt to give a flavour of this diversity, showing how the subject and the approaches of cultural geography have changed over time. Writing a chronological review, however, always runs the risk of presenting intellectual history as the inevitable replacement of one approach by another: the latter more sophisticated than the former. In fact the material history of any sub-area of geography is one of contested approaches, and often bitter struggles. Distinguishing between approaches, and placing scholars within one paradigm or another, also makes the reviewer vulnerable to charges of misrepresentation.

Accepting this risk I will outline three main sets of approaches, each with different emphases, strengths and weaknesses. First, the ideas developed by the Berkeley School in the interwar period will be discussed. Secondly, I will examine an approach to cultural geography that defines culture as sets of shared meanings expressed in social practices within a place, and then turn to the landscape school that has taken as its focus the interpretation of patterns of signification or meaning in the landscape. Finally, I shall suggest that not only cultural geographers, but social theorists in general, have a growing common interest in how the increasingly global scale of cultural production and consumption affects relationships between identity, meaning and place. Attention is focused on the ways in which symbols, rituals, behaviour and everyday social practices result in a shared set or sets of meanings that are, to greater or lesser degrees, place-specific. Thus a geographic perspective has become central to the cultural-studies project more widely (Grossberg *et al.*, 1992).

In traditional societies – in which the friction of distance is a significant social barrier and where religion, superstition and social beliefs are part of the 'social glue' that holds a people together, often in isolation from other peoples and sets of beliefs – it is easy for us to understand how place and shared sets of social meanings coincide. However the 'modern' world is vastly different. Increasingly we live in 'one world' in which the power of global capital is dominant. The same transnational companies are investing in ever-growing numbers of economies, and international-financial agencies such as the World Bank and the International Monetary Fund provide similar advice about the structural adjustment of their economies to governments in the former socialist countries and the developing countries of Africa and Latin America alike. Huge numbers of people in every part of the world now work for transnational corporations or global agencies and vast migrations for economic or political reasons have resulted in the movement of large numbers of peoples from their homelands. With the development of global telecommunications networks the same programmes are beamed around the world, millions of people watch the same films, tune in to, say, *LA Law*, and listen to 'world music', which reaches audiences widely separated in space. It thus becomes an important question whether geography, or indeed culture, matters at all. This was a question that did not overly concern the first school of cultural geography established by Sauer, despite an interest in the diffusion of material artifacts and social practices, but which has assumed enormous significance in contemporary cultural geography.

The Concept of Culture in Cultural Geography

Although the development of cultural geography as a specific perspective has been a relatively recent phenomenon in the UK (see

Philo, 1991), in the US it has a longer pedigree, drawing on the
influential work of Carl Sauer and the students he trained in Berkeley
from the 1920s onwards. Sauer's legacy to cultural geography is
huge and controversial (Cosgrove and Jackson, 1987; Gregory and
Ley, 1988; Kenzer, 1985; Price and Lewis, 1993), and Sauer and
his disciples are often criticised for the atheoretical nature of their
work. Challenges to the 'traditional' approach of the Berkeley School
have attempted to place cultural geography more centrally within
recent developments in critical social theory, adopting an explicitly
theoretical definition of culture.

Culture is, however, a notoriously slippery concept, difficult to pin
down and define. Nevertheless a broad consensus round the following
definition might not be difficult to achieve. Here is my definition:

> Culture is a set of ideas, customs and beliefs that shape people's ac-
> tions and their production of material artifacts, including the land-
> scape and the built environment. Culture is socially defined and socially
> determined. Cultural ideas are expressed in the lives of social
> groups who articulate, express and challenge these sets of ideas
> and values, which are themselves temporally and spatially specific.

As the last sentence makes clear, cultural ideas and values are linked
to *power relations.* Certain groups in society attempt to impose
their definition of culture, and other groups challenge it. As every
student knows, the main aim of youth cultures is to challenge ideas
of what is acceptable behaviour or appropriate standards of cultural expression. This may be a difficult task. The recent acrimoni-
ous debates about 'political correctness' in the US, for example,
have revealed the extent to which cultural practices are tied up with
power relations and are contested.

The Berkeley School

The centrality of contested notions of cultural meaning in geographical
scholarship has varied. 'Traditional' cultural geographers paid less
attention to contested meanings and social struggles than those dubbed
the 'new' cultural geographers, whether interested in landscape or in
questions of place-based identity. Indeed it has been suggested that
human agency, in the sense of individuals or groups making choices,
interacting, negotiating and imposing constraints on each other, was
virtually ignored by Sauer and his followers (Duncan, 1980). They

took for granted the process of production of cultural artifacts, ignoring conflict over the production and consumption of material objects, focusing instead on their dispersion throughout the landscape. Duncan (1980), Gregory and Ley (1988) and Jackson (1989), among others the key proponents of the 'new' cultural geography, have judged Sauer and his disciples harshly, criticising their emphasis on everyday objects as a 'celebration of the parochial', even as 'object fetishism' (Gregory and Ley, 1988, p. 116). Duncan and Ley (1982) have suggested that culture is seen as an all-powerful entity, subject to its own logic, which people inherit and diffuse.

The shaping of the landscape is thus attributed not to human decision makers but to culture itself as an abstraction. This notion of culture is, it has been argued by 'new' cultural geographers, superorganic in that it sees culture itself as having causal powers (see Agnew and Duncan, 1989; Duncan, 1980, 1990), detached from and determining the actions of people in a locality. As Jackson (1989, p. 14) points out, Sauer argued that 'Culture is the agent, the natural area the medium, the cultural landscape the result' (Sauer, 1925, p. 46). Culture is seen as a totality, almost as a 'black box' rather than as a pluralistic set of social practices. Price and Lewis (1993), however, have vigorously defended the traditional cultural geographers from the assertion that Sauer held to a superorganic notion of culture.

What was it that Sauer and his students were interested in? Sauer's main interests were in the ways in which people left their imprint on the landscape through their productive activities and their settlements. In one of his most influential papers, 'The morphology of landscape' (1925), Sauer argued that 'landscape' is the 'unit concept of geography'. Through the study of 'the impress of the works of man [sic] upon an area' a 'strictly geographic way of thinking of culture' would be facilitated. Sauer's focus was threefold: first, the historical reconstruction of the environmental and human forces that shaped the landscape; second, the identification of distinctive and homogeneous cultural regions defined both by material artifacts such as house types and by non-material cultural attributes such as language or religion; and third, the study of historical cultural ecology where attention is focused on how human perceptions and uses of the landscape are culturally conditioned. As you can see from this list, Sauer's interests ranged widely. Sauer himself was particularly interested in pre-European America, and many of his students also worked in 'traditional' societies. Sauer regretted what he saw as the homogenising tendencies of the modern world and 'found pleasure in "backward" lands' (Sauer, 1952, p. 4). This is one of the major differences between the 'old' and the 'new' cultural geographers, who are interested in contemporary industrial societies as well as historical landscapes, although nostalgia for earlier ways of living is still a significant theme.

To what extent are the criticisms of the 'traditionalists' justified? Are they merely mappers of the distribution of artefacts, with little theoretical sophistication? In answering this question it is important to place Sauer's work in its context. Knowledge is socially constructed and temporally-specific. Sauer was a man of his times. Critical perspectives, whether class-based or, more recently, feminist and postcolonial analyses, with a central tenet that culture is a contested concept, were not common, whether within cultural geography or the anthropology of the time that influenced Sauer. Ironically Sauer's notion of individuals as passive bearers of culture is rather similar to structuralist Marxist notions of individuals as pawns in the course of history that many of the cultural geographers who criticised Sauer also found problematic in Marxian analyses in geography in the 1970s (see, for example, Duncan and Ley, 1982; Ley, 1985).

Price and Lewis (1993), however, argue that the critics of Sauer's work have misrepresented it. While initially interested in social theory, especially that produced in Germany, they believe that Sauer deliberately turned away from the theoretical developments in the social sciences in the interwar and immediate postwar period as he disliked the positivist emphasis of the times. In this he might be seen as an early forerunner of the critique of normative social theory developed by feminist and postmodernist theorists from the 1970s. Further, Sauer was not a mere collector of mundane and descriptive detail of material artefacts but was interested in the interconnections between material and non-material cultural forms. Sauer was also an adherent of long periods of field research, very much in the manner of more ethnographic and qualitative research that is currently gaining importance in cultural geography (Jacobs, 1993). However, the weakness of Sauer's analysis in its neglect of the wider social, economic and political structures of society and the ways in which cultural practices reflect, reinforce or challenge accepted cultural norms and standards is clear.

Culture as Contested Social Practices

One of the results of geography's turn towards the social sciences and the humanities from the 1970s onwards was a new understanding of the ways in which cultures are produced and reproduced through social practices that take place at a variety of spatial scales. At the same time as this intellectual reorientation, cultural assumptions and practices themselves were challenged in a variety of left-wing or 'countercultural' movements from the late 1960s onwards. The accepted meanings of culture as 'a shared system of values and meaning' was beginning to break up and lose legitimacy. It became necessary to add the adjective 'high' to distinguish the particular, dominant definition of culture from competing notions of culture: high culture from popular culture, mass culture or youth culture, for example. Culture also became a more all-embracing term. As Rosaldo suggests

It refers broadly to the forms through which people make sense of their lives, rather than more narrowly to the opera or art-museums. Culture does not inhabit a set-aside domain. . . . [it] encompasses the everyday and the esoteric, the mundane and the elevated, the ridiculous and the sublime. Neither high, nor low culture is all pervasive (Rosaldo, 1992, p. 26).

And not only all-pervasive, which leaves us with the problem of distinguishing a specifically *cultural* geography, but also dynamic and changing, temporally and spatially specific. Cultural meanings and practices are particular to certain groups in society. Dominant or hegemonic meanings may be subverted, challenged and overthrown. This recognition of contested and dissenting meanings, and that knowledge itself is provisional and contested, is perhaps the key feature that distinguishes the 'new' cultural geographers from Sauerians. Before looking at their work, however, a glimpse backwards is in order as some of the themes identified at the end of the nineteenth century that had a crucial influence on the development of geography have a new significance as we move towards the end of the twentieth century. They raise questions that cultural geographers have returned to in the different social circumstances of the current *fin de siècle*.

Modernity and the Symbolic Order of the Metropolis

Although the 1960s were particularly significant in the deconstruction of notions of 'high' culture and 'social truths' in the social sciences and the humanities, challenges to hegemonic notions of culture were not solely a 1960s phenomenon. The history of cultural production reveals a series of challenges to conventional norms as avant-garde movements redefine cultural standards. In this history, at least as told from the perspective of the 'advanced' industrial West, modernity – that set of social and economic formations associated with the rise of industrialisation and urbanisation in the Western world – has been a crucial element in cultural production. New landscapes, new social relations and new notions about individual and social identity in industrial societies forged new ways of seeing, different ideas about the dissemination of meaning and the mode of perception and representation. Thus what we might see as preeminently the subject matter of geography – demographic and social changes associated with industrial urbanisation – is also seen by cultural theorists as of overwhelming importance in the history of cultural change in the West.

The rise of the industrial metropolis in Western Europe and North America was a decisive influence on the practices and ideas of the avant-garde movements of the second half of the nineteenth century and the early twentieth century (Williams, 1989). Vast concentrations of people from diverse backgrounds on a scale never previously experienced affected social perceptions, resulting in new forms of 'mental life' in cities (Simmel, 1909). It is difficult to exaggerate the impact of crowded city streets, new forms of transport, factories and mechanisation on people used to small settlements. Even more significantly for cultural production, these cities in England, France and the US brought together artists, painters, poets, emigrés and refugees from many different societies and made possible the cross-fertilisation of ideas that had such profound results. Williams identified the key significance of geography, location and concentration in the development of new cultural practices. The city, in its diversity and complexity, in its strangeness and sophistication, permitted new forms of expression and ways of living that were unheard of in more traditional settlements.

Despite the significant emphasis on 'natural' landscapes or preindustrial landscapes by cultural geographers, be they Sauerians or new landscape geographers (Cosgrove, 1984, 1985; Cosgrove and Daniels, 1988; Duncan, 1990), cultural geographers increasingly are turning to questions about the city and cultural life in the late nineteenth and twentieth centuries, to questions about identity, meaning and imagination: how people experience and respond to the 'urban experience' (Harvey, 1989). The work of the German critic Walter Benjamin, himself influenced by Baudelaire's analysis of modernity, is a significant influence on geographical reconstructions of contemporary ways of seeing (Buck-Morss, 1989; Gregory, 1991).

A further influence on recent geographical work that conceptual-
ises the city as a spectacle, a crowd of strangers, is a small number
of French scholars and activists writing in Paris in the 1950s and
1960s. Stimulated by their argument that spatial relations and arrangements are not fixed but changing and are differentially experienced
by social groups and individuals over time, this French 'school' links
to contemporary postmodern arguments about the particularity of
knowledge and experience. Among the key theorists recently significant in cultural geographies are Michel de Certeau (1984), Guy Debord
(1973) and Henri Lefebvre (1991). The latter's book *The Production
of Space*, originally published in 1974 in Paris but only recently translated into English (1991) has been drawn on by, among others, David
Harvey (1989), Edward Soja (1989) and Rob Shields (1991).

The work of these French theorists is important as it distinguishes
between a scientific, rational view of space, the subject matter of
urban planning and conventional geographic analysis, and an idea of
space as something that is experienced or imagined, a more ambivalent concept that is not possible to represent either in scientific discourse or in sets of social statistics. The idea of experiential or
imaginative space perhaps needs further explanation as it is still a
relatively unfamiliar idea to those of us raised on a view of geography as scientific and of the city as a 'real' and transparent object,
complex maybe but subject to definitive analysis. In *The Practice of
Everyday Life* (1984), de Certeau distinguished what he termed the
'concept city' from the 'fact' of the city. The 'concept city' is that
idea of the city familiar to us from urban planning, the writing of
urban reformers and the social geography of the Chicago school: a
city that is a grid, a circle, a set of rings with areas of poor housing,
poverty and deprivation, land-use conflicts or traffic problems. It is
a city amenable to rational planning. The 'fact' of the city, as de
Certeau uses the term, is quite different. It is a city known to us
through everyday experiences, novels and paintings, a contradictory
city, only partially known, made up of sets of fleeting experiences,
that may never be entirely captured in plans or formal representations.

As de Certeau suggested, 'Beneath the discourses that ideologise
the city the ruses and combinations of powers that have no readable
identity proliferate; without points where one can take hold of them,
without rational transparency, they are impossible to administer' (de
Certeau, 1984, p. 95). Planners are unable to exercise complete control as the city's diversity is not legible. This metaphor of reading

the city or landscapes as if they were a text is a central tenet of the practices of the 'new' landscape school (Duncan and Duncan, 1988; Agnew and Duncan, 1989; Duncan, 1990). I shall return to it later.

Rob Shields, who fits more conveniently into the first of my two categories of new cultural geography, has developed Lefebvre's threefold definition of space to discuss the range of ways these definitions produce particular landscapes and sets of spatial practices. His book *Places on the Margin* (1991) includes a fascinating range of examples of what he calls social spatialisations – how ideas of space take a concrete form both on the ground and in images. In his book he looks, for example, at the idea of the 'north' in British films and soap operas as well as the idea of the 'north' as in northern Canada, and at Brighton as a particular type of seaside resort, where sets of rather unconventional social behaviour find a place – staged battles between mods and rockers in the 1960s, for example, and its longer reputation as a place to go for a 'dirty weekend'. As the antithesis of Brighton, Shields also includes a case study of how Niagara Falls has been packaged and sold as the honeymoon capital of the world. His book is an excellent example of how the analysis both of material practices and symbolic representations produces a rich understanding of place-based meanings.

One of the most useful aspects of de Certeau and Lefebvre's work is their emphasis on the social relations of power embedded in the different ideas of space. The rational scientific discourse of urban planners includes notions of 'proper' land use, of what in the British town-planning system are called 'non-conforming' land uses. De Certeau drew attention to the ways in which the city is represented as an organism in planning rhetoric in such ways that poverty, disease or social deviance could be seen as an inevitable aspect of bodily malfunction rather than as the result of social and economic inequalities. In his superb analysis of Los Angeles, *City of Quartz* (1989), the urban critic Mike Davis has demonstrated the mechanisms of repression and control that structure the spatial practices and representations of a contemporary city. Other geographers have analysed the ways the cultural production of space reflects and reinforces dominant economic and political interests through mechanisms such as the placing and naming of buildings and streets or the division of space (Harvey, 1989).

The work of theorists such as Harvey and Davis blur the distinctions between urban, cultural and economic geography. Indeed it is only recently that their work would be included in a review of cultural geography. Sharon Zukin is another scholar whose work exemplifies the way in which cultural practices have entered the agenda of geographers that might more usually be classified as economic materialists. Zukin recently published *Landscapes of Power* (1991), a powerful account of representational strategies and socioeconomic practices that produce highly unequal spatial outcomes. Her earlier book, *Loft Living* (1988), as its subtitle *Culture and capital in urban change* indicates, was one of the earlier influential analyses of how this combination of a materialist and cultural analysis of space is proving a productive way of illuminating urban change. Significantly in her conclusion Zukin locates her text as a cultural artifact:

> The study of landscapes of economic power is a cultural artifact of its time and place. If I had written it when I began research, in 1980, it would have been part of the heated debate over deindustrialisation. In the middle of the 1980s, it might have been a critique of the cultural capital wielded by yuppies. Writing after 1985, however, I was able to recognize the extraordinary influence of a service economy, and also to lay a dispassionate emphasis on the organization of consumption (Zukin, 1988, p. 271.)

This helps us to understand that the changing emphases in cultural geography are themselves a cultural artifact, as are the boundaries of the subdiscipline. What is published and taught under the rubric 'cultural geography' changes in response to the political and economic climate of the times and the structures of disciplinary power. Current work in cultural geography reveals the growing significance of analyses of the landscapes of consumption, power and spectacle (see, for example, Glennie and Thrift's review paper [1992]; Goss, 1993; Ley and Olds, 1988; Sack, 1988; Short *et al.*, 1993; and Sorkin, 1992, for a number of examples of this contemporary focus).

While the recent emphasis on imagination, meaning and consumption may seem like a return to the concerns of a century ago, cultural geography in the postwar period took two rather different courses, with differing emphases in the UK and the US. The first took as its major focus social relations and symbolic meaning as revealed in social actions in a particular place or locality, while the second focused more specifically on landscapes *per se*. The first of these 'new' cultural geographies found its theoretical stimulus in the British school of cultural studies and social history, that developed between the 1950s and the 1970s, although its visibility in geography remained low key until the 1980s. The latter – the new landscape school – has a longer geographic pedigree and a different theoretical heritage. It too flowered in the 1980s, heavily influenced by post-structuralist and literary theory. Both, however, have a common origin in the theoretical and political changes of the late 1960s onwards, culminating in a critique of the notion of a singular or objective social science. The new cultural geographers thus concur in their recognition of what has become known as the 'positionality' of knowledge (see also Chapters 4 and 7 of this book). I shall consider the different interests and intellectual debts of the new cultural geographies in turn.

'New' Cultural Geographies. 1: Cultural Materialism

In the development of a cultural geography that addresses questions about how sets of shared meanings and social identities are linked to place, two British cultural theorists stand out as particularly significant in their influence on British cultural geography. The two are Raymond Williams and Stuart Hall. I shall show how their work lead to certain geographic questions being raised and others excluded.

Raymond Williams was the principal advocate of an approach to the understanding of cultural phenomena that emphasised the importance of the specific social, political and historical context in which cultural production takes place and meaning is created. He drew out the ways in which cultural form and meaning reinforced, or challenged, sets of power relations, focusing in particular on the development of working-class culture in areas of heavy industry and the ways in which cultural solidarity led to labourist politics. His notion of culture is, perhaps, best summarised in his argument that culture is 'the lived unity of experience' that produces certain 'structures of feeling'. These concepts point to the way in which culture is crucially bound up with local ways of living and so has become a useful stimulus to geographical investigations of locally based cultures (Jackson, 1989).

Williams himself, rather like Sauer, regretted the rise of consumer industries in postwar Britain and what he saw as their negative impact on organic working-class cultures. He deplored the rise of mass consumption and consumer culture, seeing not the oppositional possibilities of these forms but rather their adverse impact on the working class. This is a common theme among the cultural critics and social scientists, mainly sociologists rather than geographers, who analysed cultural change in postwar Britain. A large number of the community studies produced between the late 1950s and the 1970s focused on the purported disruption of solidaristic social relations and shared sets of meanings in working-class areas of cities or in single-industry towns and villages. The genre is nostalgic, romanticised and sexist (Steedman, 1986), but significant in its challenge to the perceived undervaluing of place-based working-class cultures. It includes Richard Hoggart's classic book, *The Uses of Literacy*, (1957), reflecting on his working-class childhood, the work of Young and Willmott at the Institute of Community Studies in Bethnal Green, particularly *Family and Kinship in East London* (1957), Dennis, Henrique and Slaughter's *Coal is Our Life* (1956) and the collected essays in Frankenburg's *Communities in Britain* (1966). These studies emphasised the deep sense of belonging to the local area that is created by a shared class background, resilience in the face of hardship and a geographically restricted set of social activities. Their literary counterpart are novels such as *Saturday Night and Sunday Morning* and *Love on the Dole* – the texts analysed by Shields (1989) in his work on social spatialisations and sense of place.

One of the strongest threads in the work of the community-studies school, also found in Raymond Williams' work, is a puritanical view of the just-developing opportunities for mass consumption. There was an element of anti-Americanism in their critique of the anonymity of the new, privatised lifestyle that was facilitated by improvements in housing and the growing possession of an ever-widening range of consumer durables. Hebdige, in his book *Hiding in the Light*, has summarised the disapproval thus:

> The singularity of British culture is felt to be increasingly threatened in the post-war period by the conditions under which consumption values and popular culture are disseminated. For critics pledged to defend 'authentic' British values, mass produced commodities aimed at specific target groups begin to function as symbols of decadence. They are seen to pose a threat to native traditions of rugged self-reliance, self-discipline and the muscular puritanism of the stereotypical (male) workforce, thereby leading to a softening up and 'feminisation' of the national stock (Hebdige, 1988, p. 9).

Distrust and suspicion of possessions was also a feature of US scholarship. Perhaps one of the clearest expressions of the consequences of the new, privatised lifestyle is to be found in Herbert Marcuse's *One Dimensional Man* (sic) (1964).

Interestingly, yearning for a lost authenticity has reappeared in recent texts, focusing on the 1980s and 1990s rather than on the 1950s. Thus Zukin (1991) mourns the destruction of earlier landscapes, which, she argues, were typified by their rootedness and particularity. David Harvey, too, in his overwhelmingly influential text *The Condition of Postmodernity* (1989), replays the narrative of the 'world we have lost'. This narrative not only has an anti-women strand but has a dubious right-wing as well as left-wing version, exemplified by the Nazis' link between identity and territory and in the recent significance of nationalist politics.

In British geography a sense of nostalgia for old working-class, locally based cultures, and the type of left-wing politics associated with it, found its strongest expression in the work of Doreen Massey and the 'locality school' of the 1980s. We can trace Williams' influence, albeit not explicitly acknowledged, in Massey's notion of a locality as an identifiable area marked by its own spatially specific set of social practices. Massey (1984) developed a geological metaphor to illustrate the ways in which the sedimentation of decades of regional differentiation produced a landscape of uneven development in 1970s England, even perhaps regional cultures in a gesture to Sauer. Her emphasis was predominantly economic, although there were several evocative indications of the ways in which a particular division of labour was reflected in the everyday arenas of, for example, the household and the club and in local politics. Thus the ways in which the shared dangers of heavy male manual labour was reproduced in a particular political culture and a male camaraderie in the clubs and pubs in the industrial north-east was outlined – an analysis very close to Williams' 'structures of feeling'. McDowell and Massey (1984) drew on the spatial-divisions-of-labour approach to show how distinctive gender divisions of labour are linked to locality.

However, the locality school has been severely criticised for its relative neglect of 'cultural' factors (Jackson, 1991a). Like the community sociologists, geographers too, until recently, neglected the contradictory, even positive, aspects of contemporary mass culture and the progressive possibilities of consumption-based social practices. Analysis of the ways in which material artifacts are appropriated and their meanings transformed through oppositional social practices became the focus of new work in cultural studies that is now of key importance in contemporary cultural geography.

Mass Consumption, Advertising, Popular and Counterculture

While Williams, Marcuse and Hoggart may have regretted the ravages of consumerism, at the Centre for Contemporary Cultural Studies at the University of Birmingham social and cultural analysts were developing a theoretical framework that celebrated rather than denigrated consumer culture. From the mid-1960s and through the 1970s, under Stuart Hall, who replaced Richard Hoggart, its work took a different direction. Hall and his colleagues drew attention to the ways in which consumption and style might be adopted and subverted to unite consumers in what they termed 'oppositional cultures' or 'oppositional communities' (Hall and Jacques 1983; Hall and Jefferson, 1976). Their work is stimulating as it allows geographers to work with the idea of a community that is 'imagined' in the sense of not spatially located or fixed (see also Anderson, 1983, and Mohanty, 1991).

The example of youth cultures is a useful illustration. As I indicated earlier, young people have long subverted the accepted cultural norms and codes to assert not only their independence and individuality, but also their membership of a group from which their parents are excluded. Dress, style and the possession of certain iconic consumer durables play a particularly significant part in the construction of these imagined communities. From the beatniks' black rollneck sweaters, through the leathers and motor bikes of the (masculine) rockers, the suits and scooters of the (feminised) mods to the countercultural symbols of the punks, to 'grunge' as style, consumption has been central to the construction of identity. For the members of these communities, identity is not place-specific; the locality in a strictly geographic sense plays no part in their sense of self. Style is cosmopolitan, not local, the aim is not to be placed.

Of course the staged exhibitions of these styles take place somewhere. Indeed places themselves often take on a cultural significance that reinforces cultural rituals. In the US, for example, the annual pilgrimage of students to west-coast resorts for thanksgiving is part of the image of these places. And Berkeley, despite Sauer, is forever linked in the imagination to the Grateful Dead and student riots. In the same way certain British seaside towns had symbolic significance in staged riots between different youth cultures (Shields, 1991).

One of the main achievements of the work of scholars at the Centre for Contemporary Culture was to place the investigation of youth and other oppositional cultures on the academic agenda of cultural studies, and now of geography (see Valentine, 1993, for example).

Their work revealed the ways in which consumption might be theorised as part of an oppositional politics rather than seen as an element of the 'false consciousness' of a working class duped by the shiny but meaningless symbols of consumer capitalism (McRobbie, 1991; Mort, 1988; Shields, 1992). This reassessment meant that space began to open up for new kinds of geographies that challenged the previous emphasis on the social relations of production, on the firm, the workplace or the industrial region as the geographic locii and studies of the social relations and symbolic meaning of consumption became part of geography. Reinforced by the rise of a 'new' politics of consumption in the 1980s, partly based on an insistence by some feminists, new-left intellectuals and gay men that consumption could be fun, there is interesting new work in cultural and social geography on the sites of spectacle and consumption that characterise postmodern societies (Anderson and Gale, 1992; Ley and Olds, 1988; Sorkin, 1992).

We should be careful, however, not to assume that production and consumption are entirely separate categories. As the growing corpus of feminist work has made clear, productive activities depend upon reproductive activities, a proportion of which are consumption. Pringle (1983) and Prus and Dawson (1991) remind those in danger of being carried away by ideas of pleasure that consumption is also *work*. Further, the production, advertising and marketing of goods is a crucial part of their consumption, as anyone who wears Levis knows!

In the shift towards these 'new' cultural geographies, the ideas of the Italian theorist Antonio Gramsci have had a significant influence (Jackson, 1989). Among the classical Marxist analysts, Gramsci is perhaps the Marxist scholar who has devoted the greatest attention to the politics of everyday culture. He was interested in how sets of ideas, of ideologies, about cultural standards, meanings and accepted social divisions become established and accepted within a society without the use of force, even by those who are disadvantaged by the dominant ideas and beliefs. The key concept in his analysis is that of hegemony, clearly defined by Barrett as '*the organisation of consent* (her emphasis) – the processes through which the subordinated forms of consciousness are constructed without recourse to violence or coercion' (Barrett, 1991, p. 54). Gramsci developed a hierarchy of ways of making sense of the world that differ in the extent to which they are ordered bodies of systematic and rational knowledge. These range from philosophy, through religion and common sense to folklore, and significantly Gramsci argued that there may be contradictions between the levels. Thus Gramsci's analysis of popular consciousness was more sensitive and nuanced than the 'false consciousness' of traditional Marxist theory, and also left space for the development of an oppositional consciousness. Stuart Hall drew on Gramsci in his demonstration of how cultural phenomena and the organisation of everyday life increases the dominance of capitalist control in advanced industrial societies such as Britain. As part of this work also places at its centre the notion of landscape, we must now turn to the ways in which new cultural geographers, particularly US scholars, have drawn on and diverged from the initial insistence of Sauer that landscape is the key concept of cultural geography.

New Cultural Geographies. 2: The Landscape School

The identification of landscape as the central concept, rather than social practices, by the second of the set of geographers I have classified as 'new' cultural geographers, provides a link back to Sauer's work. Influential work by geographers in the late 1960s and 1970s on environmental perception (Brookfield, 1969) and humanistic analyses of how meanings and values influence place-based behaviour (Ley, 1985; Lowenthal, 1961) is a further geographic forerunner. Thus it is possible to trace a path from descriptive analyses of material cultural artefacts through a long-standing interest in the meaning of landscape (Meinig, 1979) to studies of the cities in their cultural contexts (Agnew *et al.*, 1984; Duncan, 1990) in the landscape school. This work – as Zukin argued – reflected the theoretical considerations of its time. So, unlike the cultural materialists, the new landscape school has a more obviously geographic heritage. Recently, however, it has been towards the humanities rather than the social sciences, with the exception perhaps of anthropology, that the new landscape school has turned its attention.

One of the marked features of recent work has been a noticeable shift towards linking the analysis of cultural practices to the discursive construction of meaning (Barnes and Duncan, 1992). Unlike earlier cultural geographers, the new landscape analysts recognised that material landscapes are not neutral but reflect power relations and dominant 'ways of seeing' the world (Berger, 1972). Landscapes are not only constructed, they are also perceived through representations of ideal versions in painting and poetry, as well as in scientific discourse and academic writing. Thus the new landscape geographers have retheorised landscape as not only the material outcome of interactions between the environment and a society (the old man[sic]/land nexus), but also as the consequence of a specific way of looking. The notion of an objective, neutral or specifically geographic way of looking at the land is thus questioned. The geographer is also culturally situated and so how s/he sees the landscape is culturally and historically specific.

In their work, the new landscape geographers have drawn on a variety of traditions. In common with the social-relations/material-practices school, they were strongly influenced by the cultural materialist tradition of Gramsci and Williams, and, initially, also emphasised the class-based significance of cultural production. Thus Dennis Cosgrove, one of the dominant British members of this landscape school, argued that 'in class societies, where surplus production is appropriated by the dominant group, symbolic production is likewise seized as hegemonic class culture to be imposed on all classes' (Cosgrove, 1983, p. 5).

Recently the emphasis of the landscape school has shifted from analyses of the material production of the environment towards problematising the ways in which landscapes have been represented, whether in written texts, art, maps or topographical surveys. The pictorial metaphor was particularly suggestive. As Cosgrove and Daniels suggest in their introduction to an influential edited collection that illustrates the new emphases 'a landscape is a cultural image, a pictorial way of representing, structuring or symbolising surroundings' (Cosgrove and Daniels, 1988, p. 1). The landscape geographers have turned to work in the humanities, especially in literary theory, semiotics and discourse theory, to develop ways of reading the landscape as though it were text, utilising such concepts as intertextuality and reader reception (Duncan and Duncan, 1988; Duncan, 1990). Further, they have analysed writing about landscape in a range of forms from 'high' literature to academic texts, as well as a range of other 'texts' from architecture to cinema and painting (Aiken and Zonn, 1993; Cosgrove and Daniels, 1988; Domash, 1989; Dovey, 1992; Watson, 1991). A more recent focus is to problematise geographic writing itself, analysing the ways in which geographers have dealt with the relationship between the world and its representation (Barnes and Duncan, 1992; Duncan and Ley, 1993).

It might perhaps be useful to define the term discourse for those not familiar with its usage. Simply defined, a discourse is a way of thinking or writing about a subject. It produces meaningful knowledge within a system of thought or set of codified knowledge. All statements operate within a particular discourse, which defines or limits how we think about things. Thus, to take a simple example from economic geography, the notion of profit has a different meaning depending on whether the framework of analysis is Marxist or neoclassical. This, I think, is what Derrida implied when he argued that 'there is nothing outside the text', not that there is no material reality, sets of relations of power and exploitation or privilege but that we are not able to think about their meaning other than inside an explanatory framework. When sets of statements are linked to each other they become what Foucault termed a discursive formation, which when successfully established may be defined as a regime of truth. Thus, for example, Said's work challenges the regime of truth within which Western literature conveys images of the Orient or relations of power under imperialist rule (Said, 1978, 1992).

One of the most pronounced features of contemporary cultural geography, and of the social sciences and humanities more widely, has been the way in which dominant notions of truth have been challenged and disrupted. There is a growing recognition that knowledge is multiple and positional, that there are many ways of seeing and reading the landscape. One of the foci of contemporary cultural geography, therefore, is the investigation of multiple discourses about place and identity, uncovering previously ignored senses of place and visions of the landscape constructed by the powerless rather than the powerful. In particular, attention has been focused on what has become known as the post colonial subject, or 'other' (Spivak, 1992). A number of studies of the meaning of the landscape in indigenous cultures, including Australian (Anderson and Gale, 1992) and Southern African (Mather, 1993), are now being undertaken, which will enable the previously silenced to enter the discourses about landscape. Anderson's (1988, 1990, 1992) work on the production of the landscapes of Chinatown in Canadian and Australian cities is a particularly fine example. She shows how the distinctive landscape symbolises the exotic and inferior 'otherness' of Chinese communities, produced through specific relations of power and cultural domination by white Europeans.

As Corrigan has pointed out, one of the absences in the landscape school of new cultural geographers has been 'the valuable "Inventing/Imagining" studies of the last twenty years, and the recognition as to by whom (and how) these recognitions were made possible' (Corrigan, 1991, p. 314). In recent work, however, there is more recognition of who constructed the imaginings of landscape and also of how differently positioned subjects see it through different eyes. As well as relations of class and colonial domination, the ways in which the symbolic representation of landscapes reflect gendered power relations are also becoming the focus of examination. Landscape is frequently portrayed in terms of the female body and nature either idealised as feminine – Mother Nature – or seen as a female threat, needing domination – the rape of the earth (Fitzsimmons, 1989; Ford, 1991; Griffin, 1978; Kolodny, 1975; Merchant, 1980; Stott, 1989). Feminist scholars have shown how cultural meaning, whether in the landscape, art or architecture embody ideas of masculine superiority and feminine inferiority, as well as idealised notions of women's passivity and restriction to the 'private' sphere (Bondi, 1992; Davidoff and Hall, 1987; Deutsche, 1991; Pollock, 1988; Rose, 1993).

Work on understanding the links between the 'gaze' of the scientist and masculinist rationality, as well as links between masculinity and the pleasurable contemplation of nature and its representation, are being pursued (Keller and Grontkowski, 1983; Monk and Norwood, 1987; Rose, 1993). The position of the geographers who act as our textual guide in this work of (re-) reading and deconstructing landscape symbolism also cries out for inclusion and critical examination within these texts. The interpreter, no less than the producers and consumers of landscape, is not an innocent subject, but is enmeshed in structures of power (G. Pratt, 1992; M. B. Pratt, 1988). As Duncan and Ley recognise in their recent edited collection, 'it has usually been a white, male, elite, Eurocentric observer who orders the world that he looks upon, one whose observations and classifications provide the rules of representation, of inclusion and exclusion, of precedent and antecedent, of inferior and superior (Duncan and Ley, 1993, p. 2). Virginia Woolf put it more succinctly 65 years ago when she claimed on behalf of women, 'Though we see the same world, we see it through different eyes' (Woolf, 1938, p. 22). The recognition of this difference and also that there is a politics to different views – what is termed a 'politics of location' – has the potential to turn the social sciences, including cultural geography, upside down (Jackson, 1991b; Philo, 1991). It raises enormous questions about the validity of the representations of the world that we regard as geography that are still, in the main, produced by white men (McDowell, 1991). What exactly is it that we thought we knew about the world?

Global Cultures/a Sense of Place: Travelling Cultures?

These new questions about meaning, representation, the politics of location and the construction of a place-based sense of self in multicultural societies are currently a uniting focus in cultural geography – indeed across social and cultural geography more widely. Countries in the industrial West, especially the former colonial powers, now have to find their place in a new international division of space that is very different from the old division. In the UK, for example, migrants from the 'empire' now live in the 'old country', disrupting notions of 'Englishness' and demanding a revision in the old, shared sense of place and associated sets of cultural meanings that defined inhabitants of the country (Samuel, 1989; Wright, 1985). In the US long traditions of migration challenge old geographical distinctions between the 'first' and 'third' worlds.

Decolonisation, international migration, the globalisation of capital, trade and forms of cultural production have resulted in societies in which international trends, goods and services are changing us all and our sense of identity linked to territory. For example it is now commonplace – at least for the relatively affluent – to be able to wear Peruvian jewellery with an Italian sweater while listening to Caribbean reggae on a Japanese-made personal stereo in a Chinese restaurant in the company of Indian friends. The same types of food might be being eaten in London, New York, Toronto or Johannesburg by people wearing similar clothes and listening to the same music. Thus people separated by vast physical distances and, perhaps by ethnicity, religion and life-chances, are linked through the circuits of capital and global communications, occupying what the cultural critic Fredric Jameson (1991) calls 'hyperspace' – a 'domain in which local experience no longer coincides with the place in which it takes place' (Pred and Watts, 1992, p. 7). The material artefacts used in a place no longer have that connection to it that formed the basis of Sauer's investigation of the localisation of cultural production.

In the 'postmodern' world there is an eclecticism of style and materials that might have astonished Sauer. Different forms and styles, drawn from widely ranging times and spaces, have been mixed to challenge the notions of 'correct' form. In architecture, for example, the domestic or vernacular is mixed with hi-tech in city-centre buildings; in the shopping mall 'themed' areas divide space – a French cafe may be juxtaposed with a Mexican cantina or a US ranch – and in the city as a whole the interpenetration of spaces of play and

leisure with those of work are the features of the new financial landscapes in downtown areas from London to New York to Tokyo
(Budd and Whimster, 1992; Davis, 1990; Sassen, 1991). Images and
meanings have become detached from the real world. In the themed
areas in the shopping mall, the images of France and Spain have no
connection to the 'real' France or Spain but are created, packaged or
'imagined' for the US or UK consumer (see, for example, numerous
discussions of the West Edmonton Mall: Butler, 1991; Fairbairn, 1991;
Hopkins, 1991; Jackson and Johnson, 1991; Shields, 1989; Simmons,
1991). Further, it is argued, 'real life' begins to simulate these created
images or the images portrayed by the media. A good example here
is the way in which landscapes of the past are created for the tourist
gaze (Hewison, 1987; MacCanel, 1992; Urry, 1990; Wright, 1985) in
'heritage' museums, or in which sanitised versions of 'exotic' cultures are constructed for tourist consumption. Examples are almost
too numerous to mention – the luau of Hawaii, the mining museums
of the UK, the deserted camps of the goldrush in the US, the Bronte
landscape of Yorkshire, the wildlife 'parks' of the African veldt from
which all the local inhabitants have been cleared for the benefit of
the international tourist. Now, as Katz (1992) has suggested, it seems
that 'all the world is a stage'. Further, manufactured customs, or symbols of national pomp and circumstance, are invented in attempts to
ensure a shared sense of meaning between the increasingly diverse
occupants of a specific geographical space.

The current challenge uniting cultural geographers is the investigation of how the interconnections between global forces and local particularity alter the relationships between identity, meaning and place.
Hence we might ask a set of questions about how globally produced
and advertised goods and services, including the landscape, are differently perceived and used by people in different parts of the globe.
Despite the growing homogeneity of international cultural production,
especially in terms of ownership, there are spaces of resistance.
Appadurai's (1990) work, for example, examines the 'mediascapes'
of transnational capital and resistance to them without either romanti-
cising resistance or exalting capitalist penetration.

A second set of questions revolve around the ways in which a
sense of self, community and nationality remain rooted in place in
the so-called postmodern world. Here the research agenda shades into
questions being asked by social and political geographers, about ethnic
identity and communal violence for example. Geographers investigating these questions have begun to draw on different traditions and

different methods. The recent focus on questions about place-based identity and meaning for postcolonial subjects by Stuart Hall (1990, 1991) is once again a provocative stimulus for cultural geographers. Similarly, in anthropology, in particular in the work of the 'new ethnographers' (Clifford and Marcus, 1986; Marcus and Fischer, 1986), there is an overlap with geographical interest on place and globalisation. Anthropologists too are struggling with the relationship between the 'most local of local detail and the most global of global structure in such a way as to bring them into simultaneous view' (Geertz, 1983, p. 69). Achieving this simultaneity, however, is no easy task. It is both conceptually and methodologically complex to hold together the local and the global in geographical analyses.

In uncovering the connections between globalisation and local 'structures of feeling', in revealing the multiple senses of place held by inhabitants, in recording the ways in which global trends are interacting with locally based customs and social practices to create new layers of meaning, geographers are turning to new methods. In particular, detailed, small-scale, qualitative approaches, including those based on the recording of oral testimonies, are being utilised by growing numbers of cultural geographers, working in both the West and in 'less developed' societies (Jacobs, 1993).

Anthropologist James Clifford has argued that, at the end of the twentieth century, 'cultural analysis constitutes its objects – societies, traditions, communities, identities, in spatial terms' (Clifford, 1992, p. 97) (and he adds, 'through specific spatial practices of research' by travelling between field sites and the 'home' institution'). The field site, which used to be seen by anthropologists and geographers as a 'laboratory' in which the scholar undertook controlled observation, is now recognised to be what Clifford terms a set of complex, interactive cultural conjunctures' that are 'temporally and spatially bounded' (ibid., p. 99). What we used to understand by the term culture – a set of spatially rooted practices – is no longer an adequate conceptualisation. We need to theorise the multiple external connections – through migration, trade, exploration, tourism, research – all those 'travellers' that make a place what it is. Places are contested sites of 'constructed and disputed historicities, sites of displacement, interference, and interaction (ibid., p. 101). Further, although they are sometimes, even frequently, spatially defined, this is not always the case. Thus Anderson's (1983) notion of 'imagined communities' has become a fruitful way of theorising communities of interest, as distinct from place-based communities. Mohanty (1991), for example, uses Anderson's work in her analysis of what she terms contested cartographies, the maps of power that have constructed a 'community' of Third-World women in the cities of industrialised societies. In the postmodern world, tradition, culture, meaning and identity increasingly are related to place through the social relations of travel rather than coresidence, as in 'traditional' or even modern societies. Thus for anthropology and for cultural geography, Clifford's metaphor of 'travelling cultures' may be the most appropriate way of conceptualising that link between the local and the global that is the key relationship that unites our studies at the present time.

Acknowledgements

I should like to thank James Duncan and David Ley for allowing me to read an unpublished paper on the changing emphases in cultural geography. I drew on their assessment of the Sauerian tradition, as well as on Peter Jackson's chapter about Sauer in his book *Maps of Meaning* (1989). I should also like to thank Peter Jackson for numerous stimulating conversations about culture and geography.

References

Agnew, J. and J. Duncan (eds) (1989) *The Power of Place: Bringing together geographical and sociological imaginations* (London: Unwin Hyman).
Agnew, J., J. Mercer and D. Sopher (eds) (1984) *The City in a Cultural Context* (Boston: Allen and Unwin).
Aiken, S. and L. E. Zonn (1993) 'Weir(d) sex: representation of gender and environment relations in Peter Weir's *Picnic at Hanging Rock and Gallipoli*', *Environment and Planning D: Society and Space*, vol. 11, pp. 192–212.
Anderson, B. (1983) *Imagined communities: reflections on the origin and spread of nationalism* (London: Verso).
Anderson, K. (1988) 'Cultural hegemony and the race-definition process in Chinatown, Vancouver: 1880–1980', *Environment and Planning D: Society and Space*, vol. 6, pp. 127–50.
Anderson, K. (1990) 'Chinatown re-oriented: a critical analysis of recent development schemes in a Melbourne and Sydney enclave', *Australian Geographical Studies*, vol. 28, pp. 137–54.
Anderson, K. (1992) *Vancouver's Chinatown: Racial discourse in Canada, 1975–1980* (Vancouver: McGill-Queen's University Press).
Anderson, K. and F. Gale (eds) (1992) *Cultural Geography: ways of see-*

ing (South Melbourne: Longman Cheshire).

Appadurai, A. (1990) 'Disjuncture and difference in the global cultural economy', *Theory, Culture and Society*, vol. 7, pp. 295–310.

Barnes, T. and J. Duncan (eds) (1992) *Writing Worlds: Discourse, text and metaphor in the representation of landscape* (London: Routledge).

Barrett, M. (1991) *The Politics of Truth* (Cambridge: Polity Press).

Berger, J. (1972) *Ways of Seeing* (London: BBC Publications).

Bondi, L. (1992) 'Gender symbols and urban landscapes', *Progress in Human Geography*, vol. 16, pp. 157–70.

Brookfield, H. (1969) 'On the environment as perceived', *Progress in Geography*, vol. 1, pp. 51–80.

Buck-Morss, S. (1989) *The Dialectics of Seeing: Walter Benjamin and the arcades project* (Cambridge, Mass: MIT Press).

Budd, L. and S. Whimster (eds) (1992) *Global Finance and Urban Living* (London: Routledge).

Butler, R. (1991) 'West Edmonton mall as a tourist attraction, *The Canadian Geographer*, vol. 35, pp. 287–94.

Clifford, J. (1992) 'Traveling cultures', in L. Grossberg, C. Nelson and P. Treichler (eds) *Cultural Studies* (London: Routledge).

Clifford, J. and G. E. Marcus (eds) (1986) *Writing Culture: the poetics and politics of ethnography* (Berkeley: University of California Press).

Corrigan, P. (1991) 'My place or yours? Particular philosophies from whose stories (vernacular values revisited)', *Journal of Historical Geography*, vol. 17, pp. 313–18.

Cosgrove, D. (1983) 'Toward a radical cultural geography: problems of theory', *Antipode*, vol. 15, pp. 1–11.

Cosgrove, D. (1984) *Social Formation and Symbolic Landscape* (London: Croom Helm).

Cosgrove, D. (1985) 'Prospect, perspective and the evolution of the landscape idea', *Transactions, Institute of British Geographers*, vol. 10, pp. 45–62.

Cosgrove, D. and S. Daniels (1988) *The Iconography of Landscape: Essays on the symbolic representation, design and use of past environments* (Cambridge University Press).

Cosgrove, D. and P. Jackson (1987) 'New directions in cultural geography', *Area*, vol. 19, pp. 95–101.

Davidoff, E. and C. Hall (1987) *Family Fortunes: men and women of the English middle class 1780–1850* (London: Hutchinson).

Davis, M. (1990) *City of Quartz* (London: Verso).

Debord, G. (1973) *The Society of the Spectacle* (Detroit: Black and Red).

De Certeau, M. (1984) *The Practice of Everday Life* (Los Angeles: University of California Press).

Dennis, N., Henrique, F. and Slaughter, C. (1956) *Coal is Our Life* (London: Eyre and Spottiswoode).

Deutsche, R. (1991) 'Boys' Town', *Environment and Planning D: Society and Space*, vol. 10, pp. 5–30.

Domash, M. (1989) 'Corporate cultures and the modern landscape of New York City', in K. Anderson and F. Gale (eds), *Inventing Places: Studies in Cultural Geography* (Melbourne: Longman Cheshire).

170   *The Transformation of Cultural Geography*

Dovey, K. (1992) 'Corporate towers and symbolic capital', *Environment and Planning B: Planning and Design*, vol. 19, pp. 173–88.

Duncan, J. (1980) 'The superorganic in American cultural geography', *Annals, Association of American Geography*, vol. 70, pp. 181–98.

Duncan, J. (1990) *The City as Text: The politics of landscape interpretation in the Kandyan Kingdom* (Cambridge University Press).

Duncan, J. and N. Duncan (1988) '(Re)reading the landscape', *Environment and Planning D: Society and Space*, vol. 6, pp. 117–26.

Duncan, J. and D. Ley (1982) 'Structural Marxism and human geography: a critical assessment', *Annals of the Association of American Geography*, vol. 72, pp. 30–59.

Duncan, J. and D. Ley (1993) *Place/Culture/Representation* (London: Routledge).

Fairbairn, K. (1991) 'West Edmonton mall: entrepreneurial innovation and consumer response', *The Canadian Geographer*, vol. 35, pp. 261–7.

Fitzsimmons, M. (1989) 'The matter of nature', *Antipode*, vol. 21, pp. 106–20.

Ford, S. (1991) 'Landscape revisited: a feminist re-appraisal', in C. Philo (ed.), *New Words, New Worlds: Reconceptualising Social and Cultural Geography* (Lampeter: Department of Geography, St David's University College).

Frankenburg, R. (1966) *Communities in Britain* (Harmondsworth: Penguin).

Geertz, C. (1983) *Local Knowledge: Further essays in interpretative anthropology* (New York: Basic Books).

Glennie, P. and N. Thrift (1992) 'Modernity, urbanism and modern consumption', *Environment and Planning D: Society and Space*, vol. 10, pp. 423–43.

Goss, J. (1993) 'The magic of the mall: function, form and meaning in the contemporary retail built environment', *Annals of the Association of American Geographers*, vol. 83, pp. 18–47.

Gregory, D. (1991) 'Interventions in the historical geography of modernity: social theory, spatiality and the politics of representation', *Geografiska Annaler*, Series B, vol. 73, pp. 17–44.

Gregory, D. and D. Ley (1988) 'Culture's geographies', *Environment and Planning D: Society and Space*, vol. 6, pp. 115–16.

Griffin S. (1978) *Women and Nature: the roaring inside her* (New York: Harper Colophon).

Grossberg, L., C. Nelson and P. Treichler (eds) (1992) *Cultural Studies* (London: Routledge).

Greenwood, W. (1966) *Love on the Dole* (London: Heineman).

Hall, S. and M. Jacques (eds) (1983) *The Politics of Thatcherism* (London: Lawrence and Wishart).

Hall, S. (1988) *The Hard Road to Renewal* (London: Verso).

Hall, S. (1990) 'Cultural identity and the diaspora', in J. Rutherford (ed.), *Identity, Community, Culture, Difference* (London: Heineman).

Hall, S. (1991) 'Ethnicity: Identity and difference', *Radical America*, vol. 23, pp. 9–20.

Hall, S. and T. Jefferson (eds) (1976) *Resistance Through Rituals: Youth Sub-cultures in Post-war Britain* (London: Hutchinson).

Harvey, D. (1989) *The Urban Experience* (Oxford: Basil Blackwell).

Harvey, D. (1989) *The Condition of Post-modernity* (Oxford: Basil Blackwell).

Hebdige, D. (1988) *Hiding in the Light: On images and things* (London: Routledge).

Hewison, R. (1987) *The Heritage Industry: Britain in a climate of decline* (London: Methuen).

Hoggart, R. (1957) *The Uses of Literacy* (London: Chatto and Windus).

Hopkins, J. (1991) 'West Edmonton mall as a centre for social interaction', *The Canadian Geographer*, vol. 35, pp. 268–79.

Jackson, E. and D. Johnson (1991) 'Geographic implications of mega-malls, with special reference to the West Edmonton Mall', *The Canadian Geographer*, vol. 35, pp. 226–31.

Jackson, P. (1989) *Maps of Meaning: An introduction to cultural geography* (London: Unwin Hyman).

Jackson, P. (1991a) 'Mapping meanings: a cultural critique of locality studies', *Environment and Planning A*, vol. 23, pp. 215–38.

Jackson, P. (1991b) 'The crisis of representation and the politics of position', *Environment and Planning D: Society and Space*, vol. 9, pp. 131–4.

Jacobs, J. (1993) 'The City Unbound: Qualitative approaches to the city', *Urban Studies*, vol. 30, pp. 827–48.

Jameson, F. (1991) *Post-modernism, or the cultural logic of late capitalism* (London: Verso).

Katz, C. (1992) 'All the world's a stage', *Environment and Planning D: Society and Space*, vol. 10.

Keller, E. F. and C. R. Grontkowski (1983) 'The mind's eye', in S. Harding and M. B. Hintikka (eds), *Discovering Reality: Feminist perspectives on epistemology, metaphysics, methodology and philosophy of science* (Dordrecht: D. Reidel), pp. 207–24.

Kenzer, M. (1985) 'Milieu and the "intellectual landscape": Carl O. Sauer's undergraduate heritage', *Annals of the Association of American Geographers*, vol. 75, pp. 258–70.

Kolodny, A. (1975) *The Lay of the Land: Metaphor as experience and history in American life and letters* (Chapel Hill, NC: University of North Carolina Press).

Lefebvre, H. (1991) *The Production of Space* (Oxford: Basil Blackwell).

Ley, D. (1985) 'Cultural/humanistic geography', *Progress in Human Geography*, vol. 9, pp. 415–23.

Ley, D. and K. Olds (1988) 'Landscape as spectacle: world's fairs and the culture of heroic consumption', *Environment and Planning D: Society and Space*, vol. 6, pp. 191–212.

Lowenthal, D. (1961) 'Geography, experience and imagination: toward a geographical epistemology', *Annals of the Association of American Geographers*, vol. 51, pp. 241–60.

MacCanel, D. (1992) *Empty Meeting Grounds: the tourist papers* (London: Routledge).

Marcus, G. and M. Fischer (1986) *Anthropology as Cultural Critique* (Chicago: University of Chicago Press).

Marcuse, H. (1964) *One-Dimensional Man* (London: Routledge).

Massey, D. (1984) *Spatial Divisions of Labour* (London: Macmillan).

Mather, C. (1993) 'Oral testimony as text: knowledge, power and space in rural South Africa, paper given at the Conference of the Society for Geography, Port Elizabeth South Africa July (copy from the author at the Department of Geography, University of Bophuthatswana).

McDowell, L. (1991) 'Multiple voices: speaking from inside and outside 'the project', *Antipode*, vol. 24, pp. 56–72.

McDowell, L. and D. Massey (1984) 'A woman's place', in D. Massey and J. Allen (eds) *Geography Matters!* (Cambridge University Press).

McRobbie, A. (1991) *Feminism and Youth Culture* (London: Macmillan).

Meinig, D. W. (ed.) (1979) *The Interpretation of Ordinary Landscapes: Geographical essays* (Oxford University Press).

Merchant, C. (1980) *The Death of Nature: Women, ecology and the scientific revolution* (San Francisco: Harper and Row).

Mohanty, C. T. (1991) 'Cartographies of struggle', in C. T. Mohanty, A. Russo and L. Torres (eds), *Third World Women and the Politics of Feminism* (Bloomington: Indiana University Press).

Monk, J. and V. Norwood (1987) *The Desert is no Lady: South-western landscapes in women's writing and art* (New Haven: Yale University Press).

Mort, F. (1988) 'Boy's Own? Masculinity, style and popular culture', in R. Chapman and J. Rutherford (eds), *Male Order: Unwrapping masculinity* (London: Lawrence and Wishart).

Philo, C. (1991) *New Words, New Worlds: Reconceptualising Social and Cultural Geography* (Lampeter: Department of Geography, St David's University College).

Pollock, G. (1988) *Vision and Difference: Femininity, Feminism and the Histories of Art* (London: Routledge).

Pratt, G. (1992) 'Commentary: Spatial metaphors and speaking positions', *Environment and Planning D: Society and Space*, vol. 10, pp. 241–4.

Pratt, M. B. (1988) 'Identity: Skin Blood Heart', in E. Bulkin, M. B. Pratt and B. Smith, *Yours in struggle: Three feminist perspectives on anti-semitism and racism* (Ithaca, NY: Firebrand Books).

Pred, A. and M. Watts (1992) *Reworking Modernity: Capitalisms and Symbolic Discontent* (Brunswick, NJ: Rutgers University Press).

Price, M. and M. Lewis (1993) 'The reinvention of cultural geography', *Annals of the Association of American Geography*, vol. 83, pp. 1–17.

Pringle, R. (1983) 'Women and consumer capitalism', in C. Baldock and B. Cass (eds), *Women, Social Welfare and the State* (Sydney: Allen and Unwin) (a shorter version is in L. McDowell and R. Pringle, 1992, *Defining Women*, Cambridge: Polity Press, pp. 148–52).

Prus, R. and L. Dawson (1991) 'Shop till you drop: shopping as recreational and laborious activity', *Canadian Journal of Sociology*, vol. 16, pp. 145–64.

Rosaldo, R. (1992) *Culture and Truth* (London: Routledge).

Rose, G. (1993) *Feminism and Geography* (Cambridge: Polity Press).

Sack, R. (1988) 'The consumer's world: place as context', *Annals of the Association of American Geographers*, vol. 78, pp. 642–64.

Said, E. (1978) *Orientalism* (New York: Pantheon Books).

Said, E. (1992) *Culture and Imperialism* (New York: Columbia University Press).

Samuel, R. (ed.) (1989) *Patriotism: the making and unmaking of British national identity*, 3 vols (London: Routledge).

Sassen, S. (1991) *The Global City: New York, London, Tokyo* (Princeton NJ: Princeton University Press).

Sauer, C. O. (1925) 'The morphology of landscape', *University of California Publications in Geography*, vol. 2, pp. 19–54.

Sauer, C. O. (1952) *Agricultural Origins and Dispersals* (New York: American Geographical Society) (reprinted as *Seeds, Spades, Hearths and Herds*, 1969, Cambridge, Mass: MIT Press).

Shields, R. (1989) 'Social spatialization and the built environment: the West Edmonton Mall', *Environment and Planning D: Society and Space*, vol. 7, pp. 147–64.

Shields, R. (1991) *Places on the Margin: Alternative geographies of modernity* (London: Routledge).

Shields, R. (ed.) (1992) *Lifestyle Shopping: the subject of consumption* (London: Routledge).

Short, J., L. Benton, W. Luce and J. Walton (1993) 'Reconstructing the image of an industrial city', *Annals of the Association of American Geography*, vol. 83, pp. 207–24.

Sillitoe, A. (1975) *Saturday Night and Sunday Morning* (London: Paladin).

Simmel, G. (1909) 'The great city and mental life', reprinted in R. Sennett (ed.), 1969, *Classic Essays on the Culture of Cities* (Prentice Hall: New York).

Simmons, J. (1991) 'The regional mall in Canada', *The Canadian Geographer*, vol. 35, pp. 232–40.

Soja, E. (1989) *Postmodern Geographies: the reassertion of space in critical social theory* (London: Verso).

Sorkin, M. (ed.) (1992) *Variations on a Theme Park: the new American city and the end of public space* (New York: The Noonday Press).

Spivak, G. (1992) 'The politics of translation', in M. Barrett and A. Phillips (eds), *Destabilising Theory* (Cambridge: Polity Press).

Steedman, C. (1986) *Landscape for a Good Woman* (London: Virago).

Stott, R. (1989) 'The dark continent: Africa as female body in Haggard's adventure fiction', *Feminist Review*, vol. 32, pp. 69–89.

Urry, J. (1990) *The Tourist Gaze* (London: Sage).

Valentine, G. (1993) 'Desperately seeking Susan: a geography of lesbian friendships', *Area*, vol. 25, pp. 109–16.

Watson, S. (1991) 'Gilding the smokestacks: the new symbolic representations of deindustrialised areas', *Environment and Planning D: Society and Space*, vol. 9, pp. 59–70.

Williams, R. (1989) *The Politics of Modernism* (London: Verso).

Woolf, V. (1938) *Three Guineas* (Hogarth Press; first paperback edition 1977 – (Harmondsworth: Penguin).

Wright, P. (1985) *On Living in an Old Country* (London: Verso).

Young, M. and Willmott, P. (1957) *Family and Kinship in East London* (London: Routledge).

Zukin, S. (1988) *Loft Living: Culture and capital in urban change* (London: Radius).

Zukin, S. (1991) *Landscapes of Power: From Detroit to Disney World* (Berkeley and Los Angeles: University of California Press).

Images, Myths and Alternative Geographies of the Third World

MORAG BELL

In 1955 representatives of 29 African and Asian countries met in Bandung, Indonesia. It was the first occasion on which these recently decolonised nations had come together as a group to acknowledge their common identity and interests. They claimed to be distinct from either the capitalist or the socialist world. As a non-aligned group they represented a 'third world'. The Bandung Conference was staged to draw attention to political issues – anticolonialism and the creation of a non-aligned movement with a powerful voice in the international community. Thus the Third World, as a political concept, was born. The solidarity of this political movement can be traced through successive annual non-aligned conferences, while the effectiveness of Third-World unity has been noted in the influence it has brought to bear on the policy and practice of global institutions such as the United Nations.

The notion of the Third World is also linked to economic terms such as development and underdevelopment. Used in this economic sense, its original status as a symbol of political distinction and defiance has been subverted by Western professionals and governments to become a pejorative label associated with paternalism and dependency. International development, the aid business and the Third World are inextricably linked. The former is variously described as a goal, a set of policies and a process. Shaped and controlled by the Western industrialised countries, it is associated with the post-1945 world, the era of political independence from colonial rule, the creation of bilateral aid organisations and the formation of multilateral institutions, including the United Nations and the World Bank.

What is the geography of this Third World? Certain common features come to mind: poverty, famine, environmental disaster and degradation, political instability, regional inequalities and so on. A powerful and negative image is created that has coherence, resolution and definition. But behind this tragic stereotype there is an alternative geography, one which demonstrates that the introduction of development into the countries of the Third World has been a protracted, painstaking and fiercely contested process. The process has not been uniform between territories, and in the evolution of the concept the periphery has contributed significantly to the core.

This chapter demonstrates the following: first, that concepts of development, progress and the Third World, although associated with the post-1945 world, are long established in Western thought. The history of development forms an essential part of Europe's historical relationship with non-Western countries; a relationship with its roots in imperialism and colonialism and fraught with contradiction and conflict. Second, in the spread of Western influence to non-Western societies, while Europe would appear to be dominant, in practice colonialism was not the planned, deliberate process implied by much development theory. Control over non-Western peoples and their environments was slow to evolve and it was persistently contested. Third, in a contemporary context, our definition of, approach to and interpretation of the Third World is conditioned by the development perspective adopted by the Western social sciences in their study of non-Western societies. A negative stereotyping is characteristic of this perspective. But alternative geographies exist of these peoples and their environments that confront Third-World stereotypes.

The Western Tradition of Development and Progress

Our image of non-European societies remains ambiguous and contradictory. Deeply rooted in European thought and literature is a preoccupation with the exotic. Fascinating and intriguing in the European mind is the psychological function of non-Western cultures, including their histories, religions, philosophies and associated institutions. At the base of this interest is a preoccupation with human development, with questions of evolution and progress. Literature on these 'other' societies offers parallel commentaries on this topic.

Attempts to impose an identity on non-European cultures and territories have varied from a respect for the simple, unsophisticated virtues of the primitive, through the complex mystery of the Orient, to a vision of El Dorado in the Americas and the sinister, unknown qualities of darkest Africa. In shaping these attitudes, both environmental determinism and racism have had a significant effect (Brantlinger, 1985; Peet, 1985). Ellen Churchill Semple, an early-twentieth-century American geographer, sought to account for racial stereotypes in terms of the physical environment. She argued:

> The influence of climate upon racial temperament, both as a direct and indirect effect, cannot be doubted. . . . In general a close correspondence obtains between climate and temperament. The northern peoples of Europe are energetic, provident, serious, thoughtful rather than emotional, cautious rather than impulsive. The southerners of the sub-tropical Mediterranean basin are easy-going, improvident except under pressing necessity, gay, emotional, imaginative, all qualities which among the negroes of the equatorial belt degenerate into grave racial faults (Semple, 1911, p. 620).

But these caricatures are not exclusive to the non-Western periphery. Similar representations exist of Britain's domestic Third World; those separate social and geographical spheres occupied by the Celts, the working class and women. Here too an association has been made between environment, character and social behaviour (Porter, 1991). During the late nineteenth and early twentieth centuries writings on 'unknown England' combined personal exploration of working-class life with the rapidly developing techniques of sociological analysis. Those who lived *In Darkest England* – the title of a popular book written by the founder of the Salvation Army – were as mysterious and alien to the respectable classes as were the inhabitants of 'darkest Africa'. Thus travellers to London's East End played a similar enquiring role to nineteenth-century explorers of the dark continent. Moreover 'amateur' sociologies involving the methodological collection of social statistics, such as Charles Booth's *Life and Labour of the People in London*, initiated the systematic research of an outcast world that was to become a characteristic of professional experts in Africa from the 1930s. Contemporary equivalents of these enquiries into the geographically proximate 'unknown' can be found in the work of Bunge in Detroit (1974). They also occur in the feminist literature that seeks to expose the female world largely 'hidden from geography and history' (Kofman and Peake, 1990).

It has been argued that, historically, feelings of Anglo-Saxon uniqueness led to a sense of racial and national superiority, which promoted the misrepresentation of other societies and groups (Said, 1978). Sir Francis Younghusband, leader of the British invasion of Tibet in 1904, expressed his belief in the superiority of Western culture as follows:

> No European can mix with non-Christian races without feeling his moral superiority over them. He feels, from the first contact with them, that whatever may be their relative positions from an intellectual point of view, he is stronger morally than they are. And facts show that this feeling is a true one. It is not because we are any cleverer than the natives of India, because we have more brains or bigger heads than they have, that we rule India; but because we are stronger morally than they are. Our superiority over them is not due to mere sharpness of intellect, but to the higher moral nature to which we have attained in the development of the human race (Younghusband, 1896, pp. 396–7).

That this apparent cultural superiority was used as a justification for imperialism and colonialism cannot be denied. Early images of North America by the Pilgrim voyagers depict 'a vast and unpeopled' land 'devoid of all civil inhabitants, where there are only savage and brutish men which range up and down' (Miller, 1956, p. 12). The Indian population, characterised as 'wild beasts' did not qualify as inhabitants. This vacant territory was therefore ripe for conquest and transformation from savagery into a moral, Christian land. More than two centuries later Cecil Rhodes – mining magnate, empire builder and prime minister of Cape Province, South Africa – expressed his convictions as he travelled the South-African veld:

> As I walked, I looked up at the sky and down at the earth, and said to myself this should be British. And it came to me in that fine, exhilarating air that the British were the best race in the world (Williams, 1938, p. 55).

From the early nineteenth century emigration societies in Britain promoted the civilising role of British culture overseas. In the case of female emigration propaganda, traditional views of refined English motherhood were grafted on to notions of racial superiority to produce a concept of Englishwomen as guardians of the English race (Hammerton, 1979; Mackay and Thane, 1986). The imperial duty assigned to women, therefore, was to counteract alien assimilation – the tendency for the colonies to lose their 'imperial heritage' after the first generation of predominantly male settlers (Domosh, 1991; Chadhuri and Strobel, 1990).

By the late nineteenth century moral justfication for imperial and colonial expansion was enhanced in Britain by the belief in scientific and technical superiority. Self-styled 'enlightened specialists' such as Beatrice and Sydney Webb, representatives of a new era of scientific management, applied principles of discipline and efficiency both to social conditions in Britain and to the management of the Empire. The Coefficients Club, founded by Beatrice Webb in 1902, and of which Sir Halford Mackinder, the first director of the School of Geography at Oxford University was a member, remained united in its goal of an efficiently organised Empire based on the knowledge and skills of Western-trained experts (Semmel, 1960; Taylor, 1911).

European Civilisation Overseas – The Growth of Britain's Third World

If perceived superiority was used to justify imperialism and colonialism, then, in the case of Britain at least, neither the Empire nor indeed the 'development' of the territories acquired was initially planned in an efficient and disciplined way. The use of superior technology and organised power to secure control over non-European peoples and territories was not a purposive activity. Enthusiasm for Empire evolved only slowly in Britain. So too did the creation of an imperial philosophy. Formal intervention in the colonies through official aid did not begin until the 1930s; that is, towards the end of the colonial era. Furthermore in timing, philosophy and territorial acquisition the imperial and colonial experience of the various European powers was markedly different (Fieldhouse, 1982; Dixon and Heffernan, 1991).

The British Empire was a vast and varied collection of dependencies. It grew in a haphazard fashion. 'Religious deviationists, commercial adventurers and jailers in quest of sites for prisons were more often than not the founders of British colonial settlements' (Huttenback, 1974, p. 13). In the seventeenth and eighteenth centuries Britain's Third World overseas comprised North America and the West Indies (Figure 7.1). These original white settler 'colonies', while remaining politically dependent upon the mother country, provided a permanent home for British emigrants. Australia, initially an overseas destination for British convicts, became part of the Empire in the early nineteenth century. So too did Cape Colony and Natal in South Africa, annexed originally by the British in 1806 for military purposes as a fortress on the sea passage to the East. India was never a colony. From 1600 the English venture to India was assigned to the East India Company, when it received from the Crown monopoly rights to trade. Its acquisition and control over territory was gradual and reached its full extent only in the mid-nineteenth century.

During the last three decades of the nineteenth century geography as a scientific discipline was promoted in Europe as the tool of a more deliberate imperial enterprise that included territorial acquisition and economic exploitation. Indeed by the end of the nineteenth century Britain had acquired a new tropical Empire in Africa and the Far East, comprising some 90 million people and 750 thousand square miles. Together with the old Empire of India and the 'white' colonies, Britain was responsible for around 345 million people and 11.5 million square miles (Colls, 1986). But Britain's acquisition of the African territories was hardly achieved with the skills of scientific management and planning. The Brussels Geographical Conference in 1876 brought together geographers and explorers from across Europe to discuss the 'opening up' of Africa (Bridges, 1980; Heffernan, 1989). But the subsequent carving out of the Congo Free State in central Africa by King Leopold of Belgium was undertaken without international cooperation, and the partitioning of Africa that followed the Berlin Conference of 1884–5 was largely achieved without the benefits of detailed geographical knowledge. Costly commissions became necessary to settle subsequent boundary disputes (Hudson, 1977).

Granted, British rule imposed on these territories a new uniformity in the organisation of space. National boundaries were defined. An infrastructure of roads and railways was constructed between new centres of production, consumption and exchange – towns, ports, mines, plantations and estates (Christopher, 1988). But the concept of a united British Empire, a collection of territories with a common identity owing allegiance to the British crown, was, like the contemporary Third World, a much more powerful creation at home

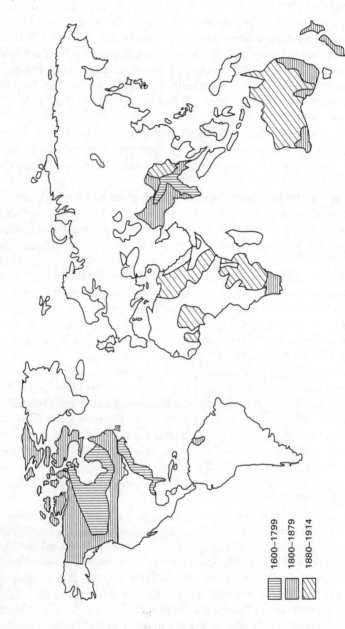

FIGURE 7.1 *British Overseas Acquisitions, 1600–1914*

1600–1799
1800–1879
1880–1914

than abroad. The sense of unity and uniformity it implies, obscures enormous variations between territories in their physical environment and social and cultural practices – variations that persist today. It also underestimates the diverse political relationships that they forged with the metropole and sought to change over time. Protectorates such as British East Africa were initially under the jurisdiction of the Foreign Office, later the Colonial Office. The self-governing colonies of Canada, Australia, the Union of South Africa and New Zealand, later known as dominions, enjoyed full autonomy with an ambassadorial representative in London.

Chartered companies played an important role as empire builders and in the early administration of overseas territories (Christopher, 1985). Not until the Government of India Act of 1858 was British power over India transfered from the East India Company to the Crown. The secretary of state for India was a political appointment based in London, but control over the government of India lay in India itself, with British viceroys and their Indian civil servants posted throughout the country. In Africa, at the instigation of Cecil Rhodes, the British South Africa Company received a royal charter in 1889 to acquire and exercise commercial and administrative rights in south central Africa. It administered Southern Rhodesia (now Zimbabwe) until 1923, when the white settlers were granted responsible government, and Northern Rhodesia (now Zambia) until 1924, when the Colonial Office assumed control.

Just as constitutional uniformity failed to exist, equally elusive was social and cultural unity. Despite the export from Britain of apparently unifying forces of race, language and cricket, Britain faced acute problems of absorbing this diverse Empire. India was deemed to be 'a burden, alien and unsettleable' (Colls, 1986, p. 45). British merchants traded in vast areas of West Africa but the unhealthy tropical climate discouraged permanent settlement. Even in the white settler colonies the overseas British were different. In the words of one Rhodesian colonist,

A Colonial child is not exactly the same as an English child, and to talk to him of loyalty and patriotism one must use a different orientation, if not a different idiom, unless one wishes to be dismissed with the half-hearing which the child gives to people who talk a language which he does not understand or which does not interest him (Jollie, 1924, p. 241).

Views expressed in the colonies revealed, on occasion, ambiva-
lence, sometimes hostility to Britain and its Empire. Nationalist
resistance towards imperial rule in India took official form after
the formation of the Indian National Congress in 1885, when increasingly militant demands were made for greater 'native' participation in the country's administration. In South Africa the African
National Congress dates back to 1912. Equally determined was the
white nationalism in the settler colonies (Eddy and Schreuder, 1988).
In the case of the United States it was warfare that finally secured
independence from Britain in 1783. Southern Rhodesia, 'fought' for
self-government less than thirty years after the Pioneer Column had
entered the country in 1890. The status of 'Responsible Government' was finally conferred after a referendum in 1923. 'Rhodesia
for Rhodesians and for the Empire', a popular battle cry in the country,
indicated the nature of local loyalties. It anticipated the later, un-
successful, struggle for white 'independence' between 1965 and 1980.

Nor was there much evidence of unity between the colonies. Indeed,
on occasion, despatches between them were marked by near hostility. Prior to securing 'Responsible Government', Rhodesians re-
fused to join the Union of South Africa. A South-African politician,
who, on a visit to Rhodesia, sought to emphasise the unity of the
white race in southern Africa as a whole, received a sharp rebuke.
To his naive and ill-judged comment, 'Remember, you are South
Africans first, Rhodesians second, and British subjects last', came
the indignant reply, 'I'm not! I'm a Rhodesian!' Despite King George
V's remark that Rhodesia was the Ulster of South Africa, Rhodesia did not wish to be associated with the racial bitterness and dis-
sension 'down South' (Jollie, 1924).

By forging and reinforcing their own separate identities, Britain's
Third-World territories ultimately achieved political independence:
India in 1947, followed by the African territories, commencing with
Ghana in 1957. Namibia finally secured its independence in 1989,
having been administered by South Africa since the defeat of Germany
in the First World War. But the watershed of political independence
should not be overstated (Crowder, 1987). Like its historical pre-
cedents, the contemporary Third World continues to be profoundly
influenced by Western thought and practices.

Contemporary Development Perspectives

In seeking to grapple intellectually and professionally with the world beyond Europe it is difficult to discard ethnocentric and metropolitan standpoints. We tend to study Anglophone areas of the world, which, though varied culturally and environmentally, share a common colonial past. Thus the countries of the Commonwealth remain Britain's entry into the Third World. We 'invade and conquer with the appropriate intellectual armoury' of the social sciences (Stokes, 1974, p. 288), including the theories of development and underdevelopment with which it is associated.

Many reviews exist of alternative approaches to and theories of development and underdevelopment (Corbridge, 1986; Hettne, 1990; Larrain, 1989; Peet, 1991). These theories seek to explain uneven regional economic conditions within and between countries and endeavour to prescribe effective interventions. Dominated by the principles of sociology and economics, they shape development geography and fix our attitudes to, and assumptions about, different societies and their environments. Three contrasting schools of thought under-pin contemporary theories and models. First, the classical tradition of modernisation and neomodernisation associated with the political right. This is based on a stylised history of the progressive evolutionary change of Third World economies and societies derived from Western free-market experience. Second, the underdevelopment school of the political left (including dependency and postdependency approaches), which, on the basis of an alternative and exploitative history of capitalist world development, presents a geography of the world economy dominated by unequal relations within and between states. Third, the liberal interventionist tradition, which stands between these two perspectives and is associated with the work of the Brandt Commission (Brandt, 1980, 1983). This school argues that in an interdependent world, contrary to the equilibrating assumptions of neoclassical economics, flows of trade and aid should be carefully managed to ensure mutual benefits to North and South.

Granted, these opposing approaches and ideological positions have undergone internal revision. With successive United Nations Development Decades and changing international political and economic circumstances, diffusionist and interventionist streams of thought have sought to redefine modernity from 'economic growth', through meeting 'basic human needs' and 'popular participation' to 'economic reform'

and structural adjustment. Likewise, within the neo-Marxist framework, proponents of the various theories of imperialism and underdevelopment have been required to question their assumptions and
methodologies (Corbridge, 1989a; Smith, 1984). Yet despite the
external impetus to internal change, these contrasting schools of
thought share a common starting point – poverty is viewed in
deprivationist terms while their different views of development have
a positive connotation (Pavlich, 1988). In terms of the geography
of the world economy, this finds expression in a spatial dualism –
North/South, core/periphery, developed/developing.

Thus statistics such as per capita gross national product, life ex-
pectancy at birth and infant mortality rate are invoked to fix our
views of the periphery. In emphasising what people are deprived of
(as is implied by poverty), they impose a negative uniformity upon
non-Western societies. As objects of study poor people become
categories and are labelled as an homogeneous group (Wood, 1985).
In contrast to the poverty of 'tradition', a vision of an ideal society is presented that – whether based on a diversified economy
within the world capitalist system or on self-sufficient autonomous
growth – implicitly prescribes, by way of solution, how people
should be living. To achieve the predefined goal, a process of carefully directed social, economic and political change is prescribed.

But the postcolonial world of the late twentieth century challenges
this crude and negative paternalism. Remnants of Empire are hidden
behind a 'high-tech' landscape of international finance, multinational
investment and free-trade zones. The cities of Abidjan, Harare, Kuala
Lumpur and Bombay, once symbols of European power and racial
superiority, share in the prosperity of a postmodern age. They form
an integrated part of a restructured global economy in which industries based on high technology replace natural resources as sources
of national wealth. Juxtaposed with this fast-moving, sophisticated
and overwhelmingly masculine world even the high-density slums
and peripheral shanty towns are symbolic of more than unequal
capitalist development. Once they were manifestations of a 'culture
of poverty' – haphazard, overcrowded and unplanned, reflecting social
disorganisation and deviance. Now their inhabitants are thought to
embody an alternative enterprise culture outside state control (Bromley
and Birkbeck, 1988).

Global economic restructuring challenges much development orthodoxy. The concept of linear progressive change is shattered by an
international economy that is unpredictable and unstable. Periods

of recession, high interest rates, falling export prices and fluctuating stock markets affect business and employment from Britain to Brazil. Nor is the political and economic response to this international instability in line with orthodox theory. In 1982 a 'debt crisis' was officially acknowledged when Mexico, burdened with massive debts, indefinitely suspended interest payments to its creditors. In 1987 Brazil and Côte D'Ivoire did likewise. Commercial banks in North America and Western Europe were paying the price of lending profligacy through the recycling of petrodollars (Edwards and Larrain, 1989; Faber and Griffith-Jones, 1990). Also in 1987 the British government removed the harsh debt-service obligations of Sub-Saharan Africa by converting loans to grants. Albeit briefly, the concept of debtor power was given practical credibility.

International integration does indeed contest the assumptions of political and economic power that lie behind a crudely drawn dualism between 'developed' and 'developing' worlds. Moreover within these geographical categories unity between states remains an elusive quality. Consider once again the 'debt crisis'. As Corbridge (1988) demonstrates, this major international event of the 1980s was the outcome of a long and complex history of capitalism, central to which was the struggle between the US, Germany and Japan for world industrial and technological leadership. These international or interimperial rivalries, and the geopolitical strategies that followed from them, demand that our analyses of development begin by 'deconstructing the received categories of North and South or core and periphery' (Corbridge, 1989b, p. 358).

The economic success of the newly industrialising countries (NICs) calls into question the concept of a unified Third World of uniform economic collapse (Harris, 1986). In 1989 the Confucian capitalists in East Asia – symbols of prudent government intervention and economic success – were joined by Malaysia, the first Moslem NIC (Figure. 7.2). Islamic revolutions in Iran, Pakistan and Afghanistan offer alternative development paths to those of Western secular society (Beeman, 1986; Halliday and Alavi, 1988). Contrary to the Third-World image of perpetual food crisis, several Asian states, including India and Sri Lanka, have emerged from the Green Revolution as net exporters of foodstuffs. Signs of demographic transition in China, Colombia, Cuba, Mexico, Sri Lanka and Thailand raise optimism about 'the end of the population explosion' (World Bank, 1984).

Evidence such as this should not obscure the struggle of many African countries to improve the living conditions of their rapidly

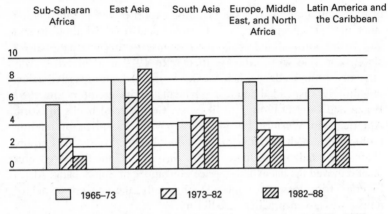

FIGURE 7.2   *Growth of Real GNP in Selected Regions, 1965–1988*

SOURCE   *World Development Report* (World Bank, 1989a).

growing populations (Table 7.1). In the postindependence era African capitalism would appear to have a similar illusive quality to African socialism, the mythical ideology that politicians sought to create in the 1960s (Sklar, 1988). Within the context of greatly enlarged bureaucratic and party structures, familiar external constraints upon indigenous enterprise have been identified and assessed – foreign competition, international terms of trade and the rise of protectionism (Kennedy, 1988). Over the last decade external debt and the imposition of structural adjustment programmes, with their faith in the superiority of market solutions, have also challenged the economic power of the state. The social effects have been severe (Marshall, 1990; Onimode, 1989). In southern Africa political struggle, drought and South Africa's policy of regional destabilisation have further constrained the achievement of economic growth and equitable development (Smith, 1990). 1990 ushered in a new era. With the end of the Cold War in Europe and the disappearance from the region of the Soviet presence and a Soviet model of development, South Africa's white-minority government launched negotiations over a new democratic constitution and southern Africa was drawn into a new world order.

As new political ideologies emerge and countries become increasingly differentiated in their economic and social performance, at the same time major international social movements seek to construct a unity between individuals and groups across national boundaries.

TABLE 7.1 *Orthodox Development Indicators for Selected Countries in Sub-Saharan Africa*

	Population (millions) mid-1987	GNP per capita, average annual growth (%)			Population average annual growth (%)		
		1965–73	1973–80	1980–87	1965–73	1973–80	1980–87
Low-income economies	397.3	3.1	0.3	−3.6	2.6	2.7	3.1
Ethiopia	44.8	1.1	0.0	−1.6	2.6	2.8	2.4
Malawi	7.9	4.3	1.4	0.0	2.8	3.0	3.8
Sierra Leone	3.8	2.3	−1.8	−2.0	1.9	2.1	2.4
Kenya	22.1	4.7	1.3	−0.9	3.4	3.8	4.1
Nigeria	106.6	5.3	1.2	−4.8	2.5	2.5	3.4
Middle-income economies	53.9	1.9	−1.2	0.3	2.8	3.3	3.3
Senegal	7.0	−0.8	−0.5	0.1	2.3	2.8	2.9
Zimbabwe	9.0	2.6	−2.0	−1.3	3.5	2.9	3.7
Côte d'Ivoire	11.1	4.5	1.2	−3.0	4.1	4.3	4.2
Cameroon	10.9	−0.4	5.7	4.5	2.4	3.1	3.2
Botswana	1.1	9.3	7.3	8.0	3.1	3.7	3.4

SOURCE World Bank, 1989b.

The late twentieth century has witnessed a revival of the environmental and the women's movements, both of which display a reluctance to accept 'difference' and contingency. Recent feminist scholarship has rediscovered shared gender as a basis for common interests across classes and cultures. Gender is socially and culturally created but, argue Momsen and Townsend (1987, p. 28), 'in the history and geography of humanity . . . women's work tends to be of less value than men's and women tend to have far less access to all forms of social, economic and political power'. This apparent continuity is reflected also in contemporary debate about the environment. Renewed concern over global resource use and depletion has prompted environmental movements to stress the mutual interest of North and South in resolving their 'common crisis' (Redclift, 1987).

This complex international landscape destroys the credibility of a unified development theory and presents new challenges to geography's two central traditions – ecological and spatial differentiation. Among the issues it raises, three are stressed here. First, in response to the world economy, countries of neither the North nor the South operate as a unified and uniform political and economic block. They construct their own histories and geographies as individual governments, albeit within constraints, seek to enhance national economic and social performance or stifle internal initiative. Second, within these diverse political and economic environments, divisions of non-Western societies based not merely on class, caste, age or ethnicity but also on gender, reveal important hidden geographies of inequality and struggle (Brydon and Chant, 1989; Momsen, 1991; Wallace and March, 1991). Third, while a return to environmental determinism is untenable, explanations of resource depletion and degradation cannot ignore local ecological conditions and the cultural patterns that shape environmental relations. Crucially, issues such as gender and the physical environment cannot merely be added to established development theory and practice. They demand that our assumptions and interpretations of development and underdevelopment be reexamined.

Radical development geography must adopt a framework that is liberated from the tyranny of dualism and allows for changes in the world economy and variations between states – one that accommodates alternative historical and contemporary geographies, cutting across the North–South divide. In the final part of this chapter selected perspectives are used to demonstrate that development is more diverse and complex than is implied by unified theory.

Contradictory Images and Alternative Geographies

Western ideologies of modernisation and development continue to impose an identity on non-Western societies. From the perspective of Europe or North America the 'outsider' interprets Third-World landscapes from the experience of an inherently 'better' place. Three powerful images reflect this vision of the 'other'. The periphery represents a source of private wealth; it remains the focus for development assistance; it is the object of pity and paternalism. In effect, crude ideologies associated with colonialism persist.

For multinational corporations in North America, Western Europe and Japan, the periphery remains a source of cheap labour, natural resources and profit. For these capitalist enterprises, apparently better and more efficient uses can be found for land and labour than the indigenous population is capable of achieving. With the support of indigenous elites, free-trade zones from Mexico to Sri Lanka provide an economic environment liberated from normal legal and financial regulations – pollution controls, trade-union laws, taxation – within which these goals are pursued.

But, like colonial capital before it, multinational investment has its own geography (Daniel, 1991; Taylor and Thrift, 1986). To date, the majority of African countries dogged by political instability and, since 1970, by low economic growth have been largely excluded from this apparently progressive investment. The 'modern' landscape that these corporations impose also brings human and physical costs. The tragedy of Bhopal in India, where several thousand people were injured or died following the release of toxic gases from the Union Carbide plant in 1984, offers a stark reminder. Equally destructive is 'ecological imperialism' in the form of exploitative short-term development projects – forest depletion, hydroelectric schemes and mining sites – that degrade natural resources (Adams, 1990). The Amazon rainforest is being aggressively destroyed on the principle that environmental deterioration is the necessary price of economic and technical progress (Hemming, 1985). In effect these are contemporary equivalents to the regressive impact of European colonial capital.

Within the aid community, equally powerful in the official mind remains a commitment to 'developing' the periphery through the modernising and progressive influence of Western science and technology. A political ideology of national unity and nation building adds weight to development projects initiated by international aid that are imbued by a spirit of scientific and professional superiority little different from their colonial predecessors. Indeed the creation of an ordered landscape, efficient economies and disciplined societies remain goals of the aid business in a manner similar to early-twentieth-century scientific management (Hancock, 1989). Thus historical studies of the 'silent violence' wrought upon indigenous peoples by apparently progressive agricultural schemes to alter the arrangement of their settlements, control their land, labour and livestock (*Journal of Southern African Studies*, 1989; Watts, 1989), have their successors in ambitious schemes of social and environmental engineering (Wisner, 1988).

Moral justification for these interventions is sought by blaming the periphery for its own apparent underdevelopment. The present is manipulated by the dehumanisation of continents such as Africa

and its peoples. Thus the inherent hostility of the African environment is perpetuated and reinforced by the Western media in images
of land degradation, desertification, famine and malnutrition. Ethnic
stereotyping continues in visions of pathetic, helpless figures – objects
of pity and paternalism or immoral sources of intractable 'exotic'
diseases (Prins, 1989; Sabatier, 1988). These images of the physical and human landscape as obstacles to progress are fused in debates
about environmental crisis and overpopulation (Patterson and
Shrestha, 1988). A negative association between environment, character and social behaviour – in effect contemporary environmental
and racial determinism – is used by aid donors to justify externally
controlled development. Equivalents can be found in the attitudes
of 'outsiders' to Britain's inner cities. Similar feelings of moral
superiority justify analysis of, and intervention in, this 'problem' space.

But the unintended impact of culturally insensitive interventions
is all too apparent. Optimistic faith in the technocratic skills of
environmental management renders invisible the disruption to local food production that accompanies irrigation schemes geared to
cash crops (Adams and Anderson, 1988). Similarly food aid – a
technical solution to international imbalances between food sur-
pluses and deficits – can threaten indigenous agriculture in the re-
cipient country, distorts diets by substituting wheat for locally grown
staples and intensify child malnutrition (Andrae and Beckman, 1985;
Maxwell, 1990; Tarrant, 1990). Even the geography of aid flows,
biased towards Europe's former colonies or America's strategic
interests, challenges the assumption that development assistance is
an exercise in altruism (Bose and Burnell, 1991; Lipton, 1986).
Evidence such as this prompts skeptical propositions that contemporary aid is little different from the much disparaged colonial
technical assistance (Blaut, 1970). But these formal interventions,
these attempts to manipulate Third-World peoples, do not go
unchallenged.

Stimulated at least in part by scholarship from the periphery and
reinforced by debate within donor countries, postcolonial texts seek
to resist the devaluation of the 'periphery' or the 'marginal' by the
metropolitan centre. They include studies that question the superiority of modern industrialisation and technological progress. The
writings of Laurens Van der Post, and the depiction by Marshall
Sahlins (1974) of hunter-gatherers as the original affluent society,
reflect this challenge. Also represented are the perspectives of
nationalist groups, ethnic interests and women (Stea and Wisner,

1984; Vail, 1989). These alternative geographies reshape our views of non-Western societies and their environments.

They demonstrate that while poverty and environmental crisis are socially and culturally created, it cannot be denied that they exist. But they are as differentiated as any other geography. Following a long tradition of cultural ecology, localised studies emphasise the diverse social, economic and agronomic strategies by which communities cope with recurrent and unpredictable food scarcity (Hill, 1986; Longhurst, 1986). The rich pool of indigenous knowledge upon which these strategies are based, renders absurd a crude dualism, long established in the colonial mind, between Western wisdom and indigenous ignorance (Richards, 1985). It demonstrates that a carefully managed rural landscape need not comprise grandiose engineering structures, complex water-extraction technologies or neatly segregated land uses (Bell and Roberts, 1990). Granted, all systems of knowledge are open to continual change, even destruction, through contact with other systems, including more powerful ones. Political ecology addresses these issues in the colonial and postcolonial context (Blaikie, 1984; Bryant, 1992). It emphasises how differential access to, and control over, resources constrains individuals and households as ecological managers (Davies and Leach, 1991; Watts, 1989). Within these constraints, among the individuals active in shaping the landscape are women.

The international women's movement has done much to bring gender issues into the development debate, while feminist theory has exposed the limitations of structural analyses of social change based on class (*Millennium*, 1988). Nevertheless many masculine and feminist outsiders perpetuate powerful myths about gender roles and relations in non-Western societies (Mohanty, 1988). Among these, two are prominent. First that women are, in the main, 'economically inactive' in non-Western societies, their 'work' being confined to the domestic sphere of child bearing, child rearing and household maintenance. Second that women are only victims of oppression and objects rather than subjects of change. The inside or private world to which women are apparently confined limits their entry to the public domain. Evidence indicates otherwise. Studies of women's economic activities, power relations between women and men, divisions among women, women's consciousness and solidarity, including their capacity to organise and struggle for change, expose these false dualities.

They demonstrate that while standard definitions of work used in censuses and surveys frequently render invisible women's activities, rural women are often major economic actors in their own right as primary food producers and traders (Boserup, 1970, 1985; White and Young, 1984). In many rural, social settings dominated by the prolonged absence of men, women handle issues of deforestation, land degradation, water scarcity and pollution as part of their daily lives. They respond to apparently well-meaning but often naive 'development' packages with skill and resourcefulness. Within the new international division of labour, women in the cities of Latin America, South and South-East Asia comprise the major source of non-unionised labour in export processing industries (Armstrong and McGee, 1985; Chant, 1991). They also play an active role in the design of self-help housing projects for low-income urban communities (Moser and Peake, 1987).

Granted women are not an homogenous group. Divisions, including those based on rural–urban location, class, household structure and age difference, cut across gender solidarity. While the introduction of rice milling in Bangladesh has liberated middle-income peasant women from arduous unpaid work, for poor and landless women with few income-generating possibilities this same technical innovation may restrict further their opportunities for paid employment (Whitehead, 1981). Gender roles and relations also vary with the cultural context (Ardener, 1981). In some Islamic societies social and geographical restrictions are imposed upon women by family and kinship obligations. But levels of restriction vary greatly; gender-defined boundaries between public and private spheres are fluid (Callaway, 1984). In Brazil's labour market, gender is one factor that can be manipulated by employers to achieve a cheap and productive labour force. It provides a basis for segregation and discrimination by skill, occupational mobility and pay scales, justified by reference to apparently 'natural' differences between women and men (Humphrey, 1987). However, in times of economic recession women are differentially affected according to their class and race (Calio, 1990).

Patterns of women's solidarity can be identified within Africa, Asia and Latin America where shared interests underlie complex and varied patterns of mutual support. These include informal groupings of women around village wells and in agricultural tasks. But these essentially cultural groupings are also political. Both at grassroots level and through international networks, women increasingly organise themselves in ways that explicitly articulate their concerns

(Dankelman and Davidson, 1988; Gale, 1990). Women are prominent in the landscape of protest. Through various forms of violent
and, more particularly, non-violent struggle, women resist the corporations and national governments that threaten to destroy their
livelihoods or infringe their human rights (Eckstein, 1988; Jacquette,
1989). Development and underdevelopment imposed from above
and outside are fiercely contested.

Conclusion

A combination of moral concern and fascination with the exotic
forms the basis of our geographical imagination and continues to
underlie much contemporary interest in non-Western societies. But
the approaches adopted are conditioned by theories in the social
sciences. It is through these theories that concepts of development,
progress, modernisation, poverty and the Third World are constructed
and defined. These theories and the labels with which they are associated fix our views of the periphery. While labelling is essential, there is no inevitable structure or destiny to our divisions of
the globe. The Third World is a more unified concept at home
than abroad. It obscures historical and contemporary divisions and
diversities within both North and South, core and periphery. The
recent collapse of the Second World in Europe raises further doubts
over its meaning and validity.

Central to the discourse on development is the status and authority of Western culture, science and technology. It is the apparent
superiority of Western systems of knowledge that has legitimised
racist and environmentalist ideologies and justified Europe's urge
to modernise the periphery. But development has traditionally shaped,
and continues to be influenced by, a reciprocal relationship between
periphery and core. Colonial cultures were persistently threatened
by alternative, indigenous systems of social and environmental organisation. The contemporary aid community and foreign private investment face similar challenges to their ethnocentric faith in the
progressive influence of Western management and technology.

Concepts of development are not uniform, unified or static.
Alternative images, myths and geographies exist that are based on
cultural and scientific systems, both complex and varied. A critical
geography of development and the Third World must challenge the
crude representations of peoples and places upon which grand theories

are based. It should demonstrate that the Third World is a contested tradition; that it is associated with widely divergent and conflicting views and practices; that these views have many historical, geographical and social contexts.

Acknowledgements

I am grateful to Denis Cosgrove, Michael Heffernan and Neil Roberts for their helpful comments on an earlier draft of this chapter.

References

Adams, W. M. (1990) *Green Development. Environment and Sustainability in the Third World* (London: Routledge).

Adams, W. M. and D. M. Anderson (1988) 'Irrigation before development: indigenous and induced change in agricultural water management in East Africa', *African Affairs*, vol. 87, pp. 519–36.

Andrae, G. and B. Beckman (1985) *The Wheat Trap: bread and underdevelopment in Nigeria* (London: Zed).

Ardener, S. (1981) *Women and Space: ground rules and social maps* (London: Croom Helm).

Armstrong, W. and T. G. McGee (1985) *Theatres of Accumulation. Studies in Asian and Latin American Urbanisation* (London: Methuen).

Beeman, W. O. (1986) 'Iran's religious regime: what makes it tick, will it ever run down', *Annals of the American Academy of Political and Social Science*, vol. 483, pp. 73–83.

Bell, M. and N. Roberts (1990) 'The politics and culture of dambo irrigation in Zimbabwe, in D. Cosgrove and G. E. Petts (eds), *Engineering the landscape* (London: Belhaven).

Blaikie, P.(1984) *The Political Economy of Soil Erosion* (London: Longman).

Blaut, J. M. (1970) 'Geographic models of Imperialism', *Antipode*, vol. 6, pp. 65–85.

Booth C. (ed.) (1889, 1891) *Life and Labour of the People in London. Vol. 1 1889. Vol. II, 1891* (London: Macmillan).

Booth W. (1890) *In Darkest England and the Way Out* (London: Salvation Army).

Bose, A. and P. Burnell (eds) (1991) *Britain's Overseas Aid since 1979. Between Idealism and Self-Interest* (Manchester University Press).

Boserup, E. (1985) 'Economic and demographic interrelationships in sub-Saharan Africa', *Population and Development Review*, vol. 11, pp. 383–97.

Boserup, E. (1970) *Women's Role in Economic Development* (London: Allen and Unwin).

Brandt, W. (1980) *North–South: A Programme for Survival* (London: Pan).

Brandt, W. (1983) *Common Crisis* (London: Pan).

Brantlinger, P. (1985) 'Victorians and Africans: the genealogy of the myth of the dark continent', *Critical Inquiry*, vol. 12, pp. 166–203.

Bridges, R. C. (1980) 'The first conference of experts of Africa', in J. C. Stone (ed.), *Experts in Africa* (Aberdeen University, African Studies Group), pp. 7–11.

Bromley, R. and C. Birkbeck (1988) 'Urban economy and employment', in M. Pacione (ed.), *The Geography of the Third World: Progress and Prospect* (London: Routledge), pp. 114–47.

Bryant, R. L. (1992) 'Political ecology. an emerging research agenda in Third World studies', *Political Geography*, vol. 11, pp. 12–36.

Brydon, L. and S. Chant (1989) *Women in the Third World. Gender Issues in Rural and Urban Areas* (London: Elgar).

Bunge, W. (1974) 'The human geography of Detroit', in R. A. Roberge (ed.), *La crise urbaine: a challenge to geographers* (University of Ottawa Press), pp. 49–69.

Calio, S. A. (1990) 'The Brazilian economic crisis and its impact on the lives of women, *Political Geography Quarterly*, vol. 9, pp. 415–23.

Callaway, B. J. (1984) 'Ambiguous consequences of the socialisation and seclusion of Hausa women, *Journal of Modern African Studies*, vol. 22, pp. 429–50.

Chadhuri, N. and M. Strobel (eds) (1990) 'Special issue on western women and imperialism', *Women's Studies International Forum*, vol. 13, no. 2.

Chant, S. (1991) *Women and Survival in Mexican Cities. Perspectives on Gender, Labour Markets and Low-Income Households* (Manchester University Press).

Christopher, A. J. (1985) 'Patterns of British overseas investment in land, 1885–1913', *Trans. Inst. Br. Geogr.*, vol. 10, pp. 452–66.

Christopher, A. J. (1988) *The British Empire at its Zenith* (London: Croom Helm).

Colls, R. (1986) 'Englishness and the political culture', in R. Colls and P. Dodd (eds), *Englishness: Politics and Culture 1880–1920* (London: Croom Helm), pp. 29–61.

Corbridge S. (1986) *Capitalist World Development. A Critique of Radical Development Geography* (London: Macmillan).

Corbridge S. (1988) 'The debt crisis and the crisis of global regulation', *Geoforum*, vol. 19, pp. 109–30.

Corbridge S. (1989a) 'Marxism, post-Marxism and the geography of development', in R. Peet and N. Thrift (eds), *New models in geography, the political-economy perspective* (London: Unwin Hyman), pp. 224–53.

Corbridge S. (1989b) 'Debt, the nation-state and theories of the world economy', in D. Gregory and R. Walford (eds), *Horizons in Human Geography.* (London: Macmillan), pp. 341–60.

Crowder, M. (1987) 'Whose dream was it anyway? Twenty-five years of African Independence', *African Affairs*, vol. 86, pp. 7–24.

Daniel, P. (ed.) (1991) 'Foreign investment revisited', *IDS Bulletin*, vol. 22, no. 2.

Dankelman, I. and I. Davidson (1988) *Women and Environment in the Third World: Alliance for the Future* (London: Earthscan).

Davies, S. and M. Leach (1991) 'Food security and the environment', *IDS Bulletin*, vol. 22, no. 3.

Dixon, C. and M. J. Heffernan (eds) (1991) *Colonialism and Development in the Contemporary World* (London: Mansell).

Domosh, M. (1991) 'Towards a feminist historiography of geography', *Trans. Inst. Br. Geogr.*, vol. 16, pp. 95–104.

Eckstein, S. (ed.) (1988) *Power and Popular Protest: Latin American Social Movements* (Berkeley: University of California Press).

Eddy, J. and D. M. Schreuder (1988) *The Rise of Colonial Nationalism* (London: Unwin Hyman).

Edwards, S. and J. Larrain (eds) (1989) *Debt, Adjustment and Recovery: Latin America's Prospects for Growth and Development* (Oxford: Blackwell).

Faber, M. and S. Griffith-Jones (eds) (1990) 'Approaches to Third World debt reduction', *IDS Bulletin*, vol. 21, no. 2.

Fieldhouse, D. K. (1982) *The Colonial Empires, a comparative survey from the eighteenth century*, (2nd edn) (London: Macmillan).

Gale, F. (1990) 'The participation of Australian Aboriginal women in a changing political environment', *Political Geography Quarterly*, vol. 9, pp. 381–95.

Halliday, F. and Alavi H. (eds) (1988) *State and Ideology in the Middle East* (London: Macmillan).

Hammerton, A. J. (1979) *Emigrant Gentlewomen, Genteel Poverty and Female Emigration, 1830–1914* (London: Croom Helm).

Hancock, G. (1989) *Lords of Poverty* (London: Macmillan).

Harris, N. (1986) *The End of the Third World. Newly Industrialising Countries and the Decline of an Ideology* (London: Tauris).

Hayford, A. M. (1974) 'The geography of women: an historical introduction, *Antipode*, vol. 2, pp. 1–19.

Heffernan, M. (1989) 'The limits of utopia: Henry Duveyrier and the exploration of the Sahara in the nineteenth century', *Geographical Journal*, vol. 155, pp. 342–52.

Hemming, J. (ed.) (1985) *Changes in the Amazon Basin*, vols 1 and 2 (Manchester University Press).

Hettne, B. (1990) *Development Theory and the Three Worlds* (London: Longman).

Hill, P. (1986) *Development Economics on Trial: the anthropological case for the prosecution* (Cambridge University Press).

Hudson, B. (1977) 'The new geography and the new imperialism: 1870–1918', *Antipode*, vol. 9, pp. 12–19.

Humphrey, J. (1987) *Gender and Work in the Third World. Sexual Division in Brazilian Industry* (London: Tavistock).

Huttenback, R. A. (1974) *Racism and Empire. White Settlers and Coloured Immigrants in the British Self-Governing Colonies 1830–1910* (Ithaca: Cornell University Press).

Jacquette, J. S. (ed.) (1989) *The Women's Movement in Latin America: Feminism and the Transition to Democracy* (London: Unwin Hyman).

Jollie, E. T. (1924) *The Real Rhodesia* (London: Hutchinson).
Journal of Southern African Studies (1989) vol. 15, no. 2, special issue on the politics of conservation in Southern Africa.
Kennedy, P. (1988) *African Capitalism. The Struggle for Ascendancy* (Cambridge University Press).
Kofman, E. and L. Peake (1990) 'Into the 1990s: a gendered agenda for political geography', *Political Geography Quarterly*, vol. 9, no. 4, pp. 313–36.
Larrain, J. (1989) *Theories of Development* (Cambridge: Polity Press).
Lipton, M. (ed.) (1986) 'Aid effectiveness', *IDS Bulletin*, vol. 17, no. 2.
Longhurst, R. (ed.) (1986) 'Seasonality and poverty', *IDS Bulletin*, vol. 17, pp. 27–35.
Mackay, J. and P. Thane (1986) 'The englishwoman', in R. Colls and P. Dodd (eds), *Englishness: Politics and Culture 1880–1920* (London: Croom Helm).
Marshall, J. (1990) 'Structural adjustment and social policy in Mozambique', *Review of African Political Economy*, no. 47, pp. 28–43.
Maxwell, S. (ed.) (1990) 'Food security in developing countries', *IDS Bulletin*, vol. 21, no. 3.
Millennium (1988) special issue: *Women and international relations*, vol. 17, no. 3.
Miller, J. (ed.) (1956) *The American Puritans* (New York: Anchor Books).
Mohanty, C. (1988) *Third World Women and the Politics of Feminism* (Indiana University Press).
Momsen, J. (1991) *Women and Development in the Third World* (London: Routledge).
Momsen, J. H. and J. Townsend (eds) (1987) *Geography of Gender in the Third World* (London: Hutchinson).
Moser, C. and L. Peake (1987) *Women, Human Settlements and Housing* (London: Tavistock).
Onimode, B. (1989) *The IMF, the World Bank and the African Debt*, volumes I and II (London: Zed).
Patterson, J. G. and N. R. Shrestha (1988) 'Population growth and development in the Third World: The neocolonial context', *Studies in Comparative International Development*, vol. 22, pp. 3–32.
Pavlich, G. (1988) 'Re-evaluating modernisation and dependency in Lesotho', *Journal of Modern African Studies*, vol. 26, pp. 591–605.
Peet, R. (1985) 'The social origins of environmental determinism', *Annals of the Association of American Geographers*, vol. 75, pp. 309–33.
Peet, R. (1991) *Global Capitalism. Theories of Societal Development* (London: Routledge).
Porter, D. (1991) '"Enemies of the race": Biologism, environmentalism and public health in Edwardian England', *Victorian Studies*, vol. 35, pp. 159–78.
Prins, G. (1989) 'But what was the disease? The present state of health and healing in African Studies', *Past and Present*, no. 124, pp. 159–79.

Redclift, M. (1987) *Sustainable Development. Exploring the Contradictions*, (London: Methuen).

Richards, P. (1985) *Indigenous Agricultural Revolution: Ecology and Food Production in West Africa* (London: Hutchinson).

Sabatier, R. (1988) *Blaming Others. Prejudice, Race and Worldwide AIDS* (London: Panos).

Sahlins, M. (1974) *Stone Age Economics* (London: Tavistock).

Said, E. (1978) *Orientalism* (London: Routledge and Kegan Paul).

Semmel, B. (1960) *Imperialism and social reform. English Social-Imperial Thought 1895–1914* (London: George Allen and Unwin).

Semple, E. C. (1911) *Influences of Geographic Environment on the Basis of Ratzel's System of Anthropo-Geography* (New York: Russell and Russell).

Sklar, R. (1988) 'Beyond capitalism and socialism in Africa', *Journal of Modern African Studies*, vol. 26, pp. 1–21.

Smith, N. (1984) *Uneven Development. Nature, Capital and the Production of Space* (Oxford: Blackwell).

Smith, S. (1990) *Front Line Africa. The Right to a Future. An Oxfam Report on Conflict and Poverty in Southern Africa* (Oxford: Oxfam).

Stea, D. and B. Wisner (1984) 'The fourth world: A geography of indigenous struggles', *Antipode*, vol. 16, no. 2.

Stokes, E. (1974) '"The voice of the hooligan": Kipling and the Commonwealth experience', in N. McKendrick (ed.) *Historical Perspectives. Studies in English Thought and Society in Honour of J. H. Plumb* (London: Europa), pp. 285–301.

Tarrant, J. R. (1990) 'Food policy conflicts in food-deficit developing countries', *Progress in Human Geography*, vol. 14, pp. 467–87.

Taylor, F. W. (1911) *The Principles of Scientific Management* (London: Harper & Bros).

Taylor, M. J. and N. J. Thrift (eds) (1986) *Multinationals and the Restructuring of the World Economy* (London: Croom Helm).

Vail, L. (ed.) (1989) *The Creation of Tribalism in Southern Africa* (London: Currey).

Wallace, T. and C. March (eds) (1990) *Our Work is Just Beginning. A Reader on Gender and Development* (Oxford: Oxfam).

Wallace, T. and C. March (eds) (1991) *Changing Perceptions: Writings on Gender and Development* (Oxford: Oxfam).

Watts, M. J. (1989) 'The agrarian question in Africa: debating the crisis', *Progress in Human Geography*, vol. 13, pp. 1–41.

White, C. P. and K. Young (eds) (1984), 'Research on rural women: feminist methodological questions', *IDS Bulletin*, vol. 15, no, 1.

Whitehead, A. (1981) 'A conceptual framework for the analysis of the effects of technological change in rural women', *World Employment Paper* (Geneva: ILO).

Williams, B. (1938) *Cecil Rhodes* (London: Greenwood).

Wisner, B. (1988) *Power and Need in Africa. Basic Human Needs and Development Policies* (London: Earthscan).

Wood, G. (1985) *Labelling in development policy, Essays in honour of Bernard Schaffer* (London: Sage).

World Bank (1984) *World Development Report* (New York: Oxford University Press).

World Bank (1989a) *World Development Report* (New York: Oxford University Press).

World Bank (1989b) *Sub-Saharan Africa, from Crisis to Sustainable Growth* (Washington DC: World Bank).

Younghusband, F. E. (1896) *The Heart of a Continent* (London: Murray).

8
Taking Aim at the Heart of the Region

NIGEL THRIFT

Introduction

Only a very few human geographers nowadays would lay claim to being 'regional geographers', and in quite recent times regional geography has been described as if it was in need of exhumation rather than resuscitation. Even worse, it has sometimes seemed as though it has become an acceptable form of professional nostalgia, conjuring up memories of a golden age, now (thankfully) defunct. Yet in the last few years regional geography has made something of a comeback. A flurry of publications and projects have put regional synthesis back on the map (Gregory, 1978; Gilbert, 1988; Pudup, 1988; Sayer, 1989; Thrift, 1983, 1990b, 1991, 1993).

In this chapter I too want to go back to regional geography. My suggestion will be that this act of going back can also point the way forward. In particular I want to argue that grouped around the practice of doing regional geography can be found most of the important problems that human geography faces today. The invocation of regional geography cannot solve these problems but it certainly brings them into focus and, in that act of focusing, it shows us how far we still have to go.

The chapter is in three sections, beginning with a study of the work of Paul Vidal de la Blache (1845–1918). Why choose Vidal's work as an introduction to the dilemmas of modern regional geography? Three main reasons stand out. The first of these is that certain elements of his thinking on regional geography have persisted to the present. We need to examine these different elements and how they are present in modern regional geography. The second reason is that I want to claim that we are now living in a period rather similar to that through which Vidal lived, one in which an old order is in its death throes and the main contours of a new order are just becoming apparent. Like Vidal, we too have to cope with a changed world and the changed nature of regions in that world. A third reason is that we seem to be entering a new period of localism and the comparisons with the localism of Vidal's time are both instructive and important.

The next section considers the work of Karl Marx (1818–83). I have chosen to concentrate on Marx for two main reasons. The first is that, like Vidal, Marx lived through a time of flux. He was both a critic and a celebrant of the birth pangs of the new capitalist order and of the emergent industrial city region that lay at its heart. The second is that Marx's writings have been a major influence on the human geography of the last twenty years. In the struggle to understand Marx's insights into modern capitalist societies and how they can be applied to the study of regions, geographers have been able to discover their own insights that point to both the strengths and the weaknesses in Marx's work.

In the last section I outline the work of Fredric Jameson (1987, 1988a, 1988b, 1991). I have chosen Jameson for three reasons. The first is that his is an attempt to set out changes in our own time, which are, in their own way, as epic and far-reaching as the changes that Vidal and Marx lived and thought. The second is because, in principle at least, Jameson is intent on establishing a key role for space in these changes. The third reason is because Jameson still wants to take Marx's work forward and his manner of attempting this task points to what still remains to be understood about (post) modern regional geographies and what cannot be understood through Marx.

In Table 8.1 have attempted to sketch out some of the main ways in which I have drawn distinctions between these three authors' geographies. The table is not exhaustive, but it acts as a rough guide to the terrain I will cover. A number of caveats need to be entered. First, and importantly, I will be talking about the regional geography of Western capitalist countries. Many of my generalisations and strictures do not apply, or do not apply equally well, in other kinds of country. The reason for the seemingly orientalist omission of a good part of the world is a simple one; space is limited. Second, I do not enter into the problems of regional definition and taxonomy. In part this is again because of limited space, but also because the idea that

TABLE 8.1   *Three Authorities: Vidal, Marx and Jameson*

	Vidal	Marx	Jameson
Chief imaginary	peasant France	industrial England	suburban United States
Dominant mode of production	Feudalism	Industrial capitalism	Late or multinational capitalism
Main classes	Peasants/ landowners	Proletarians/ capitalists	Middle classes
Dominant experience	Being	Producing	Consuming
Dominant mode of cultural representation	Speaking	Writing	Images
Chief means of cultural interpretation	Story-telling/ natural metaphors	Meta-narrative/ science/ universals	Local narratives/ hermeneutics/ difference
Chief spatiality	Return/ reenactment homogenisation	Explosion/ colonisation/ heterogeneity	Implosion/ colonisation/ mobility
Chief sites	Village/field	Home/factory	Home/shops

there can be just one definition or taxonomy is naive (Lakoff, 1988). Finally, as will become clear, it can hardly be said that I have covered all regional geography in this chapter. In particular I feel the omission of the vast number of 'popular' regional geographies that appear each year, although, as will also become clear, the increasing popularity of these kind of works is, I believe, one indicator of a new kind of region. I have restricted myself to 'academic' regional geography, but in doing so it is with no sense of the automatic superiority of this product – in some cases quite the reverse in fact!

The Political Unconscious of Paul Vidal de la Blache

In so many accounts it is Paul Vidal de la Blache who is supposed to trigger off the classical period of regional geography, and so it is only appropriate to begin with this well-known yet surprisingly enigmatic figure (Wrigley, 1965; Buttimer, 1971; Lacoste, 1979; Andrews, 1984). Some authors have described a Vidalian theoretical system of an almost unworldly elegance and symmetry that I simply cannot find in his works (for example, Buttimer, 1978; Berdoulay, 1978), however, so I feel free to bring to the fore ·what I see as the two main features of Vidal's work. Both of them involve in different ways the legitimation of the idea of France and a French nation.

The first of these features, and the one for which he is best known, consists of an appreciation of, even a hymn to, peasant France. For Vidal the peasant landscapes of France were proof of the power of the physical environment as 'an underlying principle of causation' (Vidal de la Blache, 1903, p. viii). At the same time they also showed the power of social groups to both adapt to and mould the physical environment down through the centuries.

> It is man who reveals a country's individuality by moulding it to his own use. He establishes a connection between unrelated features, substituting for the random effects of local circumstances a systematic cooperation of forces. Only then does a country acquire a specific character differentiating it from others, till at length it becomes, as it were, a medal struck in the likeness of a people (ibid.)

In France this process of interdigitation of land and people resulted in the evolution of a series of '*pays*', 'consecrated by no official acceptance but handed down from one generation to another among the peasant folk, who are geologists after their fashion' (ibid., p. 14). The *pays* were a set of places in which repeated agricultural and other practices (what Vidal called a 'community of habits') had lain hold of the land. However this emphasis on the 'disciple of the soil' (ibid., p. viii) and what she or he wrought was but one feature of Vidal's work on regions. Vidal was also concerned with the other ways in which France might be defined.

Thus Vidal was active throughout his career in giving consideration to France's influence on other races. In the wake of the defeat of France at the hands of the Prussians in 1870 he was an enthusiastic advocate of the 'habit of geography' as a tool in France's geopolitical armoury (see Hudson, 1977). It is no surprise to find that he actively supported colonisation. Vidal's later work tended to become even more geopolitical in character. Especially in *La France de l'Est*, published in 1916 (Vidal de la Blache, 1916, 1979), Vidal gave detailed consideration to geopolitical factors. Given the region he had chosen to study – Alsace Lorraine – and the symbolic potency it derived from the competing French and German claims to it, it could hardly be otherwise.

Vidal has often been taken to task for his emphasis on the 'little local communities' that made up peasant France and certainly, with the benefit of hindsight, such an emphasis seems misplaced. Throughout the time he was writing, the distinctive ways of life of the French peasantry were flickering out of existence under the onslaught of capitalism and the French state. Only three years after Vidal's birth, in 1848 the last major revolt of the peasantry took place, 'protesting against the emergence of private capitalist agriculture in defence of traditional, community rights' (Baker, 1984, p. 25). The cohesion of the French peasantry was under attack from all sides: from colonisation of its own people by a more and more acutely rationalised and centralised French state (with its military service, its system of mass education, and so on) determined to turn *le paysan* into *le Français* (Weber, 1977); from the individualism engendered by the cash economy in the countryside; from new transport investments, such as the railways; and from the associated pull of rapidly growing cities – most especially Paris. 'Paris is centralisation itself' proclaimed the emperor Louis Napoleon. Haussmann called Paris 'the head and heart of France' (Harvey, 1985).

But this was not all. For once they reached the cities the peasants were subjected to new forces. In their local communities they had been cocooned in their representations of themselves.

> The life of a village, as distinct from its physical and geographical attributes, is perhaps the sum of all the social and personal relationships existing within it, plus the social and economic relations – usually oppressive – which link the village to the rest of the world. But one could say something similar about the life of a large town. What distinguishes the life of a village is that it is also a living portrait of itself: a communal portrait, in that everybody is portrayed and everybody portrays. As with the carvings on the capitols in a Romanesque church, there is an identity of spirit between what is shown and how it is shown – as if the portrayed were also the carvers. Every village's portrait of itself is constructed, however, not out of stone, but out of words, spoken and remembered: out of opinions, stories, eye-witness reports, legends, comments and hearsay. And it is a continuous portrait; work on it never stops (Berger, 1979, p. 33).

But now the peasants had to bend to new works of interpretation, interpreting the lives they lived in the cities. For many the city was both a 'liberation from tradition and routine, but also the locus of interpersonal estrangement and fragmented experience' (Berman, 1983, p. 38). In other words the peasants had to confront head on the explosive experience of capitalist modernity. The shock must have been great. Here were bright gas lights; the play of fashion; highways, speed, change and movement, celebrated in Baudelaire's Parisian poetry (and then sacralised in Benjamin's interpretations of Baudelaire's Paris). In the process of confrontation with modernity, the peasants were changed.

> The archetypical modern man, as we see him here, is a pedestrian thrown into the maelstrom of modern city traffic, a man alone contending against an agglomeration of mass and energy that is heavy, fast and lethal. The burgeoning street and boulevard traffic knows no spatial or temporal bounds, spills over into every urban space, transforms the whole modern environment into a 'moving chaos'. The chaos lies here not in the movers themselves – the individual walkers or drivers, each of whom may be pursuing the most efficient route for himself – but in their interaction in the totality of their movement in a common space. This makes the boulevard a perfect symbol of capitalism's inner contradictions, leading to anarchic irrationality in the social system that brings all these units together (ibid., p. 159).

Of course it was not just the French peasantry who found modernity hard to bear. So too did many other Frenchmen, including those from a bourgeois background like Vidal. Thus Vidal's work on peasant France should be seen not just as an elegy to a vanished way of life (Miller, 1987), partly wistful, partly reactionary, but also as an attempt to come to terms with the modern urban world in which he lived.

> Vidal de la Blache regretted what he could not help but observe. He considered that much that was best in the life of France arose out of the range and balance of original communities to be found there. He considered, like many of his contemporaries that the moral qualities of rural life were important to the nation and feared their decay (Wrigley, 1965, p. 11).

But it is to Vidal's credit that he did not bury his head in the sands of the past. He was willing to take account of the changes coming about in the make-up of the French regions after the middle of the nineteenth century. Thus the first and longer part of *La France de L'Est* consists of a conventional paean to rural France set in the style of his earlier work. But the second part of the book proceeds to confront the tidal wave of industrial capitalism that was sweeping across Alsace-Lorraine, dissolving many of its previous, locally based economic and social ties. Vidal takes to heart the need to address not only the uniqueness of the region but also its growing inter-dependence

> The advent of the steam-engine, the railways, the coal-carrying canals and of the new Alsatian cotton mills did not mean the super-imposition of a few new strands upon an old-established pattern but was the first stage in the dissolution of the traditional, rural, local, regional pattern of life. The new industries represented a new type of society. The new society was able to produce indus-trial goods on a vastly bigger scale, and was formed round cheap and speedy communications. Food, clothing, building materials, tools, all soon ceased to be locally made and different in one re-gion from its neighbour (ibid., p. 10).

Thus, Vidal lived and wrote a dilemma. He inhabited a France that was becoming more rationalised, more modern by the moment, but he looked back to a world peopled by peasants living off the soil in local communities. As *La France de L'Est* shows he did adjust to the new reality: 'the idea of the region in its modern form is a conception to do with industry: it is associated with the industrial metropolis' (Vidal de la Blache, 1916, p. 163, cited in Wrigley, 1965, p. 11). But it would be difficult to claim that he wholeheartedly suc-ceeded in the task of modernising his regional geography so that it could cope with the modern world of industrial capitalism and, es-pecially, with the nodal city-based industrial region.

It is easy to be dismissive of Vidal's ideas now. I want to make a more measured response. The most important and progressive ele-ment of Vidal's ideas was his conception of geography as a social science. This was always a halting and occluded conception but it still bears examination. First, it was a social science based on the model of the natural sciences. For Vidal, geography was the science of landscape. Thus, 'Vidalian geography takes its model from the taxonomic dream of the natural sciences and is resolutely turned towards description, the geographer finds himself facing a landscape: the perceptible, visible aspect of space' (Ross, 1988, p. 86). Second, Vidal's idea of geography as a social science was often less than systematic in its character.

> The presentation of arguments by Vidal frequently followed a fairly consistent pattern involving a cascade of illustration drawn from diverse regions of the World, as if the litany of illustrations were proof enough of the correctness of the preceding position or associations. Causal connections are simply asserted or implied, suggested and made to appear plausible, but rarely demonstrated through such an appeal (Andrews, 1984, p. 327).

But towards the end of his life Vidal's views did become firmer and more coherent. In 1903 he wrote, 'modern geography is the scientific study of places' (Vidal de la Blache, 1903, cited in Andrews, 1984), and the example of *La France de l'Est* bears out the degree to which that dictum was being adhered to. Third, Vidal's idea of social science was never fully social. His notions of spatial structure were generally impressionistic while people rarely figure at all, except as representative types. In too much of Vidal's work, 'if humans appear at all they must do so in such a way as to reinforce the natural harmony of the region, the native . . . is part of the landscape in a . . . relationship of décor' (Ross, 1988, p. 87).

In summary, Vidal was not driven to examine very closely the idea of what a social science was or might be. His ideas of a social science were generally loose, non-reflective and too often posed space as a frozen, natural referent. The comparisons with contemporaries such as Durkheim and Reclus are still instructive. Thus Durkheim's idea of social science was highly systematic in character, partly influenced by Comtean positivism, and he had well-founded views on how spatial structure influenced social life, and vice versa, encapsulated in the branch of sociology he called 'social morphology' (Gregory, 1978). Reclus' ideas were just as definite. For him, geography was 'nothing but history in space' and the relationship between space and social life was a reflexive one: 'geography is not an immutable thing. It is made, it is remade every day; at each instant it is modified by men's actions' (cited in Ross, 1988, p. 23; see also Stoddart, 1986).

However there are some mitigating factors that can be put in the balance that give weight to the view that Vidal was no naïf. If his views on social science were blinkered in some ways, they were far-seeing in others. For undoubtedly part of the reason for Vidal's un-clear view of social science came from a commitment to the 'depth' of the spatial. If Vidal is unclear (and undoubtedly he sometime is) then his problems of clarity seem to me to come in part from his attempts to appreciate, take into account and describe differences be-tween regions that are not just drawn from a set of 'universal' forces that come together in combination in different places, but also de-pend upon the personality of the places themselves. That is, univer-sal forces have to be lived by people, and they can often be put together in all kinds of unexpected ways. These different ways of living, sedimented over the ages, contain their own powers to react back on universal forces, changing them, even producing new forces.

Thus, some at least of what Vallaux, writing in 1925, saw as a 'vagueness and haziness' in Vidal's thought, 'prone to take hold of opposing or contradictory things at the same time' (cited in Andrews, 1984, p. 328) might be more usefully seen as the notorious difficulty of trying to describe and explain contextual causality. Many of Vidal's most awkward themes – enchainment of phenomena, connectivity and so on – can be interpreted as attempts to allow the singular a place in science. Here Vidal was trying to acknowledge that places could have a value as more than a case study illustrating or confirming a more general law, trying to show that their singular existence was not just so much cannon fodder for science.

Of course this contextual casuality was much easier to trace in amongst the *pays* where a local order predominated:

> Each small region might conduct a trade with other areas in special communities but the basic stuff of life and work was to be local. This naturally gave rise to typical regional foods and dishes, styles of domestic and farm architecture, clothes and so on. Especially, it must be rural, rooted in the land, with the bulk of the popula-tion either working on the land or serving those who did. Even the bourgeosie and the local landed gentry might find it difficult to break free from local rural patterns of life. The peasant was deeply embedded in them. Hence Vidal's interest in the minutiae of the material culture of each small area. He dwelt at some length on the importance to the geographer of ethnological museums in this connection (Wrigley, 1965, p. 8).

It was much more difficult to perceive (at this time) amongst the spreading industries of Nancy and Mulhouse.

The history of regional geography spreads out all over the world and for reasons of space I cannot speak of it in detail. There are certainly some high points – Demangeon's Picardy, Spate's India and Pakistan, Darby's Fenlands, Meinig's Texas, Chombart de Lauwe's Paris, Lewis's New Orleans (Pudup, 1988). Yet in retrospect it is possible to portray the history of regional geography as only fulfilling part of the promise held out by Vidal's writings. Two examples will suffice to illustrate this point.

First, the broad range of Vidal's ideas were not developed. Instead geographers concentrated on a few of his ideas, narrowing his message and constraining his project. In France it has been argued that much of the substance of Vidal's system was more ably taken on board by the Annales school of historians, with their embrace of the region, their interest in *mentalité* and their insistence on large-scale perspective. Meanwhile French regional geographers produced regional monographs that concentrated on but a few of Vidal's ideas.

As French geography turned in upon itself, the regional monographs which it produced tended to become decreasingly interpretative and increasingly factual, with academic reputations being made by collecting more bricks rather than by building better bridges. The geographer's equivalent of the 'sin of eventism' was celebrated in fundamentally factual monographs recording the geography of place 'as it really was' (Baker, 1984, p. 16).

Second, there is the example of what happened when geographers turned to the city region. Too often they became trapped in a taxonomic amber, listing the formal characteristics of the city and assiduously avoiding the most important point about the modern city, the rough and tumble of constant economic, social and cultural *change*, generated by capitalist modernity.

In Anglo–American geography this strategy of formalisation was particularly apparent, as were its consequences. In the 1920s and 1930s geographers took on board the Chicago School of Sociology's models of the city but ignored its elegant enthnographic work (and subsequently a whole important tradition of American sociology). In the 1940s and 1950s geographers became obsessed by defining regions with various elegant measures. It was no wonder that by the 1960s some geographers effectively decided that the study of formulae could replace the study of regions. The pursuit of simplicity had led to the death of the region.

It is difficult to decide why regional geography so rarely fulfilled Vidal's promise. But four interrelated reasons stand out. First of all there seems little doubt that the theoretical backdrop to most regional geography was weak, weak enough to be edged aside in the 1960s even by a flimsy philosophy such as positivism. The debates around regional geography too quickly collapsed into simple oppositions: 'idiographic' versus 'nomothetic', 'systematic' versus 'synthetic', 'functional' versus 'formal' and so on. Even where discussions on regional geography attained sophistication they were too often bedevilled by their authors' seeming lack of knowledge of social theory, which would have allowed them to anchor what they argued within the broader reaches of social science. Second, and following on from this, regional geography was continually dogged by the naturalism implicit in Vidal's work. From notions of human ecology (whether those of Barrows or Hägerstrand), through environmental determinism to simple biological analogies, writers of regional geography continually shied away from the idea of society as being like, well, society. As a result they never properly conceptualised the social and cultural realms, or connected them with its endemic problems of description. Third, the region has changed its nature over the course of history. Vidal noted one change from a rural, locally based spatiality to the region whose motor is urbanised industrial capitalism. There have been other changes as well. These changes in the nature of regions are not well served or captured by a conceptual base that too often consists of simple, ahistorical concepts. Fourth, too few regional geographers ever turned their attention to the problem of how to *write* regional geography. Regional geography could be described as 'the highest form of the geographer's art' (Hart, 1982), but remarkably little attention was ever focused on what that art was (with a few exceptions, such as Darby, 1962).

However in the 1970s some of these objections to the practice of regional geography began to be met as a result of various Marxist-inspired perspectives on the region. It is to these perspectives that I now want to turn, via a consideration of Marx himself.

The Political Unconscious of Karl Marx

Karl Marx was born before Vidal and died when Vidal was still in his thirties. Yet in so many ways Marx now appears as the more original and prescient thinker. His intellectual achievements were understandably aided by his experience of a geography of capitalist transformation that was in advance of that of France (see Shanin, 1983; Corrigan and Sayer, 1983). For Marx, England was the 'metropolis of capital'. Long before Vidal he was able to observe within England's borders the transformation of the peasant into the proletarian. In the cauldron of England's emergent industrial city regions he was able to fix his gaze on greater and greater numbers of factory labourers massing together and becoming 'new-fangled men' (sic) in the process. As the new modes of transport and communication compressed English time and space (Harvey, 1989), so economic, social, political and cultural centralisation on the new city regions became increasingly apparent, not just at the national but also at the international scale.

For Marx it was clear that the motive force behind this radical transformation of England's geography was the 'whirlpool' of industrial capitalism, the 'great revolutioniser of all social conditions and relationships', and that in time it would occupy 'the whole surface of the globe'. But capitalism would not stop there. In order to survive it would have continually to smash the barriers to accumulation that it itself had built up; it would have to feed on itself.

The truth of the matter, as Marx sees, is that everything that bourgeois society builds is built to be torn down. 'All that is solid' – from the clothes on our backs to the looms and mills that weave them, to the men and women who work the machines, to the houses and neighbourhoods the workers live in, to the firms and corporations that employ the workers, to the towns and cities and whole regions and even nations that embrace them all – all these are made to be broken tomorrow, smashed or shredded or pulverised or dissolved, so that they can be recycled or replaced next week, and the whole process can go on again and again, hopefully forever, in ever more profitable forms (Berman, 1983, p. 122).

This state of continual apocalypse knits the world together economically, socially and culturally.

In place of the old wants, satisfied by the production of the country, we find new wants, requiring for their satisfaction the products of distant lands and climes. In place of the old local and national self-sufficiency, we have intercourse in every direction, universal interdependence. And, as in material, so in spiritual production. The spiritual creation of individual nations becomes common property. National one-sidedness and narrow-mindedness becomes more and more impossible, and from the numerous national and local literatures there arises a world literature (Marx, 1952, pp. 476–7).

It perhaps comes as no surprise to find that Marx did not give great attention to geographical difference in his work, which is not to say that he was insensitive to it, especially in his later writings. But it is clear that for Marx capital was essentially an *homogenising* and a *centralising* influence. Given the times through which he lived, these must have seemed quite reasonable conclusions to draw. In the first rush of capitalist development, the homogeneity represented by mass production, mass markets, mass culture and the growth of the masses must have seemed likely far to outweigh any tendencies to heterogeneity. Similarly the 'annihilation of space by time' (Schivelsbuch, 1987), coupled with the scale of rural to urban migration and the gradual urbanisation of the countryside, must have seemed to describe a trajectory in which the world's population, figuratively at least, would end up dancing on the head of a pin.

However there are other, more deep-seated problems in Marx's system that made it difficult for him to incorporate geographical difference. First, he did not foresee the degree to which local variety might become a part of capitalism's dynamic. For example the system of nation-states has waxed rather than waned since Marx's time and these states constitute both barriers (to the free flow of commodities, money, capital, labour, power and so on) and opportunities (as markets, pools of labour power and so on) for capital accumulation. Again, local variation within and between states has become a source of profit and consequently something to be nurtured by capital. Differences between regions can become economic opportunities precisely because of their differences, as the growth of the modern capitalist tourist industry eloquently attests.

Second, Marx did not develop (as he meant to) his explanation of the 'reproduction of labour power', in other words the production of people fit and able to take their part in the capitalist system. That must involve the explanation of how a complex system of social institutions (such as schools, factories and offices) are set up and which have to be laid over social divisions (such as gender, ethnicity and religion) that more often than not predate capitalism. These divides have their own often quite distinctive histories and geographies with which this system of social institutions interacts.

> It is the difficulty and even the impossibility of producing from one day to the next, or in the space of a few years, 'capitalist people' (as capitalists, properly speaking, and as proletarians) – that is to say, of socially fabricating individuals for whom what does and does not count, what does and does not have a signification, for whom the signification of a given thing or a given act are henceforth defined, posited and instituted. Men [sic] for whom space and time are organized, internally articulated and imaginarily represented in a different manner; men whose own body is not merely subjected to other external disciplines but caught up in another relation to the world, capable of touching, grasping, manipulating other objects and in other ways; men for whom the relations between individuals are overturned, traditional collectives and communities crushed, attachments and corresponding loyalties destroyed, men for whom, finally, an eventual economic surplus . . . is destined not to be spent for prestige, distributed among members of the extended family or clan, used for a pilgrimage or hoarded, but *accumulated* (Castoriadis, 1987, p. 358).

Third, Marx's lack of appreciation of regional difference can be traced to his notion of social science. His notion of a science of structural relations is quite clearly very sophisticated, especially when compared with the stumblings of writers such as Vidal. Yet, with the benefit of hindsight, it is not without problems born out of the time and place in which it was originated. Three of these problems, each related to the other, are particularly important.

Nowadays Marx's work sometimes seems to be dangerously close to a totalising system; that is, a system 'as full and as tightly closed as an egg' – an evolutionist master-narrative of big and generally bad Capital versus the good proletariat accounts for all there is of social life (Jay, 1984; Terdiman, 1985). The messiness of local spatial variation is a challenge to this kind of theoretical system because it disputes the degree to which a unified system exists to be mapped, the degree to which one theoretical system can explain and map out all the different geographies of modern society. Thus it comes as no surprise to find that nowadays many writers want to see 'society' not as a coherent 'thing', a single clearly defined 'structure' or 'system' but as a series of overlapping and intersecting networks of power/social integration/discourse (see Foucault, 1977; Giddens, 1985; Mann, 1986).

One might well object to a depiction of Marx as a singer of 'the great hymn of history' (except in his polemical mode) (Shanin, 1983; Corrigan and Sayer, 1983). After all, 'no discourse – as Marx himself was at pains to insist – can totalise history, if only because the sociohistorical dialectic to which discursive strategies are responsive is not played out... within the world of words alone' (Terdiman, 1985, p. 253). Certain it is that many of the versions of Marxism that have come after Marx have tried to escape any taint of totality by developing other sides to Marx's writings. It is rather more difficult to escape Marx's rationalism. For all his commitment to praxis, Marx retained a belief in the power of reason, in an ability to keep a critical distance and to distinguish between what is real and what is imaginary. Thus one of his chief intentions was to turn bourgeois rationality against itself, to use its insights to abuse its conclusions.

But the discoveries of psychology and anthropology, which began to impinge on social scientific thought in the 1860s and 1870s have made rationality a more and more difficult premise to uphold. Most recently the attack on this kind of thinking has been led by a poststructuralist appreciation of difference and incommensurability: people and society simply do not 'add up', they do not reproduce themselves in such a way as to produce the kind of coherent knowledge that would be needed to provide objects for rationalist theory to grasp (see Dews, 1987; Derrida, 1978). The best that can be hoped for are degrees of certainty, what Lakoff (1988) calls 'radial knowledge'. Again space is a vital ingredient of the critique of rationality. People and societies are increasingly stretched over space and time, fragmented, differentiated; modern geography makes difference (Thrift, 1985). (It is noticeable, I think, that the current key defender of the notion of rationality in the social sciences, Habermas, is also one of the few modern social theorists who has not incorporated space into his theories).

The third problem in Marx's system stems from the remorselessly increasing circulation of *meanings* that has taken place since Marx's time. Marx lived in a world in which the mass media and mass communications had, in hindsight, developed only a small part of their potential (Terdiman, 1985; Thrift, 1990a; Giddens, 1984, 1987; Gregory, 1989; Habermas, 1962). Marx could not foresee that the increase in the production and circulation of capital would be accompanied by a vast increase in the production and circulation of information and communication. The apparently seamless circuit of symbolic exchange in which we now appear immersed had yet to be completed (Terdiman, 1985). But since Marx's time it is not surprising to find that the study of the production, circulation and interpretation of meanings within this circuit of symbolic exchange has become a key to modern social science. Some commentators have depicted the spread of a vast network of communications, of writing and texts and latterly images, that has no identifiable origin or end (and so no location from which it is possible to establish a critical distance). In this network meanings multiply themselves indefinitely. Seen in this way, the 'imaginary' becomes the real and the 'real' becomes the imaginary. The 'commentator' becomes the commentary and the 'commentary' becomes the commentator. There is no eyrie left from which to view the passing parade of society.

The attention to meanings has meant that much greater attention is now being paid to matters of description. How can we represent the world when it has become so decidedly inter-textual? Thus the search for inspiration from the arts and humanities, from subjects such as literary theory, asthetics and rhetoric. For, if the master-narratives of Marx and others are to be written off, what is to replace them? Is it to be a series of stories about localities, revealing the modern world through intertextuality (for example, Cooke, 1989)? Is it to be an archaeology, bent upon digging up the effects of the old master-narratives, still there engrained in the way we think about contexts, but buried by present scepticisms (Foucault, 1977; Lentricchia, 1987)? Or is it to be the free play of all manner of textual devices, a time of wild experimentation (Eagleton, 1986)? Further, can the new textual strategies avoid the fate of the old modernist ones that finally became assimilated into capitalism?

If a way had to be found to summarise these three lacunae in Marx's system, it would be by pointing to the lack of the contextual dimension that Vidal strove, however hazily, to inject into his work. For Marx, local difference is a problem for both theory and capitalism to overcome, not to play on (or with).

The neglect of regional difference in Marx made it difficult for Marxist geographers, as they appeared on the Anglo–American scene in the 1960s and 1970s, to talk about geography. Certainly too many of the early attempts by the new Marxist geographers ended up looking like crude forms of economic determinism. At the same time it is easy to see why this might be: there is the stress on capital as a protean force, unconstrained by any barriers; there is the lack of attention to the reproduction of that unique commodity – labour power; and there is the difficulty of introducing contextuality into Marx's system, with its consequences for notions of totality, rationality and description.

The idea of uneven development, a concept borrowed from Lenin presaged the first attempt at a Marxian regional geography. Of course it would be difficult to deny that regions are unevenly developed and that capital has had a hand in the business. But the problem is to go beyond these insights. The responses to this problem have produced a rich and varied literature, which I shall not detail here (but see Gilbert, 1988; Pudup, 1988). Instead I want to concentrate upon one attempt to respond to the problem of uneven development (and redevelopment) that, more than any other, took hold of the geographical imagination, namely Massey's (1984) idea of the 'spatial division of labour'. More than any other Marxist geographer, Massey tried to produce a set of principles for doing Marxist regional geography. Massey's basic contention was that different levels of production require different qualities of labour power. Firms search for the appropriate quality of labour to satisfy their needs amongst the available regional alternatives and locate accordingly, producing, in aggregate, a spatial division of labour. In different rounds of capital accumulation these needs will change so that some region's labour forces will be discarded by capital, others will be adapted, still others will be opened up to new forms of exploitation. At the end of the process of struggle between capital and labour, the state of play can be summarised as a spatial division of labour. Industrial restructuring leads to regional restructuring. In time, as successive cycles of capital accumulation come and go, so the successive spatial divisions of labour they engender will combine with one another to form a rich and complex palimpsest of 'plant and person' (see Gregory, 1989).

Massey's 'geological' metaphor, consisting of layer upon layer of sedimented outcomes of struggle between capital and labour, is striking for its simplicity and economy of explanation. It is also notable that it finds a way of doing Marxist regional geography that can be

connected back to Vidal's tentative attempts to consider the emergence of the industrial city region in the nineteenth and early twentieth centuries as well as Marx's explorations and that can carry the
story forward. In Massey's scheme of things places such as Nancy
or Mulhouse in this early period form the nuclei of a region that
represents an outcome of the first round of capital accumulation, a
region based upon 'spatial sectoral specialisation'. Regions such as
these began to be broken upon the wheel of a new round of capital
accumulation in the 1920s and 1930s as Fordist methods of mass
production altered the state of play between capital and labour and
ushered in a new spatial division of labour. Then, some time in the
1960s or 1970s the wheel turns again; new spatial divisions of labour
begin to appear, laying waste to some regions and rejuvenating others,
based upon new more flexible methods of production and new more
flexible demands for labour (see Massey, 1988; Harvey, 1987; Scott,
1988; Lash and Urry, 1987).

Massey's depiction of the constant restructuring of industry, regions and labour forces is a brilliant metaphor of a cumulative and
accumulative modernity. But it is not without its problems. Most
particularly it has been pointed out that the geological metaphor of a
sedimented capitalism acts, by its very nature, as a means of simpli-
fying complex processes. Thus Massey herself points out that the
metaphor blocks out 'broader structures of community, changing
patterns of consumption, the restructuring of spatial forms, the changing national ideological and political climate, and the market patterns of geographical cultural differentiation' (Massey, 1984, p. 58).
Warde (1985) has extended the list of elisions even farther. Again,
the movement from one spatial division of labour to another, which
is usually hard-fought and tentative, tends to be represented as a fore-
gone conclusion, a kind of Marxist game of musical chairs. There is
also the problem of identifying truly 'regional' processes in the
modern internationalised web of multinational corporations and
communications.

But one thing is clear and that is that a new Marxist-inspired
regional geography was engendered by Massey's work, a regional
geography symbolised by the word 'locality'. This new geography of 'localities' has been the butt of numerous criticisms (summar-
ized in Jonas, 1989; Warf, 1989), but these criticisms are revealing in
themselves. For example the work on localities has been criticised
by Duncan and others (Duncan, 1989; Duncan and Savage, 1989) for
being unable to produce evidence of autonomous spatial effects

(locality effects), distinctive ensembles of social relations that emanate from the region. It has been criticised by Harvey (1987) and others for draining away the power of the metanarrative of Marxism in its insistence on investigating the local. It has been criticised by Gregory (1989) and others for the conservatism of its textual strategies.

These criticisms seem to me to be symptomatic of wider questions that need to be asked about the nature of modern capitalist regions and how that nature can best be represented. Thus, to answer the three criticisms set out above, it might be argued that modern media and communications, combined with the process of commodification, are altering the context and meanings of local contexts, perhaps irrevocably. Again it might be argued that this new sense of the local must be a crucial element of metanarratives such as Marxism if they are to survive (Doel, 1991). Finally, it might be argued that textual strategies will have to change if these points are accepted. Thus Sayer (1985, 1989) has moved from a narrow position on what constitutes regional geography, based on causal explanation, combined with case studies, to a more wide-ranging position that incorporates problems of interpretation and acknowledges the importance of new textual strategies and the uses of rhetoric.

In the next section I want to entertain the possibility that these debates are indeed symptomatic by focusing on the work of Fredric Jameson. For Jameson, the rules of the game have been changed dramatically by a new form of capitalism, so dramatically that, as in Vidal's and Marx's time, the region is being redefined. As a result regional geography must redefine itself.

The Political Unconscious of Fredric Jameson

It is something of an irony that as Marxist geographers began to construct a new kind of regional geography – one that did not see the natural environment as the exemplar of the social, one that did not consist of simple ahistorical concepts, one that was theoretically sophisticated – so the nature of society and (by implication) the region seemed to be changing, almost as if history wanted to underline the lessons that needed to be learnt.

It is no easy thing to fashion an account of the new order; what it is and what it means are still contested. But perhaps its foremost explorer is the Marxist literary critic, Fredric Jameson, and it is to his work that I will turn for guidance. Jameson is useful because of his connections to Lefebvre (1971), to situationist 'psychogeographers' such as Debord (1977), and to poststructuralist (and ex-Marxist) authors such as Baudrillard (1988a, 1988b) and Lyotard (1984) (see Jameson, 1988a, 1988b, 1991).

What, then, is the nature of Jameson's synthesis? For Jameson, following Mandel, from the 1960s we entered the age of late multinational capitalism in which multinational corporations hold sway over the globe. It is an era in which capitalism has become fully established on the world stage: 'it is not that this is no longer the capitalism analysed by Marx, but that it is a much closer, *purer* version of capitalism' (Jameson, 1987, p. 38). Jameson's landscape of capitalism is both sweet and sour.

First of all, it is based upon the sheer economic power of multinational corporations backed up by 'dizzying edifices of credit and power' (ibid., p. 42). Second, that power is organised and transmitted by electronic means. 'This is the age of the signal and the wire, of instantaneous communication, of a global network of microcircuits and blinking lights' (Jameson, 1988b, p. 38). Third, there is the absolute preeminence of the commodity form. The logic of the commodity has reached its apotheosis, an apotheosis based not on an homogenous but on a heterogeneous market that thrives on a difference and incommensurability fuelled by the cut and thrust of 'symbolic rivalry, of the needs of self-construction through acquisition (mostly in commodity form) of distinction and difference, of the search for approval through life-style and symbolic membership' (ibid., 1988b, p. 84). Fourth, this drive to commodification has been made possible by the development of the media, especially television. Advertising and design companies have produced, in conjunction with the media, an enormous machine for generating a desire for commodities. Fifth, and in turn, these pressures have produced a new spatial order. The old tensions between city and country, centre and periphery, have been replaced by the suburb, the shopping centre and the freeway. This is 'shopping centre capitalism' (Jameson, 1987, p. 33) in which the commodity and the power of the media have conspired to produce emblematic spaces (or simulacra, a term that Jameson borrows from Baudrillard) that are carefully designed to stimulate people to consume, little toy countries where context and consumption feed on one another. In these simulated spaces and in the 'hyperspace' of the media and communications, pseudo-events (spectacles) are staged that all contribute to the effect. To update

Shelley, 'Look on my works, ye mighty, ... and shop' (see Bonnett, 1989, and Marcus, 1989, for the clear connections to situationist rhetoric).

Thus we find a culture that has become dependent on commodities for meaning and expression. 'The commodity is its own ideology: the practices of consumption and consumerism ... are enough to reproduce and legitimate the system' (Jameson, 1984, p. 9). For Jameson this postmodern culture is the 'cultural dominant' of late capitalism. It forms a marked contrast to the modernist era of Vidal and Marx with its notions of a high culture of single authentic works of art, set off from the culture of the masses, a culture that was itself a reaction to the early growth of mass consumption. But in the latest phase of capitalism we find that, in 'a sick joke' (Eagleton, 1986), such aesthetic production, however bizarre it might have seemed, has been integrated into commodity production: 'the frantic economic urgency of producing ever more novel-seeming goods (from clothing to airplanes), at ever greater rates of turnover, now assigns an increasingly structural function and position to aesthetic innovation and experimentation' (Jameson, 1984, p. 56). The commodity has been out hunting and the alternative aesthetic currency of modernist high culture has been captured and incorporated: all images have been devalued in the pursuit of profit. 'With the eclipse of culture as an autonomous space or sphere, culture itself falls into the world, and the result is not its disappearance but its prodigious expansion, to the point where culture becomes coterminous with social life in general ... in the society of the spectacle, the image or the simulacrum, everything has at length become cultural' (ibid., p. 87), which is to say, 'a potential text, an exchange value, and a commodity all at the same time' (ibid., p. 88).

Finally, there is the effect that these developments have had on the experience of modernity. For Jameson, these are so great that we have crossed the divide into a new era of postmodernity in which a new kind of 'new-fangled man' has appeared, what Derrida (1987) calls both playfully and seriously, the post-man, a subject lost in the web of communication without end, without an inside or an outside. Thus Jameson notes a loss of coherent human expression consisting of the loss of (1) affect, caused by the dispersal of feeling for 'others' into the web of 'referential depth'; (2) interpretations that allow us to imagine that there is something inside an image, a sign, or a person that is trying to get out; and (3) historical time – the modernist ideas of history and of a logic of history have been replaced by a spatial logic. In other words the past is no longer a vertical, depth dimension. It has been rotated into the present and has become a horizontal, surface collection of images whose chief function is to aid commodity differentiation by acting as the inspiration for present-day copies. Hence the nostalgia boom – the past becomes a going concern. In summary, postmodernity consists of a blurring of the old boundaries, between self and other, inside and outside, and history and geography.

For Jameson, postmodern culture and the experience of postmodernity are simultaneously a solution and problem. Whilst they provide a solution to the problem of consumption they attenuate our critical impulses. In the world of electronic media, we may have more *information* about the world but we have less *knowledge* of ourselves. So we use information as a substitute for knowledge, we plunder history for images, we paste and stick, make collages, create pastiches. Our older systems of perception are foundering and, in a very real sense, we have lost ourselves. In the poststructuralist lexicon, we have become 'decentred subjects' (see Hebdige, 1989). It is this sense of disconnection and confusion that leads Jameson to call for new 'cognitive maps', for a cartography that will allow us 'to again begin to grasp our positioning as individual and collective subjects' (Jameson, 1984, p. 88), our sense of place.

This new order of late or global capital can be summarised in one word: *decentred*. Power resides in the collectivity itself, which can be entered from any number of terminals. This is a 'hyperreality' of decentred corporations, decentred cities, decentred subjects that is difficult to grasp and therefore difficult to contest (see Kearney, 1989; Hebdige, 1989: Journal of Communications Inquiry, 1986; Theory, Culture and Society, 1988).

It is clear that Jameson's writings add up to a powerful vision of the world and one that clearly has an heuristic value. They connect back to Vidal. Jameson also has a vision of colonisation, but now it is of the colonisation of society by capitalist culture as well as the capitalist economy, and of that capitalist culture reaching out into the rest of the world, leaving no room for critical distance. In turn, his writings connect back to Marx. But this is now a world in which all that is solid has melted in the heat of constant symbolic exchange. We are left swimming in the sea of signs.

There are powerful reasons for taking seriously Jameson's vision of modern capitalist society. But there are equally powerful reasons for being suspicious. Three reasons stand out. First, Jameson's body of writings are a 'view from the top' (especially, from the US). They are the sales executive's success story. In narrative terms the electronic web has been spun by the capitalist spider and the proletarian fly has been trapped. Of course this kind of vision of mass culture as the 'final inauthentic state' (Miller, 1987; Thrift, 1983) has a long history and the reasons for its revival by French and American academics in the 1980s would no doubt bear closer examination (and not just as a prime example of Eurocentrism) (see Ahmad, 1986; Said, 1978). But it is simply too negative a vision of life in modern capitalist countries. It ignores powerful evidence that suggests consumers can make their own cultures out of commodities: terms of use are not always dictated by capital (Miller, 1987; Willis, 1977; Hebdige, 1989). Indeed, sometimes commodities are used as symbols of resistance. It ignores powerful evidence to suggest that the reception of meanings by people from the media is not a passive process but a transformative one: 'media messages are not received and interpreted in isolation, the very activity of receiving them is a social practice which may have its own significance for recipients' (Thompson, 1988, p. 378; see also Morley, 1986). It ignores powerful evidence to suggest that the media are not simply a tool for reproducing the dominant order but constitute their own Estate (Habermas, 1962) and can be used positively (witness the example of Band-Aid). It ignores powerful evidence that consumers can function as bodies of opinion that can change the type of commodities on offer (Mennell, 1985; Morley, 1986). It ignores powerful evidence that suggests that the announcement of the death of narrative is premature. Outside elite cultures, narrative still seems to do the job (Williamson, 1986). The list could be extended almost indefinitely. The point is that the view from the top obscures all the emergent activity going on at the bottom.

Second, although Jameson follows Lefebvre in attaching great importance to space in the reproduction of modern capitalism, he too often ignores Lefebvre's equal and opposite stress on space as an arena of contest and conflict (Ross, 1988). Jameson's spaces are the spaces of the city centre and the shopping centre: 'vivariums for the upper middle classes' in Davis's (1985) memorable phrase. But in other spaces outside these enclosures (and sometimes in them), people are still struggling, still escaping, still taking refuge, still making symbolic takeovers of space like a carnival, still disputing the right to the city (Lefebvre, 1968; Bakhtin, 1968; de Certeau, 1984).

Third, there is Jameson's view of doing social science. As has been pointed out by a number of authors, Jameson's is a relatively conventional Marxist view of science (drawn through Lukacs) but it is one that is certainly aware of the criticisms of Marx's thought. Both as a way of drawing the teeth of these criticisms and as a way of analysing modern capitalism, Jameson takes on board much of the apparatus of poststructuralist thinking – the stress on difference and incommensurability, the recourse to local narrative, the loss of critical distance, the importance of rhetoric, the decentred subject. He does not do this naively. He is well aware that many of these motifs can be seen as symptoms of the prevalence of commodity culture (as used in advertising, for example). But, it can be argued that in doing so he takes a tiger by the tail. For he is surely affected by the sense of pessimism and alienation ('to the second power', as Eagleton [1986] puts it) that informs much poststructuralist thinking about modern society. He produces what is, in effect, a totalising system that is so tightly drawn and projects so bleak an outlook that he is effectively left having to assert that there are ways out of it. Why should this be? To begin with, Jameson takes the processes he describes in modern society to be the apotheosis of capitalism when, as Davis (1985) points out, they may just as well be interpreted as the symptoms of crisis, of an excremental society in its final phase of dissolution of the kind that Gibson (1985, 1986a, 1986b, 1988) depicts so well in his 'cyberpunk' science-fiction stories. Then he too often ignores what look suspiciously like outbreaks of critical distance in modern society (such as the women's movement or the ecological movement), partly, I suspect, because he too often equates, as a literary theorist, intertextuality with the world. To paraphrase Mallarmé, the whole world is made to end up on TV (in distinct opposition to the situationist critique of everyday life) (see Jameson, 1981). Finally, he allows his sense of space to desert him when it is most needed. For distribution in geographic space, however blurred by the media and community, is still great enough to provide evidence of selves and others, insides and outsides, other histories and geographies (as indeed Jameson's interests in Third-World literature make clear). There are still distances, and some of them are critical.

Finally then, Jameson provides an important problematisation of modern capitalist society and space by taking on many of the motifs of poststructuralist thought. But he follows poststructuralist thinkers too far, and ends up repeating their mistakes. In particular, at the final hurdle of the contextual dimension his historical sense fails him (so that he ends up caught in the web of a totally ordered system), and so does his geographical sense (so that he equates difference with incommensurability). In summary, and in contrast with Marx, Jameson pays insufficient attention to local difference as a source of resistance to the simulations of capitalism, and too much attention to it as a resource for capitalism to play on.

How then can regional geography be carried forward in postmodern times? It is clear that a start has already been made in the Marxist-inspired regional geographies. But it is equally clear that these geographies do not go far enough. Jameson's ideas, for all their flaws, at least give us the key to what problems need to be addressed.

Three problems seem particularly pressing. The first of these is that the region is, in some senses, fragmenting, becoming not so much disorganised (as Lash and Urry [1987] would have it) as *displaced* in the terms that we tend to think of regions, as continuous, bounded areas. That fragmentation has taken place in a number of registers. For example, in the register of the economy the growth of multinational corporations made up of networks of offices and plants spread over the globe has integrated far-flung pockets of space. In the register of society and culture there is the proliferation of different lifestyle groupings, the members of which both want a particular locality and increasingly have such areas served up to them, ready-made or renovated, by a capital intent on maximising its rewards by promoting the fragmentation of space into more and more 'place market' segments (Harvey, 1989). (As a result, particular kinds of people become more and more prominently represented in particular localities as this process of sorting takes effect, exaggerating its effects still further.) Third, in the register of culture there is the spatialisation of culture remarked upon by Jameson and the consequent growth of simulacrums that provide affective anchors for fragmentation.

Thus we see a new 'globalised' localism emerging, a systematised, rationalised localism aimed at soaking up commodities by producing and reproducing consumers. This new globally local society is obviously very difficult for the regional geographer to come to terms with. In contrast with Vidal's time, when myriad different local communities each had different ways of life associated with them, linked to the nature of the environment and the different economic, social and cultural strategies evolved over many years to cope with the exigencies of that environment, what we now see is a series of localities scattered through the megalopolis that will have the *same* lifestyles associated with them (but for varying local signatures) (Thrift, 1989). The need now is to speed up turnover time, not the plough, and global capital is therefore manufacturing heterogeneity, commodifying place at an ever increasing pace.

Of course this process has limits. Spatial fixes still abound. Consumers are also pools of labour. Buildings have to earn returns before they can be pulled down. Images must be continually remade out of known histories and geographies. But one things is sure – contexts may be locally consumed (although even that is at issue) but they are less and less often locally produced.

Second, there is the problem of how to deal with community in this world of manufactured context. Vidal's peasants knew only their region and perforce 'identified' with it, insofar as this kind of identification has the same meaning as now. Then, through the nineteenth century, Western society developed more conscious levels of community identification with places, based primarily on the growth of media and travel. Now communities are wider spread and often nomadic by historical standards. Their affective ties, even their subjectivities are based upon communications and the media as well as face-to-face interaction (Kirby, 1988). Their social networks run down wires as well as roads. Thus their sense of identity with a community (or communities) is often obtained at a distance, is 'imagined' (Anderson, 1983). 'While people's actual community identification may have declined, their imagined community identification may have increased' (Savage, 1988, p. 267). Thus the urge to identify with localities seems to have become stronger, if anything. The enormous upsurge in local literatures and heritage histories suggests an attachment to locality, but one mediated by the media (and incidentally providing a vital affective hum for the new manufactured contexts). Again a 'global' localism holds sway.

Third, there is the problem of how to represent this artful new world, when we are no longer sure what 'context' or 'community' or 'local' means. The latest generation of locality studies are at their most profoundly conservative here. In the age of television and video they offer snapshots. In the age of movement they offer stasis. In the age of diffuse communities, identities and subjectivities they offer boundaries. Their textual strategies leave a lot to be desired (Carter, 1987).

Conclusions: The Road to Nowhere?

Society and space have changed since Vidal's time, and people have changed with them. We need to be careful not to overstate the changes. Many people still live in poverty, in dreadful conditions. Not for them the luxuries of conspicuous consumption in sculpted contexts and the pleasures of hypermobility (but most of them have a television).

Yet changes there have been, and these changes have increased the problems of doing regional geography rather than lessened them. If we are to understand the modern region then four areas of research have to be investigated in much greater depth than has been the case so far. First, we need more extensively to investigate the circulation of symbolic exchange over space, and most especially what Habermas (1962) calls the 'public sphere' the whole complex of (increasingly electronic) texts and media that frames debates, forms opinions and is increasingly the hope for informed political solutions in a world of symbols. Second, and related, we need to be much clearer how particular contexts influence the way particular kinds of people receive, negotiate and are made by meanings (Thrift, 1986). Third, we need to theorise more clearly how the process by which context has been commodified can be connected back into economic relations, especially those of consumption, and money and debt (Thrift and Leyshon, 1992). Fourth, we need to find new ways of representing regions. To do that we need to hone our tools of writing *and* reading. Certainly the glimmerings of this new kind of regional geography can be seen in the upsurge of social and cultural work that is currently taking place around issues such as gender, sexuality and ethnicity. The strength of this work is its attention to the construction of localised spaces of meaning out of global relations of power and knowledge. Perhaps this provides the text for regional geography's future. Certainly it promises a new period of exploration for regional geography, the exploration of the limits of the text and the possibilities of other means of representing the other (Clifford and Marcus, 1986; Jackson, 1989).

Whatever else, I hope to have shown that regional geography is central to the practice of doing human geography. It poses questions about the world in which we live in a way that is important because it is contextual. In this chapter, I have tried to pose some of these questions, if only in the broadest of terms. I have had to leave out much. In particular I remain uneasy with some of the social and cultural analysis I have offered. It is undoubtedly much too sweeping; thus it tends to the epic, even as it extols the local (but see some examples of feminist writing and writing on racialisation, for example Steedman, 1986; Gilroy, 1987). But this is one of the important functions of *doing* regional geography, perhaps its most important. By interrogating *particular* everyday contexts it reveals just how important the contextual is. The contextual cannot be swept under the carpet by grand social theories, for it remains where we actually live. It is the margin that constitutes the centre (Lefebvre, 1971; Derrida, 1982; de Certeau, 1984).

Finally, I want to come back to where I started, to Vidal de la Blache. Vidal's nostalgia for little local communities tied to the soil may seem naive, even misplaced. But as we move towards little local communities whose sole purpose is to provide contexts for conspicuous consumption, or dumps for those without the wherewithal to consume, it is worth reflecting on just how reprehensible such a view is. For, as we move towards an horrendous ecological crisis that is tied to the very nature of global capital's culture of excess, Vidal, and nature, may still have the last laugh. As Lacoste (1979) would have it, 'A bas Vidal . . . Viva Vidal!'.

Acknowledgements

The title of this chapter is taken from Habermas, 1986. A first draft was completed in summer 1987. The revision, which benefited enormously from the comments of Derek Gregory, was completed in summer 1989. The opportunity for revision came as the result of a sojourn at Macquarie University, Sydney, for which my thanks are in order.

References

Ahmad, A. (1986) 'Jameson's rhetoric of otherness and the national allegory', *Social Text*, vol. 15, pp. 65–88.

Anderson, B. (1983) *Imagined Communities* (London: Verso).

Andrews, H. (1984) 'The Durkheimians and human geography', *Transactions, Institute of British Geographers*, NS9, pp. 315–36.

Baker, A. R. H. (1984) 'Reflections on the relations of historical geography and the *Annales* School of History', in A. R. H. Baker and D. Gregory (eds), *Explanations in Historical Geography* (Cambridge University Press), pp. 1–27.

Bakhtin, M. (1968) *Rabelais and His World* (Cambridge, Mass: MIT Press).

Baudrillard, J. (1988a) *Jean Baudrillard: Selected Writings* (trans. M Poster) (Cambridge: Polity Press).

Baudrillard, J. (1988b) *America* (London: Verso).

Berdoulay, V. (1978) 'The Vidal-Durkheim debate', in D. Ley and M. Samuels (eds), *Humanite Geography* (London: Croom Helm), pp. 77–90.

Berger, J. (1979) *Pig Earth* (London: Writers and Readers).

Berman, M. (1983) *All That is Solid Melts into Air. The Experience of Modernity* (London: Verso).

Bonnett, A. (1989) 'Situationism, geography, and poststructuralism', *Environment and Planning D. Society and Space*, vol. 7, pp. 131–46.

Buttimer, A. (1971) *Society and Milieu in the French Geographic Tradition* (Chicago: Rond McNally).

Buttimer, A. (1978) 'Charism and context. The challenge of la geographie humaine', in D. Ley and M. Samuels (eds), *Humanistic Geography* (London: Croom Helm), pp. 58–76.

Carter, P. (1987) *The Road to Botany Bay. An Essay in Spatial History* (London: Faber).

Castoriadis, C. (1987) *The Imaginary Institution of Society* (Cambridge: Polity Press).

Clifford, J. B. and G. Marcus (eds) (1986) *Writing Cultures* (Berkeley: University of California Press).

Cooke, P. (ed.) (1989) *Localities* (London: Unwin Hyman).

Corrigan, P. and D. Sayer (1983) *The Great Arch* (Oxford: Blackwell).

Darby, H. C. (1962) 'The problem of geographical description', *Transactions and Papers. Institute of British Geographers*, no. 30, pp. 1–14.

Davis, M. (1985) 'Urban renaissance and the spirit of postmodernism', *New Left Review*, no. 151, pp. 106–14.

Debord, G. (1977) *The Society of the Spectacle* (Detroit: Black and Red).

de Certeau, M. (1984) *The Practice of Everyday Life* (Berkeley: University of California Press).

Derrida, J. (1978) *Writing and Difference* (University of Chicago Press).

Derrida, J. (1982) *Margins of Philosophy* (Chicago University Press).

Derrida, J. (1987) *The Postcard* (Chicago University Press).

Dews, P. (1987) *Logics of Disintegration* (London: Verso).

Doel, M. A. (1991) '(In)stalling deconstruction', unpublished manuscript.

Dreyfus, H. and Rabinow, P. (1983) *Michel Foucault. Beyond Structuralism and Hermeneutics.* (Berkeley: University of California Press).

Duncan, S. (1989) 'What is a locality?', in R. Peet and N. J. Thrift (eds), *New Models in Geography*, vol. 2 (London: Unwin Hyman).

Duncan, S. and M. Savage (1989) 'Space, scale and locality', *Antipode*, vol. 21, pp.179–206.

Eagleton, T. (1986) *Against the Grain* (London: Verso).

Foucault, M. (1977) *Discipline and Punish* (London: Allen Lane).

Gibson, W. (1985) *Neuromancer* (London: Gollancz).

Gibson, W. (1986a) *Count Zero* (London: Gollancz).

Gibson, W. (1986b) *Burning Chrome* (London: Gollancz).

Gibson, W. (1988) *Mona Lisa Overdrive* (London: Gollancz).

Giddens, A. (1984) *The Constitution of Society* (Cambridge: Polity Press).

Giddens, A. (1985) *The Nation and State and Violence* (Cambridge: Polity Press).

Giddens, A. (1987) in A. Giddens and J. Turner (eds), *Social Theory Today* (Cambridge: Polity Press).

Gilbert, A. (1988) 'The new regional geography in English and French-speaking countries', *Progress in Human Geography*, vol. 12, pp. 208–28.

Gilroy, D. (1987) *There Ain't No Black in the Union Jack* (London: Hutchinson).

Gregory, D. (1978) *Ideology, Science and Human Geography* (London: Hutchinson).

Gregory, D. (1989) 'The crisis of modernity? Human geography and critical social theory', in N. J. Peet and N. J. Thrift (eds), *New Models in Geography*, vol. 2 (London: Unwin Hyman), pp. 348–85.

Habermas, J. (1962) *Strukterwandel der Offentlichkeit* (Berlin: Leuchterhand).

Habermas, J. (1986) 'Taking aim at the heart of the present' in D. C. Hoy (ed.), *Foucault: A Critical Review* (Oxford: Blackwell), pp. 83–155.

Hart, J. F. (1982) 'The highest form of the geographers art', *Annals of the Association of American Geographers*, vol. 72, pp. 1–29.

Harvey, D. W. (1985) *The Urbanisation of Consciousness* (Oxford: Blackwell).

Harvey, D. (1987) 'Flexible accumulation through urbanisation: reflection on post-modernisation in the American city', *Antipode*, vol. 19, pp. 200–36.

Harvey, D. (1989) *The Condition of Postmodernity* (Oxford: Blackwell).

Hebdige, D. (1989) *Hiding in the Light* (London: Routledge).

Hudson, B. (1977) 'The new geography and the new Imperialism: 1870–1918', *Antipode*, vol. 9, pp. 12–19.

Ingham, G. (1984) *Capitalism Divided?* (London: Macmillan).

Jackson, P. (1989) *Maps of Meaning* (London: Hutchinson).

Jameson, F. (1981) *The Political Unconscious. Narrative as a Socially Symbolic Act* (London: Methuen).

Jameson, F. (1984) 'Postmodernism or the cultural logic of late capitalism', *New Left Review*, vol. 146, pp. 52–92.

Jameson, F. (1987) 'Regarding postmodernism – a conversation with Fredric Jameson', *Social Text*, vol. 17, pp. 29–54.

Jameson, F. (1988a) *The Ideologies of Theory*, vol. 1 (London: Routledge).

Jameson, F. (1988b) *The Ideologies of Theory*, vol. 2 (London: Routledge).

Jameson, F. (1991) *Postmodernism, or the Cultural Logic of Late Capitalism* (London: Verso).

Jay, M. (1984) *The Dialectical Imagination* (London: Heinemann).

Jonas, W. (1989) 'A new regional geography of locality studies', *Area*, vol. 20, pp. 101–10.

Journal of Communication Inquiry (1986), special issue on postmodernism.

Kearney, R. (1989) *The Wake of Imagination* (London: Hutchinson).

Kirby, A. (1988) *Journal of Communications Inquiry*, vol. 12, pp. 121–76.

Lacoste, Y. (1979) 'A bas Vidal. . . . Viva Vidal!', *Hérodote*, no. 16, pp. 68–81.

Lakoff, G. (1988) *Women, Fire, and Dangerous Things* (Chicago University Press).

Lash, S. and J. Urry (1987) *The End of Organised Capitalism* (Cambridge: Polity Press).

Lefebvre, H. (1968) *Le Droit à la Ville* (Paris: Anthropos).

Lefebvre, H. (1971) *Everyday Life in the Modern World* (Harmondsworth: Penguin).

Lentricchia, F. (1987) *Ariel and the Police* (Brighton: Harvester Press).

Lyotard, J. F. (1984) *The Postmodern Condition* (Manchester University Press).

Mann, M. (1986) *The Sources of Social Power*, vol. 1 (Cambridge University Press).

Marcus, G. (1989) *Lipstick Traces. A Secret History of the Twentieth Century* (London: Secker and Warburg).

Marx, K. (1952) *The Communist Manifesto* (Moscow: Progress Publishers).

Massey, D. (1984) *Spatial Divisions of Labour* (London: Macmillan).

Massey, D. (1988) 'Uneven development: social change and spatial divisions of labour', in D. Massey and J. Allen (eds), *Uneven Re-Development* (London: Hodder and Stoughton), pp. 250–76.

McLellan, D. (1973) *Karl Marx* (Oxford University Press).

Mennell, S. (1985) *All Manners of Food* (Oxford: Blackwell).

Miller, D. (1987) *Mass Consumption and Material Culture* (Oxford: Blackwell).

Morley, D. (1986) *Family Television* (London: Comedia).

Pudup, M. B. (1988) 'Arguments within regional geography', *Progress in Human Geography*, vol. 12, pp. 319–40.

Ross, K. (1988) *The Emergence of Social Space. Rimbaud and the Paris Commune* (London: Macmillan).

Said, E. W. (1978) *Orientalism* (London: Routledge and Kegan Paul).

Savage, M. (1988) 'Spatial differences in modern Britain', in C. Hamnett, L. McDowell and P. Sarre (eds), *The Changing Social Structure* (London: Sage), pp. 244–68.

Sayer, A. (1985) 'Realism in geography', in R. J. Johnston (ed.) *The Future of Geography* (London: Methuen), pp. 159–173.

Sayer, A. (1989) 'The new regional geography and the problem of narrative', *Environment and Planning D. Society and Space*, vol. 7, pp. 253–76.

Schivelsbuch, W. (1987) *The Railway Journey* (Berkeley: University of California Press).

Scott, A. J. (1988) *New Industrial Spaces* (London: Pion).

Shanin, T. (ed.) (1983) *Late Marx and the Road to Capitalism* (London: Routledge and Kegan Paul).

Steedman, C. (1986) *Landscape for a Good Woman* (London: Virago).

Stoddart, D. (1986) *On Geography* (Oxford: Blackwell).

Terdiman, R. (1985) *Discourse, Counter-Discourse* (Ithaca, NY: Cornell University Press).

Theory, Culture and Society (1988) vol. 5, nos 2–3, special issue on postmodernism.

Thompson, J. B. (1988) 'Mass communication and modern culture', *Sociology*, vol. 22, pp. 359–83.

Thrift, N. J. (1983) 'On the determination of social action in space and time', *Environment and Planning D. Society and Space*, vol. 1, pp. 23–57.

Thrift, N. J. (1985) 'Flies and germs. A geography of knowledge', in

D. Gregory and J. Urry (eds), *Social Relations and Spatial Structure* (London: Macmillan), pp. 366–403.

Thrift, N. J. (1986) 'Little games and big stories', in K. Hoggart and E. Kofman (eds), *Politics, Geography and Social Stratification* (London: Croom Helm), pp. 86–143.

Thrift, N. J. (1987) 'No perfect symmetry: a response to David Harvey', *Environment and Planning D. Society and Space*, vol. 5, pp. 400–7.

Thrift, N. J. (1989) *Images of Social Change* (Open University course D314: 'Restructuring Britain') (London: Hodder and Stoughton).

Thrift, N. J. (1990a) 'Transport and Communication, 1770–1914', in R. Dodgshon and R. Butlin (eds), *A New Historical Geography of England and Wales* (London: Academic Press).

Thrift, N. J. (1990b) 'For a new regional geography 1', *Progress in Human Geography*, vol. 14, pp. 272–9.

Thrift, N. J. (1991) 'For a new regional geography 2', *Progress in Human Geography*, vol. 15, pp. 456–65.

Thrift, N. J. (1993) 'For a new regional geography 3', *Progress in Human Geography*, vol. 17, pp. 92–100.

Thrift, N. J. and A. Leyshon (1992) *Making Money* (London: Routledge).

Vidal de la Blache, P. (1903) *Tableau de la Geographie de la France* (Paris), references to English part-translation (1928), *The Personality of France*, trans. H. C. Brentnall (London: Christophers).

Vidal de la Blache, P. (1916) *La France de L'Est* (Paris: Armand Colin).

Vidal de la Blache, P. (1979) 'La France de L'Est' (Lorraine-Alsace)', *Hérodote*, no. 16, pp. 82–96.

Warde, A. (1985) 'Spatial change, politics and the division of labour', in D. Gregory and J. Urry (eds), *Social Relations and Spatial Structures* (London: Macmillan), pp. 190–212.

Warf, B. (1989) 'Locality studies', *Urban Geography*, vol. 10, pp. 178–85.

Weber, E. (1977) *Peasants into Frenchmen: the Modernisation of Rural France 1870–1914* (London: Chatto and Windus).

Williamson, J. (1986) *Consuming Passions* (Edinburgh: Marion Bayers).

Willis, P. (1977) *Learning to Labour* (Farnborough: Saxon House).

Wrigley, E. A. (1965) 'Changes in the philosophy of geography', in R. Chorley and P. Haggett (eds), *Frontiers in Geographical Teaching* (London: Methuen), pp. 3–20.

9

Urban Geography in a Changing World

SUSAN J. SMITH

Traditional urban geography has its roots in early-twentieth-century Chicago. Undergraduates can still be found drawing rings and sectors, correlating social indices across spatial units and, on occasion, assessing the ambience of 'townscape'. Yet the subdiscipline has grown rapidly and ranged widely during the last half century. Cities have been celebrated for their role in the transition from feudalism to industrialism, assigned a place on the economic trajectory from organised capitalism to flexible accumulation, participated in the industrial transition from Fordism to post-Fordism and infused the cultural dynamic of postmodernism. There are vast literatures on the urban consequences of capitalism and socialism, on the urban impact of liberalism and conservatism, and on the effects of class conflict and cultural change on the conduct of urban life. A single chapter cannot do justice to the diverse and changeable material packaged as Urban Geography. I begin, therefore, at a moment when the integrity of urban studies was called into question. However most of my comments dwell on the even greater excitement generated by geography's spirited response.

In his book *Social theory and the city*, Peter Saunders (1981) claims that there is nothing distinctive about cities that justifies the development of specifically *urban* studies. His reasoning is persuasive: cities may once have played a role in the transition to industrialism (by prising the actors in a new economic order away from the feudal regime of the countryside), but this role has long become redundant; if cities were once characterised by a distinctive administrative system, this is no longer the case; if the size, density and

232

heterogeneity of cities was once thought to give rise to uniquely 'urban' cultures, there are many grounds on which such an assumption can now be questioned; if urbanism was once delimited by the built form of cities, suburban sprawl and the 'urbanisation of the countryside' now deny even this spatial rationale for a distinctively urban focus. In short, from Saunders' perspective, there is nothing to be gained theoretically by continuing to label some parts of the economic, political, social or spatial order as 'urban' simply because we have always thought of them as cities in the past. Of course, if we accept this argument, there is also no logical reason for retaining urban geography on the teaching or research agenda.

Not surprisingly Saunders' critique has attracted some spirited refutations, especially from geographers. Some of this debate appears in the early pages of *Environment and Planning D: Society and Space*. Yet, while many dispute his reasoning, few question the fundamental point that, with the economic and welfare restructurings of the late twentieth century, the old order of urban studies is ripe for replacement: all disciplines with their foundations in the social and spatial structure of the city are being forced to reconsider their roots and rationales. This is as true of urban geography as it is of any other field of urban studies, and it is a time of excitement as well as agitation as analysts seek to find a way forward, by building on their own disciplinary strengths and by exchanging inspiration with related fields. In an attempt to capture this excitement, what follows is not about the history of a subdiscipline; nor is it, in any more than a passing way, about urban geography's recent crisis of identity. Rather it is about what urban geography is becoming as it renegotiates its position vis-à-vis social science generally and within the broad field of urban studies in particular.

It is necessary, before proceeding, to rehearse again the well-worn arguments that knowledge and interests are linked, and that the outcomes of urban analysis (and therefore the content of urban theory and urban policy) will reflect the presuppositions and value judgements of the research environment. The chapter is structured, therefore, around four distinctive (politically loaded but not mutually exclusive) perspectives on the subject matter of urban studies. First, the contribution to urban theory made by left-wing political economy is outlined. This prefaces an outline of the political and theoretical significance of the feminist and antiracist challenges to conventional urban analysis – challenges which themselves have come primarily from the left. Third, I consider briefly the implications

for urban geography and urban policy of the philosophy and practice of the so-called New Right. The chapter concludes with some
thoughts about the significance of culture for an understanding of
city life in an era preoccupied with the 'postmodernisation' of the
built and social environments.

Urban Theory and the Left

In the last 20 years urban theory has undoubtedly gained its major
impetus from the left, and, notwithstanding some significant attempts to place Max Weber's legacy in a central position (Elliott
and McCrone, 1983), it is Karl Marx whose writings have been
most effectively extended into urban geography. From a neo-Marxian
perspective there are at least two distinctive 'urban questions' that
have preoccupied researchers.

The first concerns the role of space in the process of capital
accumulation; and in linking this to urban analysis, geographers
have always been at the leading edge. The presupposition of such
an approach is that the role of the urban system is to realise profits
for industrial capital (such profits would be created by the scale
economies associated with agglomeration, and by an associated
stimulus to the service sector). As Scott (1986) shows, in fulfilling
this role, distinctively 'urban' space can be conceived of as a phenomenon created by economic processes. This view is important and
well reasoned, but it is also necessary to recognise that urbanism
has an ideological as well as an economic dimension. This is taken
up by Henri Lefebvre, whose concern, in works such as *La Révolution
Urbaine* (1970) and *The Survival of Capitalism* (1976), was to explain how the inequalities generated by capitalism, and encapsulated in cities, are largely accepted or ignored by citizens. Lefebvre's
quest, therefore, has been to formulate a theory of urbanism able
to sweep away the ideological veil that enshrouds 'common-sense'
understandings of urban life. In an important two-volume study of
The Urbanization of Capital and *Consciousness and the Urban Experience* David Harvey (1985a, 1985b) has put these two dimensions – the economic and the ideological – together in an attempt
to account for the structuring of urban economic and social space
by the processes associated with capital accumulation. These works
trace out the ways in which capitalism shapes both the form and
organisation of cities and the consciousness of their inhabitants.

A second neo-Marxian 'urban question' focuses on cities as an arena for the reproduction of labour power. The fundamental processes in this respect relate not to the means of production and capital accumulation, but to the *consumption* of goods and services. In tackling this theme geographers have looked for inspiration outside their own discipline, drawing particularly from the work of Manuel Castells (1977, 1978, 1983). Castells originally focused on consumption because, on the basis of his Althusserian reading of Marx, he identified this process (unlike, in his view, those associated with the economy, ideology or politics) as distinctively urban. One of Castells' main achievements, therefore, has been to use urban studies to turn attention to the crises of capitalism associated not with production, but [*Manuel Castell*] with consumption. He points out in a number of his works that the principle of profit maximisation is not compatible with maintaining the urban infrastructure, or the standards of living associated with it, at levels adequate to secure either workers' satisfaction or the reproduction of labour power. His reasoning feeds into two important themes in urban geography: the study of urban social move- [2 *important*] ments as an expression of struggles over collective consumption; [*themes in urban geography*] and the analysis of specifically *urban* policies as the form of state intervention required to maintain the labour force.

Urban social movements have probably received more attention in the literature than they deserve. They were initially conceptualised as the new cutting edge of social change, with the potential to augment, and perhaps replace, labour movements as a source of collective action with revolutionary potential. In the light of their limited achievements in practice, however, this view of urban social movements has had to be revised. Now they tend to be seen as a [*Urban*] more limited vehicle for expressing interests outside party politics, [*social*] and they have been interpreted both as a symptom of social re- [*movement*] adjustment to economic and political change (Ceccarelli, 1982) and as the foundation for more decentralised forms of urban management (Castells, 1983).

At a theoretical level nevertheless, the study of urban social movements has been important in focusing attention on at least three issues of particular relevance to geography. First, such work draws a distinction (and establishes a relationship) between conflicts concerning production and those concerning consumption. Second, it seeks to specify the factors mediating and controlling social conflict; and, third, a preoccupation with social movements directs attention to the importance of exploring the distinctively urban sources of political power. Lowe (1986) considers these three areas of concern at greater length. In the last twenty years, an explosion of interest in the political realignments associated with postmodernism, and in the accompanying flexibility and negotiability of identity has given fresh impetus to these lines of enquiry.

Peter Saunders has also taken up the theme of collective consumption (which he continues to regard as a more valid analytical category than either cities or urbanism). He has, however, avoided the lure of debates on urban social movements, and instead developed the analysis of collective consumption along a second route: that concerned with the role of state intervention in the distribution of goods and services. He has been concerned especially with the widening rift between those able to consume via the market and those dependent on the state for provision in cash or kind. Two elements of this work are particularly important. First, his approach forces analysts to acknowledge the extent to which the politics of consumption differ from the politics of production, and to recognise that this might require new theories of state intervention. Secondly, his reasoning suggests that consumption-sector cleavages can be more salient and more entrenched, and therefore more important politically, than class cleavages as more conventionally defined. If so (and this has proved difficult to confirm empirically), urban studies will require new or extended theories of public participation in politics.

More recently Saunders has extended his work on the politics of consumption. In the most recent edition of his book he expresses particular excitement about the concept of 'self-provisioning', which he contrasts with consumption via the market and consumption that is directly subsidised by the state. It is clear, however, that the policies required to promote self-provisioning – emphasising an 'enabling' rather than a welfare state – are more in line with strategies of the right than with those of the left. They are, therefore, most appropriately considered in a later section.

Broadly, the restructuring of urban geography initiated by the left is based on an appreciation of the 'new' international division of labour, which has, on the whole, not so much prompted authors to reject the urban focus as required them to contextualise it within a wider political–economic framework than has been usual in traditional urban geography. Fothergill *et al.* (1988) thus explain how the process of deindustrialisation – one corollary, in the developed world, of the internationalisation of capital and labour – affects urban, suburban and rural areas in different ways. Many large cities face a disproportionate loss of manufacturing industries and sustain disproportionately high rates of unemployment. Others have accumulated a disproportionate share of the capital concentrated in the world's financial markets, tying local space – not least through large-scale capital investment into the built environment – firmly into the global economy. This world economy has, it seems, a very marked urban dimension: the newly flexible forces of production have internationalised and localised all at once.

flexible accumulation internationally & localized all at once

The centrality of urban analysis in an internationalising economy is well illustrated in Rees and Lambert's (1986) commentary on *Cities in crisis*. These authors expose some shortcomings of traditional urban studies, criticising their failure to relate processes in particular cities to the broader social system driving local change. Focusing on the links between capitalist production, class relations and the state, Rees and Lambert are able to contextualise but not dilute the urban focus, and they argue convincingly that state intervention, as well as market economics, has a territorial component and that this is the domain of the urban-policy analyst. A similar argument is advanced by John Short (1984) in *The Urban Arena*, where a systematic analysis of capital, state and community as factors influencing city structure and organisation suggests that there are particular, localised sets of interests that have to be dealt with by a distinctively 'urban' level of political intervention, and analysed by those with expertise in urban studies. Similar examples can be drawn from the developing world and the Pacific rim: both McGee's (1988) study of Malaysia and Douglass's (1988) work in Japan draw out the urban dimensions of the internationalisation of capital. The topic has also been reviewed by Leitner (1986).

Geographers on the left, then, have acknowledged the importance of setting urban studies within the framework of both national politics and an international economy. This is particularly important at a time when analysts in many disciplines are trying to come to grips with the advent of post-Fordism and its place in the transition to disorganised capitalism (Lash and Urry, 1987) or flexible accumulation (Harvey, 1987). The left has also, and increasingly, assented to the importance of examining both production and consumption in the urban arena. For the most part this school of thought has retained its urban focus, not only by recognising a distinct role, still, for cities in the process of capital accumulation, but also by demonstrating that the fact that legislators and administrators treat

Left's contributions to the domain of urban analyses
① transformation from Fordism → Post-Fordism
② equal attention paid to production & consumption

the urban as 'real' gives cities a political dynamic of their own. What is nevertheless largely missing amid all this concern for the urban dimensions of production and consumption, industrial restructuring and the transition to post-Fordism, is some appreciation of the extent to which urban life is both gendered and racialised. The analysis of patriarchy and racism has yet to be fully integrated into urban geography, though, as the next sections illustrates, some important foundations have been laid.

The Feminist and Antiracist Challenge

Urban geography has always been preoccupied with how the class structure and status order are reflected in, and shaped by, the organisation of urban space. The study of 'racial' segregation, as a spatial index of the state of 'race relations' has also been a traditional concern. Until recently, however, race categories were taken for granted in urban geography and the salience of gender was often ignored. On the one hand, therefore, urban theory has utilised 'race' as an explanatory variable (rather than as a social construct that has itself to be explained). On the other hand urban theory has been gender-blind, developing generalisations largely from observations of male heads of households.

For instance, urban geography's interest in 'racial segregation' has often been fuelled by the tautologous assumption that 'ethnic status' is what explains the spatial clustering of minority or immigrant groups. In fact this clustering often occurs within the worst parts of the housing stock, and is primarily a consequence of residents' marginal position in the labour market (which in turn limits their achievements in the housing market), and of their exclusion from many welfare benefits (which limits their access to housing subsidies and a decent home in the public sector). 'Ethnic status' is not, then, a package of attitudes, aspirations and behavioural traits that accounts for where people live; it is rather a label testifying to some important socioeconomic and political divisions within the population. It is these divisions which must be explained by analysts, usually with reference to the discriminatory operation of urban markets and housing institutions.

A different kind of error is contained in much of conventional urban economics, where family behaviour is subsumed to the activities of male heads of households. Trade-off models of urban structure, for instance, claim to make generalisations about the activities of the population as a whole, but they are based only on the male journey to work. These approaches ignore the behaviour and aspirations of more than half the population, but they inform the majority of urban theory. As a consequence such theory is in urgent need of revision, as Pratt and Hanson's (1988) work clearly shows. Likewise ethnographic studies, which have produced a welcome insight into the meaning of urban life and the negotiation of urban culture, are overwhelmingly preoccupied with male-dominated street-life or with waged work in the male-dominated professions. Even the more critical neo-Marxist analyses of collective consumption tend to ignore the sphere of family life and of women's roles within it by viewing the cities as a whole, rather than their gender-differentiated populations, as a vehicle for the reproduction of labour power. Such gender-blind approaches also concentrate primarily on the analysis of waged labour, implicitly devaluing the contribution of unwaged domestic labour to the maintenance of the urban system.

[handwritten margin note: appreciate of women and their unwaged reproductive work]

These theoretical and empirical gaps in the literature of urban geography have been gradually filled during the last decade. Studies of 'race', 'racial segregation' and 'race relations' are being replaced by analyses of racial ideologies, racism and discrimination (Jackson, 1987; Smith, 1989), while feminist geographers have largely succeeded in their attempts not only to make women visible but also to build a concept of gender relations into urban theory, both in the West (Little *et al.*, 1988) and in the developing world (Momsen and Townsend, 1987).

For an antiracist urban geography, the challenge is to reject the concept of 'race' as an explanatory category and to concentrate instead on explaining how the reproduction of material inequalities is structured around scientifically indefensible ideas about the social significance of somatic (phenotypic and genetic) variety. The emphasis should be placed not on describing where different 'races' live and how they behave, but rather on accounting for the socio-economic and political processes of 'race' formation. This will require us to pay attention to the organisation of labour migration (Miles, 1982), the pattern of economic restructuring (Cross, 1983), the exercise of social policy (Rex, 1986) and the conduct of political democracy (Gilroy, 1987). Some of these ideas have been developed more recently in the collection edited by Cross and Keith (1993).

From feminist theory, an early challenge to urban geography was simply that of making women visible. This raised questions relating to women's place in the division of domestic labour, their limited access to urban space, and their unrecognised requirements for undersubsidised services such as child-care facilities. This focus produced explanations of the differences between women's and men's behaviour in terms of gender roles and role expectations. Subsequently, however, this 'women and . . .' perspective has been eclipsed by a concern with gender *relations*, gender inequality and, above all, with patriarchy. Patriarchy is that particular, most typical, form of gender relations in which men dominate women, and which produces a distinctive form of gender inequality in which women are disadvantaged relative to men in terms of access to material resources, status and political power. We are seeking, then, to find ways of conceptualising and analysing the urban dimension of power struggles between men and women, and to link them with the power struggles associated with class conflict and racism. One imaginative approach to this is developed by Elizabeth Wilson (1991) who argues that women's visions can be instrumental in rescuing the ideal of the city and in humanising the urban landscape.

These feminist and antiracist perspectives provide important new dimensions to the theories underpinning urban geography. We are forced, for instance, to reinterpret the role of cities in the transition to industrialism in order to take into account the ways in which urban labour markets require (in order to secure the reproduction of labour power) new patternings of gender roles, as well as new sources of cheap (racialised) labour. More immediately, the transition to post-Fordism and the spatial restructuring of the economy that goes with this, directs our attention to how gender relations are shaped, how social relations are racialised and how patriarchy and racism are reproduced in the modern urban arena. We are seeing, therefore, analyses of urban housing systems that reveal a bias against non-family households; that is, against households that are frequently female headed and least likely to reproduce the patriarchal structures associated with traditional nuclear-family life (Watson, 1988). Analysts have demonstrated the relevance of gender to theories of gentrification (Bondi, 1991), conceptions of the housing system (Madigan *et al.*, 1990) and to ideas about the reproduction of urban inequality (Smith, 1990). We are seeing, too, analyses of urban economies that marginalise racialised minorities (Harris, 1987), and we are uncovering evidence of citizenship entitlements that are not only racist (Smith, 1989) but also implicitly exclude women (Pateman, 1988). In short, the feminist and antiracist challenge to urban geography requires us to develop new analytical tools to accommodate not only a spatial restructuring of the political economy, but also the importance of space in reproducing patriarchy and in perpetuating the legacy of imperialism. While this requirement may seem self-evident to many readers, it is frequently denied by analysts on the 'New Right' – a body of views which, as the next section shows, carries some new imperatives for the subject matter and conduct of urban geography.

Urban Problems and the Right

The work of Chicago's early twentieth-century urban economists and social ecologists is generally associated with the liberal political right, and this has not escaped the critical eye of modern urban geography. It is therefore ironic that the subdiscipline has, as yet, paid scant attention to the intellectual significance of New Right thinking during the 1980s. This reworking of liberal economics, authoritarian politics and conservative morality nevertheless demands a place within urban geography.

Whereas traditional conservatism has its roots in political philosophy and in the principles of tradition and hierarchy, the impetus behind the New Right comes from economics and is founded on the principles individualism and market forces. However a number of right-wing governments succeeded, during the 1980s, in combining liberal monetary policies (which were expected to arrest economic decline) with a revival of authoritarianism and moralism (which were thought necessary to preserve the social fabric of the nation). In principle these twin arms of the New Right coexist uneasily. The proponents of neoliberal economics, and of associated libertarian views, eschew state intervention, while moral authoritarians tend to demand a strong state, at least in the sphere of social control. In practice, however, these combined economic and ideological elements of the New Right have proved politically expeditious. Most importantly for our purposes, they have played a key role in managing (and in legitimising the management of) what Gottdeiner (1986) terms the modern urban crisis. This crisis is signalled above all by the fiscal stress experienced by urban (local) governments, and by the escalation of urban unrest. These problems might, from a left-wing perspective, be linked directly with the processes of global economic restructuring, and with the crisis of legitimacy experienced by states whose welfare expenditure can no longer secure the reproduction of labour. Analysts on the right, however, tend to portray urban problems as more discrete (and potentially more manageable) by depicting them, on the one hand, as a symptom of over-intervention by the state and, on the other hand, as a consequence of declining moral standards. Defined in this way the problems of local government finance and civil disorder appear to have obvious solutions in the urban policies promoted by neoconservative governments.

Although the political right does not have a monopoly on urban management in the 'new times', right-wing governments have presided over the economic and cultural restructurings of the last decade in both Britain and the US. Taking the example of Britain, which experienced both of Gottdeiner's symptoms of urban crisis during the 1980s, the remainder of this section illustrates how the impact of the two strands of New Right philosophy – neoliberal economics and conservative authoritarianism – is manifest at the urban scale. I shall argue that, during the last decade, this package of ideas has had a powerful influence on how urban problems are conceptualised, has affected the strategies comprising urban policy, and has left its mark on the conduct of urban life and the interpretation of urbanism.

Economic policy fuelled the initial political success of the New Right, and I consider this first. Neoliberal economics relies on the efficiency of market forces and is founded on the premise that free markets are more effective, and at least as just, as state intervention as a means of delivering goods and services to citizens. State intervention in the processes of production and consumption is rejected on the grounds that it rarely achieves its stated aims and has undesirable (and uncontrollable) unanticipated effects. It follows that the only sense in which politics should be allowed to impinge on economy is to maintain conditions that are conducive to the workings of a free market. This reasoning has led governments to cut public spending by reducing state provisioning in cash and in kind and (in theory) using savings to reduce taxation. In Britain this has resulted in, among other things, the sale of public companies and the sale (or commodification) of council housing. Additionally there are three areas in which this neoliberal thinking has a direct bearing on the fiscal crises of local governments which have recently dominated British urban geography.

First, in order to contain the crisis of deindustrialisation facing the inner cities (which is discussed at greater length by Fothergill *et al.*, 1988), urban policy was, throughout the 1980s, geared increasingly to the project of economic regeneration. The route to success was defined in terms of the 'liberation' of free enterprise from state control. This goal infused most areas of urban policy: it underpinned the changing emphasis of the Urban Programme (which has dropped its early social concerns in favour of an almost-exclusive focus on urban regeneration), the creation of urban development corporations, the advent of urban task forces, the popularity of initiatives such as Business in the Community and the Financial Institutions Group, and a host of more recent political strategies to boost investment in the inner cities. The spirit of such ideas may, however, be illustrated with reference to the notion of enterprise zones, which were first provided for in the 1980 budget. Within these zones (there were eleven in the first instance) industrial developers were guaranteed, for a ten-year period, incentives including exemption from rates and from land tax on site disposal, tax allowances on the costs of building construction and various relaxations of local planning controls. The aim, then, was to 'free up' the market by releasing small tracts of urban land from a web of bureaucratic (state-inspired) planning and taxation rules. Eventually 25 enterprise zones were designated in the rundown areas of the old industrial cities. Many achieved substantial successes in property redevelopment and, to a lesser extent, in generating jobs. Nevertheless the 'cost' to the state (in terms of lost revenues) has been enormous, and in many areas it is argued that the bulk of regeneration would have occurred without the establishment of an enterprise zone. What cannot be denied is the extent to which an emphasis on free enterprise and private investment has changed the form and organisation of many large British cities.

Second, in parallel with providing incentives to private enterprise, a series of attempts have been made by central government to curb the spending of local governments, which in high-spending urban areas have tended to be Labour-controlled. High-spending authorities clearly do not conform to the requirements of neoliberal economics since they continue to mobilise state intervention rather than market forces to provide for citizens' needs. In order to reduce spending (and thereby 'free up' the local economy) local governments have been prevented from investing the capital receipts from council-house sales back into public housing, they have been rate- or change-capped where their spending on services and welfare has exceeded government targets, and for a short period they were required to abolish domestic rates in favour of a community charge, or poll tax, which was designed (among other things) to encourage the public to vote for low- rather than high-spending politicians. This curbing of public expenditure requires financially successful cities to depend increasingly on attracting private investment, skilled labour and high-income consumers. This brings me to my third example.

While the notion of urban management dominated urban policy and urban theory during the 1960s and 1970s, reflecting the prevalence of large public bureaucracies in the delivery of goods and services, in the neoliberal climate of the 1980s the watchword became urban entrepreneurialism. As Harvey (1987) points out, cities are now in competition with each other for investment, prestige and labour. They must appear safe, pleasurable and profitable. This is achieved by 'the mobilisation of the spectacle' – the construction of luxurious shopping malls, the adoption of festivals or the promotion of sporting events, the notion of European Cities of Culture and so on. Such spectacles perform the multiple roles of appearing to unite class-divided communities, attracting investors and generating jobs. They may make the difference between failure and success in the post-Fordist urban economy.

Neoliberal economic policy has left its mark both on the organisation of urban life and on our interpretations of it. However the impact of the New Right is also felt through a revival of neo-conservative authoritarianism and moralism. This is a movement concerned with arresting perceived moral decline by strengthening shared social values and imputing a stabilising role to traditional institutions (such as the family) and to the sense of common heritage accompanying a 'national way of life'. Tory economic strategy has therefore amounted to more than a switch from 'social-consumption capital' (provision in cash or kind of resources usually purchased by wages) to 'social-investment capital' (spending on projects channelling resources into the private sector by stimulating the business climate) in the sense outlined by O'Connor (1973). It has also involved a massive investment of 'social-expenses capital' to support the services responsible for law and order and so contain that second symptom of urban crisis: the escalation of civil unrest. In Britain, for instance, outbreaks of rioting in the early 1980s – especially in 1981 and 1985 – help explain why, in the first few years of Conservative government (following 1979) expenditure on law and order doubled, the size of the police force relative to the public increased, there was a marked centralization – some would say virtual nationalisation – of the policing process, and police accountability seemed minimal (Fyfe, 1989; Smith, 1986). Cities seem to have been divided, for policing purposes, into respectable and disreputable zones, on the assumption that if the latter cannot be 'cured' they can at least be contained, so that they do not tarnish the image required to secure urban investment from private capital.

For the New Right the urban crises linked by the left to international economic restructuring are held to originate instead in the economic and political failings of the welfare state, in the ascendancy of interest-group politics, in the disruption to free-market forces caused by union-related disturbances, and in a loss of national pride. Defined as such, these crucial urban problems are expected to be resolved by policies that free up the market while maintaining the forces for social control. This is producing an urban geography steeped in the ideals of economic growth rather than in the principles of social justice, a structuring of space more dependent on mobilising citizens' obligations than on extending their rights, and an environment built around inequalities in personal prosperity that has little interest in promoting collective social welfare.

Culture, Capital and Urban Change

It is obvious from the perspectives already discussed that although the content and organisation of city life has changed dramatically in the last half century, the interpretation of urbanism is essentially a political rather than an ontological question. Urban geography is as much a contest of ideas as a quest for reality; as much a statement of how things ought to be as an account of how they are. This is well-illustrated by recent attempts within urban geography to make sense of postmodernism – a cultural form that has become an increasingly pervasive element of urban life in the last 20 years.

Postmodernism is a complex and contested notion that is associated with trends in art, literature and architecture as well as with developments in philosophy and social theory. It is a cultural condition that, in cities, finds expression in the built environment, in the organisation of consumption, in the conduct of social life and in the negotiation of personal identity.

Architecturally, postmodernism represents a shift away from the modern, international styles associated with the work of Frank Lloyd Wright, Corbusier and Mies Van Der Rohe, and epitomised in the monotonous greys of the concrete-slab skyscraper and the residential estate composed of flats. Instead postmodern architecture adopts a plurality of forms, colours and textures; it demands the return of symbolism and ornamentation; and its hallmarks are eclecticism and pastiche produced by the free combination of past architectural styles. The postmodern cityscape is thus a collage of local traditions, historic references and vernacular allusion. The aim, epitomised in the work of Charles Jencks and Robert Venturi, is to create a socially and culturally relevant environment, catering to a variety of tastes and capturing the plurality of contemporary urban life (see Relph, 1987). Postmodern architecture now dominates many a central city skyline (downtown San Francisco is the most widely quoted example), postmodern designs inspire the dwelling-construction industry, and postmodern built environments are the new hallmark of successful neighbourhood and community planning. But the urban impact of postmodernism is not restricted to architecture. Jameson (1984) characterises postmodernism as the transformation of consumption of urban goods and services as in the production of urban form.

Coffee, cars, clothes, food, furniture, home extensions: today none of these are sold, or bought, simply for their use value. Consumer goods are packaged into an image – of romance, machismo, elegance or affluence – as if, by purchasing a product, the buyer is expressing or absorbing the exclusive, often elite, lifestyle that envelopes it. This is vividly illustrated by Mills' (1988) study of gentrification in Vancouver. In this way postmodernism encourages the renegotiation of social boundaries, facilitating the emergence of new political identities (through feminism and antiracism for instance); it marks the dissolution of traditional class boundaries and it signals the transmutation of consumption-sector cleavages, so that a key social distinction in cities today is that dividing 'those who spend time to save money' from 'those who spend money to save time' (Ignatieff, 1989).

In short, postmodernism may be regarded as the cultural character of the so-called 'new times' (times that also embrace both the advent of flexible accumulation and post-Fordism in the economy and the success of neoconservative politics). As such the spirit of postmodernism feeds into a longer-lived preoccupation among urban geographers with the analysis of urban culture. This preoccupation was first established in Louis Wirth's seminar paper on 'Urbanism as a way of life' (1938), and it has been revived many times in the interests of developing a cultural theory of the city. To this end there have been two schools of thought.

The first derives directly from the work of the Chicago School and is taken up by Ulf Hannerz, whose fine book *Exploring the City* (1980) portrays urbanism not as the determinant of social identity, but as a symbolic product of social life. In the words of Jonathan Raban

> the city goes soft; it awaits the imprint of an identity . . . it invites you to remake it, to consolidate it into a shape you can live in. . . . Decide who you are and the city will again assume a fixed form around you. . . . Cities, unlike villages and small towns, are plastic by nature. We mould them in our images: they, in their turn, shape us by the resistance they offer when we try to impose our own personal form on them (Raban, 1974, pp. 9–10).

From this perspective, cities do not infuse people with a set of cultural norms that condition their behaviour and psyche. Rather people create cities, infusing them with symbolism and social significance.

A second approach to the analysis of urban culture argues that the form of cities affects the structure and meaning of social relations and impinges on the development of individual and social personality. This kind of reasoning is laid out in Smith's commentary on *Social Theory and the City* (1980), partly in the chapter on Louis Wirth, but most poignantly in the critique of writings by Theodore Roszack and Richard Sennett, both of whom were concerned with the cultural consequences (rather than causes) of urbanisation. More recent studies in this vein have been concerned with the effects on human personality and consciousness of new forms of economic development and increasing technological complexity.

These perspectives have confronted one another time and again in the history of urban cultural studies. It is not surprising that we should find them at the heart of geographers' debates on the significance and impact of postmodernism. Few authors dissent from the view that postmodernism, flexible accumulation and neo-conservatism have, so far, been closely interlinked. Where disagreement arises, it centres on the question of whether, and in what way, these are causally related – and, in the urban context, how these relations are expressed in the built and social environment of cities.

On the one hand there is the view most closely associated with the work of Phil Cooke, that postmodern culture is at least partly autonomous, and may even help drive economic and political processes. This places an optimistic (or, in Cooke's [1990] own terms, pragmatic) gloss on postmodernism, allowing us to interpret postmodernism as a humanising force. This dimension is apparent, for instance, in the 'liberal' landscapes of Vancouver as described by David Ley (1987). It is also manifest in the opportunities Cooke identifies for the 'democratisation and opening up of culture', the development of 'maximum feasible local control', and the advent of cities that are 'increasingly cosmopolitan, diverse, fragmentary but communicative' (Cooke, 1990, pp. 29–30). Here the vision is clearly one in which cultural priorities shape the meaning and use of urban space, harnessing at least some economic and political forces to the traditions, needs and aspirations of an heterogeneous local public.

On the other hand there is a more critical view, advanced above all by David Harvey (1989) who regards postmodernism as little more than the 'cultural clothing' of flexible accumulation. Postmodern culture is, from this perspective, a product of the organisation of the economy. Cityscapes have become a screen for the projection of corporate image; postmodern architecture embraces the ideals of commerce and the commodification of living space. These landscapes are not responsive to culture – they shape it, as systems of meaning, images and lifestyles are bought and sold in the shape of location, neighbourhood and architectural form. According to this interpretation, the postmodern city is preoccupied with market forces: pluralism, choice and democracy of taste are notions relevant only to those with significant disposable income. The postmodern way of life is only available to those eager to 'spend money to save time', and a steep socioeconomic and political gradient separates them clearly from those – often just a stone's throw away – whose lifestyles revolve around the less conspicuous, early modern concept of spending time to save money. Thus it is that Short describes the postmodern built environment as 'bunker architecture' – a form 'concerned more with security than display, personal safety more than show and the exclusion of indigenous communities rather than their incorporation' (Short, 1989, p. 187).

My aim in summarising these argument is not to force a choice between them. Indeed, some of the very best of today's scholarship transcends them both (for example Zukin, 1991). The point, however, is that cities are important to social theory precisely because urbanism has cultural as well as economic and political components. Cities are soaked in symbolism, reproduced and recreated in the public mind and entrenched in the political cultures that determine public policy.

Conclusion

Urban geography has a rich and complex past, but this chapter has been concerned primarily with its future. First, I have argued that the subdiscipline does have a future: urban places are significant for their role in capital accumulation, information dissemination, the consumption of goods and service and the reproduction of waged and unwaged labour. Cities are also important, still, as a way of life. Perhaps increasingly in these turbulent 'new times', the *idea* of the city is a powerful cultural and political symbol. Second, I have suggested that the kind of future in store for urban geography does not rest on the collection and coordination of ever-more detailed and precise sets of data. Rather its future will be shaped by political debates – debates in which urban geographers could and should be involved – concerning how cities should be organised, how urban problems are defined and what form urban policy can take. Finally, I showed that the conduct of urban geography cannot take place around concepts such as capital, class and culture in the abstract. The influence of feminism and antiracism already show how inequality and discrimination take particular, systematic forms in different contexts, and the postmodern debate reminds us of the importance of a sense of place in the shaping of urban identities in a changing world.

References

Bondi, L. (1991) 'Gender divisions and gentrification: a critique', *Transactions, Institute of British Geographers* NS16, pp. 190–8.
Castells, M. (1977) *The Urban Question* (London: Edward Arnold).
Castells, M. (1978) *City, Class and Power* (London: Macmillan).
Castells, M. (1983) *The City and the Grassroots* (London: Edward Arnold).

Ceccarelli, P. (1982) 'Politics, parties and urban movements: Western Europe', in N. I. Fainstein and S. S. Fainstein (eds), *Urban Policy Under Capitalism* (Beverly Hills: Sage).

Cooke, P. (1990) 'Modern urban theory in question', paper presented to the annual conference of the Institute of British Geographers, Glasgow.

Cross, M. (1983) 'Racialised poverty and reservation ideology: blacks and the urban labour market', paper presented to the fourth conference on Urban Change and Conflict, Clacton-on-Sea.

Cross, M. and M. Keith (eds) (1993) *Racism, the City and the State* (London: Unwin Hyman).

Douglass, M. (1988) 'The transnationalization of urbanization in Japan' *International Journal of Urban and Regional Research*, vol. 12, pp. 425–54.

Elliott, B. and D. McCrone (1983) *The City: Patterns of Domination and Conflict* (New York: St Martin's Press).

Fothergill, S., G. Gudgin, M. Kitson and S. Monk (1988) 'The deindustrialisation of the city', in D. Massey and J. Allen (eds), *Uneven Redevelopment. Cities and Regions in Transition* (London: Hodder and Stoughton), pp. 68–90.

Fyfe, N. (1989) 'Policing the recession', in J. Mohan (ed.), *The Political Geography of Contemporary Britain* (London: Macmillan).

Gilroy, P. (1987) *There Ain't no Black in the Union Jack* (London: Hutchinson).

Gottdeiner, M. (1986) *Cities in Stress: A New Look at the Urban Crisis* (Beverley Hills: Sage).

Hannerz, U. (1980) *Exploring the City* (New York: Columbia University Press).

Harris, C. (1987) 'British capitalism, migration and relative surplus – population: a synopsis', *Migration*, vol. 1, pp. 47–96.

Harvey, D. (1989) *The Condition of Postmodernity* (Oxford: Blackwell).

Harvey, D. (1985a) *The Urbanization of Capital* (Oxford: Blackwell).

Harvey, D. (1985b) *Consciousness and the Urban Experience* (Oxford: Blackwell).

Harvey, D. (1987) 'Flexible accumulation through urbanization: reflections on 'post-modernism' in the American city', *Antipode*, vol. 19, pp. 260–86.

Ignatieff, M. (1989) 'Cleverness is all', *The Independent*, 7 January, p. 25.

Jackson, P. (ed.) (1987) *Race and Racism* (London: Allen and Unwin).

Jameson, F. (1984) 'Postmodernism, or the cultural logic of late capitalism', *New Left Review*, vol. 146, pp. 53–94.

Lash, S. and J. Urry (1987) *The End of Organised Capitalism* (Cambridge: Polity Press).

Lefebvre, H. (1970) *La Révolution Urbaine* (Paris: Gallimard).

Lefebvre, H. (1976) *The Survival of Capitalism* (London: Allison and Busby).

Leitner, H. (1986) 'Urban geography: the urban dimension of economic, political and social restructuring', *Progress in Human Geography*, vol. 13, pp. 551–65.

Ley, D. (1987) 'Styles of the times: liberal and conservative landscapes in inner Vancouver 1968–86', *Journal of Historical Geography*, vol. 13, pp. 40–56.

Little, J., L. Peake and P. Richardson (1988) *Women in Cities* (London: Macmillan).

Lowe, S. (1986) *Urban Social Movements* (London: Macmillan).

Madigan, R., M. Munro and S. J. Smith (1990) 'Gender and the meaning of the home', *International Journal of Urban and Regional Research*, vol. 14, pp. 625–647.

McGee, T. G. (1988) 'Industrial capital, labour force formation and the urbanization process in Malaysia', *International Journal of Urban and Regional Research*, vol. 12, pp. 356–74.

Miles, R. (1982) *Racism and Migrant Labour* (London: Routledge and Kegan Paul).

Mills, C. (1988) '"Life on the upslope": the postmodern landscape of gentrification', *Environment and Planning D: Society and Space*, vol. 6, 169–89.

Momsen, J. and J. Townsend (eds) (1987) *The Geography of Gender in the Third World* (London: Hutchinson).

O'Connor, J. (1973) *The Fiscal Crisis of the State* (New York: St Martin's Press).

Pateman, C. (1988) *The Sexual Contract* (Cambridge: Polity Press).

Pratt, G. and S. Hanson (1988) 'Gender, class, and space', *Environment and Planning D: Society and Space*, vol. 6, pp. 15–35.

Raban, J. (1974) *Soft City* (London: Collins Harvill).

Rees, G. and J. Lambert (1986) *Cities in Crisis* (London: Edward Arnold).

Relph, E. (1987) *The Modern Urban Landscape* (London: Croom Helm).

Rex, J. (1986) *Race and Ethnicity* (Milton Keynes, Open University Press).

Saunders, P. (1981) *Social Theory and the Urban Question* (London: Hutchinson) (2nd edn, 1986).

Scott, A. J. (1986) 'Industrialization and urbanization: a geographical agenda', *Annals, Association of American Geographers*, vol. 76, pp. 25–37.

Short, J. (1984) *The Urban Arena* (London: Macmillan).

Short, J. (1989) *The Humane City* (Oxford: Blackwell).

Smith, M. P. (1980) *The City and Social Theory* (Oxford: Blackwell).

Smith, S. J. (1986) *Crime, Space and Society* (Cambridge University Press).

Smith, S. J. (1989) *The Politics of 'Race' and Residence* (Oxford: Polity Press).

Smith, S. J. (1990) 'Income, housing wealth and gender inequality', *Urban Studies*, vol. 27, pp. 59–78.

Watson, S. (1988) *Accommodating Inequality. Gender and Housing* (Sydney: Allen and Unwin).

Wilson, E. (1991) *The Sphinx in the City* (London: Virago).

Wirth, L. (1938) 'Urbanism as a way of life', *American Journal of Sociology*, vol. 44, pp. 1–24.

Zukin, S. (1991) *Landscapes of Power* (Berkeley: University of California Press).

10
History, Geography and the 'Still Greater Mystery' of Historical Geography

CHRIS PHILO

Introductory Remarks

> Some look upon the geographer as a kind of intellectual rag-and-bone [collector] content to cull ill-assorted bits and pieces of information from many other disciplines.... Historical geography is a still greater mystery; few go further than a belief that it is about 'old' maps, and perhaps concerns itself too with the tales of ancient mariners, medieval travellers and merchant adventurers. Some feel that it is an unsound attempt by geographers to explain history, and think that the historical geographer is most certainly trespassing and probably should be prosecuted. This is not so, the historical geographer is a geographer first, last and all the time (Mitchell, 1954, pp. 1–2).

'Historical geography' is a term that has long been employed in the English-speaking world to describe certain varieties of topographical writing, and it is a term that in more recent years has come to identify a seemingly distinctive subdiscipline of academic geography. Certain difficulties attach to this subdiscipline, however, and students first encountering courses on historical geography are often bemused by precisely how these courses are to be distinguished from others given in departments of history and geography. Indeed, historical geography – unlike the more systematic geographies designated as 'economic', 'social', 'political', 'urban', 'agricultural', 'medical' and so on – cannot claim a clearly defined object of study, for what does it mean to say that 'history' is this object when history itself is so heterogeneous and can be studied in so many different aspects (and when historians themselves divide up their inquiries into boxes labelled 'economic', 'social', 'political')? Moreover, it is evident that researchers who call themselves historical geographers concentrate upon a diversity of substantive issues, and also tend to deploy a diversity of philosophical and methodological toolkits upon a diversity of primary and secondary sources. The situation is not so much one of a unitary academic enterprise spurred on by a commonality of interest, theory and practice, then, as of a loose and eclectic collection of inquiries adding up to what Mitchell (1954) described as the 'still greater mystery' of historical geography.

Of course, such an observation might fuel the conclusion that there is no point in speaking about historical geography, but I want to oppose such a conclusion on the ground that probing Mitchell's 'still greater mystery' permits an understanding of how the complex geography of the world is intimately bound up with what happens in its history. I could develop this claim in several directions, but my key argument here is that the importance of historical geography lies in bringing a geographical sensitivity to bear upon the study of all those past phenomena – economic, social, political or whatever – that are the very 'stuff' of history and which have attracted the attention of historians (as well as of other scholars from the social sciences and the humanities). Consider, for instance, an historical occurrence such as the Newport 'massacre' of autumn 1839 (see Williams, 1959, pp. 234–41) when a number of Welsh Chartists, agitators for political reform, were shot and killed by soldiers during an uprising in the South Wales town of Newport. The fact that a region such as South Wales experienced Chartist activity reflected a peculiar combination of economic distress with a certain style of political radicalism; the fact that an uprising was to occur at all depended upon the coming together in one place of disaffected individuals from three different and disjoint centres (Blackwood, Ebbw Vale and Pontypool); and the fact that the uprising broke up in disarray and with loss of life was partly due to the failure of the Pontypool men to get to Newport on time, a failure itself related to both the distance that they had to travel over rough terrain and the bad weather of the preceding night. This is obviously only a thumbnail example, but it illustrates how a handful of geographical factors – the economic and political characteristics of a specific region, the coordination of people in different places, the movement of people and information across space – were central to the working out of a small 'piece' of history.

These claims may not initially appear all that strong or exceptional, but stating the importance of a heightened geographical sensitivity in the face of an entrenched 'historicism' – a tendency for scholars of almost all persuasions to interpret the social world in terms of temporal relations (usually chains of cause-and-effect chasing themselves 'down the ages') – is a vital but onerous task (and for a sustained theoretical treatment of such matters see Soja, 1989, especially Chapter 1). Furthermore, whilst my claims here would not appear alien to older generations of both historians and geographers, many of whom were alert to the role of geography in history, they actually run against the grain of what has more recently been taken as the niche of historical geography in the intellectual 'division of labour'. To be more precise, the alternative niche that I envisage for historical geography amongst the social sciences and the humanities is one that scholars once referred to not as historical geography but as 'geographical history' (and I will explain this term shortly), and in advancing this suggestion I am not so much arguing against today's historical geographers as swimming with the tide of what they really do in their substantive research. In the second section of my paper I hence examine older discriminations that have been made between history and geography, and through this examination I recover the notion of geographical history as a lens through which to view current work in historical geography. In the third section I develop a more detailed example of geographical history, and in this case the history in question is that of 'madness': of people who have been designated as 'mad', of the institutions that have housed them and of the doctors who have treated them. And in the final section I reflect upon the 'spatialised' history of Michel Foucault, the renowned French intellectual who often wrote on historical subjects, and in so doing I introduce both a 'feel' for historical inquiry and a handful of concepts – to do with such intangible phenomena as knowledge and power – that inform my broader vision of historical geography (or geographical history) and also figure in my more focused historical geography of 'madness'. Taken together, I hope that the various elements of my chapter amount to a theoretical and substantive demonstration of why something that can still be called 'historical geography' (even if I personally would prefer to recover the term 'geographical history') should remain central to the intellectual arena.

Historical Geography and Geographical History

> History . . . is not the story of successive events or an account of change. It does not deal with events as such. It consists of a study of the processes of thought which have motivated human actions in the past, and is not simply considering phenomena in their time relationships. The content of the field of history is limited to particular objects, namely human actions which are the consequences of conscious thought (Beaujeu-Garnier, 1952, p. 6).

> [T]he material, or objects, of geographical study [are] the features which characterise different parts of the earth's surface. By features I mean those phenomena which are capable of being observed either directly by the naked eye or indirectly by means of an instrument or statistics. We can see such things as houses, railway lines, clouds, plants and hills; we can observe by instruments temperature, rainfall or solar radiation; we can measure statistically the number of people in a place or the density of crops in a given area. All these together make up the features of the earth's surface which can reasonably constitute the material of geography (ibid., p. 7).

These passages are taken from an address that the French geographer Jacqueline Beaujeu-Garnier delivered at Ibadan University College, Nigeria, in 1952, and – whilst it may seem strange to unearth this long-forgotten lecture – it strikes me that Beaujeu-Garnier makes explicit here a set of discriminations that has shaped much thinking about historical geography both then and more recently. More particularly, she taps into a wider development whereby a number of mid-century geographers were seeking to establish the boundaries between history and geography, and were in the process effectively picking apart the more seamless and holistic approach to conjoint historical–geographical inquiry displayed by (say) Vidal de la Blache and the *Annalistes* in France or by H. J. Fleure and the Aberystwyth School in Wales. The result of this picking apart was to compartmentalise knowledge in an unhelpful fashion, so I would argue, and to produce a situation in which the avowedly historical subdiscipline of geography – namely, historical geography – ended up strangely divorced from the concerns, theories and methods of history.

It is not enough to make this claim, however, because it is vital to understand the precise nature of this separation (if only to appreciate better the possible terms for reconciliation). It is sometimes suggested that the crucial manoeuvre was the analytical separation between history as the science of 'time relations' and geography as the science of 'space relations' that Richard Hartshorne (drawing upon earlier German geographers and philosophers) introduced into the Anglo–American geographical literature (Hartshorne, 1939, pp. 134–44):

> 'Description according to time is History, that according to space is Geography' ... 'History differs from Geography only in the consideration of time and area. The former is a report of phenomena that follow one another and has reference to time. The latter is a report of phenomena beside each other in space' (Kant, 1802, quoted in Hartshorne, 1939, p. 135).

Hartshorne thus declared that for geography 'time in general steps into the background' (ibid., p. 184), and stated that geographical studies emphasising the temporal dimension risked becoming studies in history (ibid., pp.177–84). This meant that his understanding of historical geography involved a determined distancing from the factor of time – a distancing that led him to use the term 'historical' to mean merely 'of the past' rather than to imply any connection with the field of history (ibid., p. 185) – and he thereby confined the subdiscipline to reconstructing the geography of the 'historical present', a 'cut' taken through a particular and preferably short period of time (ibid., pp. 184–8).

But doubt must be cast upon Hartshorne's separation as the basis for the actual practice of mid-twentieth-century historical geography, particularly given that at much the same time Carl Sauer – who is often claimed as an historical geographer (Williams, 1983) through his centrality to the Berkeley School of historical and cultural geography – was quite explicit in his emphasis upon long-term historical mutations in the realm of material culture (and even described his studies as part of a broader 'cultural history': see Sauer, 1941). Sauer hence had few qualms about placing a concern for history as 'temporal relations' at the heart of his historical–

geographical practice, and even the British historical geographer H. C. Darby, who certainly worried about the logical compatibility of history and geography, was prepared to accept Sauer's commitment to 'the dimension of time in geography' (Darby, 1989). It is therefore revealing that in her 1952 address Beaujeu-Garnier outlined Hartshorne's separation of history and geography (Beaujeu-Garnier, 1952, pp. 2–4), but then criticised it for failing to specify the objects – the content or the material – making up 'the field of geographical inquiry' as opposed to that of historical inquiry (ibid., pp. 4–7). She drew upon the ideas of the historian R. G. Collingwood, who delimited history as the study of 'processes of action which have an inner side, consisting of processes of thought' (quoted in ibid., p. 5: see also Guelke, 1982), and used his definition as a springboard for delimiting geography as the study of much more permanent, tangible and observable phenomena. This distinction is clearly laid down in Beaujeu-Garnier's two passages quoted earlier, and in summary it is evident that she regarded history and geography as separated not so much in terms of a concern either for 'temporal relations' or for 'spatial relations', as separated because the one concentrated on immaterial (or 'ideal') objects such as human thoughts and actions whilst the other concentrated on material objects such as 'houses, railway lines, clouds, plants and hills'.

I would suggest that human geographers in general have often been uneasy about dealing with phenomena lacking an obvious materiality, and that a whole history remains to be written about the fear of 'the immaterial' in geographical inquiry (but see Philo, 1991; Watson, 1957). It also appears that the sort of distinction identified by Beaujeu-Garnier has led many historical geographers to close their research around material objects, and in so doing to distance themselves from historians who talk more readily about immaterial phenomena, not just the 'ideas' present in the heads of historical people (Collingwood's focus) but also a whole range of fleeting events (wars, famines), abstract entities (political institutions, intellectual movements) and deeper structures (the 'laws' of capitalism, the 'logic' of class struggle). Indeed, if we think of various traditions and 'schools' in historical geography we can see this predeliction for the material world, and this is as true of North Americans such as Carl Sauer and Fred B. Kniffen (with their focus upon material culture and such 'homespun' things as barns and fenceposts) as it is of British researchers concerned with the morphologies of past settlements and field systems. Moreover, if we reconsider Darby's classic theoretical paper of 1953 (reprinted 1957) we can see that he regarded the task of the historical geographer as at bottom 'to explain the landscape' – by which he meant the configurations (the distributions and the associations) within the landscape – if necessary by the mud and sweat of field work (Darby, 1957, p. 650).

It is helpful to stay with Darby's classic paper for a moment, since here he codified three possible ways of conjoining the disciplines of history and geography, and in the process arguably lent a direction to historical geography that took it away from much that was interesting in the field of history (which is certainly *not* to decry the substance of his own research). Firstly he identified the study of 'past geographies', in which the landscapes of human artefacts and activities associated with particular periods of time (temporal 'cross-sections') were to be reconstructed (ibid., pp. 643–54); and secondly he identified the 'history behind geography', in which long-term developments boasting significant landscape impacts (the 'vertical themes') were to be traced over tens and even hundreds of years (ibid., pp. 646–9). The first of these possibilities he apparently regarded as historical geography 'proper', with the second possibility playing an important supporting role, but the third of his triad – which he referred to as the 'geography behind history' – was seen as rather alien and as something that could not be incorporated 'within even the broad embrace of Geography' (ibid., p. 643). What Darby meant by the 'geography behind history' were those studies in which the course of human history was related to controls exerted by the natural and human attributes of a given region's 'geographical basis' (ibid., pp. 640–3), and in identifying this species of intellectual inquiry and then banishing it from the field of geography he voiced a theme that had been present in British geography ever since a meeting of geographers and historians in 1932, when C. B. Fawcett – capturing the mood of the meeting – stated that any attempt to use 'geographical facts' to explain 'historical events' comprised an exercise of 'History, geographical history, and not Geography' (Geographical Association/Historical Association, 1932, p. 40). The object of discussion in this respect was indeed referred to by some writers as 'geographical history', and a concise summing up of the conclusion commonly arrived at here was provided by F. J. Monkhouse in 1955:

[T]he relationship between Geography and History may be examined in terms of geographical history and of historical ge-

ography. Geographical history is the work of the historian, pursuing his [sic] own interests with his own methods; he makes
use of the 'geography behind history' in order to give a precise
location to the web of events with which he is concerned. . . .
But, conversely, historical geography is within the direct province of the geographer. The historical geographer is concerned
with the reconstruction of the geography of the past, the history
of the landscape. . . (Monkhouse, 1955, pp. 19–20).

In other words, so long as researchers anchored their studies in the
material objects of past landscapes (and thereby investigated where
these objects were located and how they were combined) the result
was proper historical geography: but if they diverted their attention
to the more immaterial events, entities and structures of history,
and if they perhaps sought to say something about the geography
behind this history, then the result was a geographical history that
belonged to history and not to geography. And such a manoeuvre
effectively debarred many older studies – by the likes of Ellsworth
Huntington, Ellen Churchill Semple and, more recently, Gordon
East (1938) – from the geographical corpus, and in so doing also
exaggerated the disciplinary distance between geographers and the
intriguing writings of historians such as H. B. George (1901) and
Lucien Febvre (1932).

It may seem a little odd to be worrying now about these older
arguments and discriminations, but the point of the above account
is to recover a series of oppositions that were once taken seriously –
between history and geography; between geographical history and
historical geography – and which can usefully illuminate what is
actually going on in historical geography today (and perhaps in human
geography more generally: see also Driver, 1988). To put matters
simply, it occurs to me that much of what currently passes for
historical geography no longer respects the older closures, and that
study after study now actually proceeds in the vein of a geographical history where the focus has shifted from the materiality of 'geographical facts' to the immateriality of historical phenomena. This
is not to imply that no current historical geographers tackle phenomena with an indelible expression on the surface of the earth – such
as deserted villages, churches, temples, factories, ghettos and so on –
but it is to claim that at least as much research has turned to phenomena with at best a minor or tangential impact upon 'the soil'. And
in this latter connection consider research on subjects as diverse as
the diffusion of innovations, the migration of peoples and their

ideological systems, the growth of fraternal and political associations, the clash of social classes, the operations of state machineries,
the artistic representations of land and labour, and so on. The
motivation behind this research is transparently not a straightforward
desire to reconstruct the materiality of 'past geographies': rather
attention has strayed from these geographies as the terminus of
inquiry towards an agenda set by historians (and by other scholars)
dominated by issues and themes thought to be significant in the
transformation of past ecological, economic, social, political, cultural and ideological systems. This is not to imply that the material
geography of the world has disappeared from the studies conducted:
instead it is to emphasise that this geography is no longer investigated as an 'end in itself', but is introduced to indicate the crucial
difference that the geography in history makes to the issues and
themes specified on the (at first sight 'ageographical' and 'aspatial')
agenda of the historians. In other words, from being the things
to be explained 'past geographies' have become part of the
explanation being given for something else, and here this 'something else' is to be found in the range of more immaterial events,
entities and structures conventionally dealt with in the field of
history.

This manoeuvre must be interpreted very carefully, though, for
what it involves is not a return to the crass geographical history
written into the 'environmental determinism' of Huntington, Semple
and others, nor any sympathy for statements such as 'history is
governed by geography' or 'history is geography set in motion' (Darby,
1957, p. 642). In this sense I agree with Darby that we should be
wary of trading in geographical history, but I can see no reason to
suppose that all attempts at writing geographical history are mis-
guided in their ambitions and achievements. And if recent works of
historical geography are consulted, there can be little doubt that the
tendency is not towards some simple environmental determinism,
but towards a cautious account of how the realities of space and
place – town–country contrasts and relations, regional patterns in
agricultural and industrial practices, ways of seeing and acting in
landscapes, internal layouts and external environments of institutions such as workhouses and prisons, local geographies of ethnic,
gender, occupational and class groupings (to give but a few examples) – have all entered centrally into the shaping of such fundamental historical happenings as the rise of capitalism, the agricultural
and industrial revolutions, the upsurge of urbanism in the Western

world, the making of nations and states, the formation of modern senses of human self-identity, and the production of racial, sexual and class-based conflicts (see, for instance, Cosgrove, 1984; Daniels, 1993; Dennis, 1984; Dodgson, 1987; Driver, 1993a; Dunford and Perrons, 1983; Gregory, 1982; Harvey, 1985; Langton and Morris, 1986; Mackenzie, 1989; Rose, 1988). The conclusion to be drawn from these works is not that the happenings of history can be reduced to the complexities of geography, but that it is possible to enrich and to shed fresh light upon these historical happenings by injecting them with a measure of geographical sensitivity. This is the promise of the new geographical history: it is the promise of studies that refuse to close themselves around the arrangement of objects in the material world, but which are prepared to rework the concerns of such 'masters' as Darby and Sauer in an attempt to create a subdiscipline attuned to the broader interests of the contemporary social sciences and humanities. It is also the promise that I must now endeavour to illustrate more substantively, although it must be admitted that the following discussion can do little more than gesture towards the potential of a carefully pursued geographical history.

Space and Place in the History of Madness

Until comparatively recently much research in the mental health field has been both ahistorical and aspatial. We feel that the comprehensive treatment of both the historical and geographical settings of mental health subjects is particularly important (Smith and Giggs, 1988, p. viii).

In recent years work on the history of 'madness' has become quite common, and it is possible to find all manner of historical inquiries concerned with mentally distressed individuals of past ages – the 'mad people', 'lunatics' and 'insane' of older parlances – and with both the institutions that have sometimes housed them and the doctors (and other specialists) who have sometimes treated them. These inquiries have thereby recovered the thoughts and experiences of past mad people; have pieced together past interpretations of madness and associated proposals for dealing with it; have discussed the actual practices pursued in asylums and in other institutional spaces; have encountered the 'mad-doctors' and their backgrounds; and have teased out the demographic, economic, social and political contexts in which specialist 'mad-businesses' (systems of institutions and practices directed at the object of madness) have appeared. Some of these studies have been narrow 'psychiatric histories' written by psychiatrists celebrating the achievements of their predecessors, but most of the more recent studies have tended to situate their findings against a canvas of broader socioeconomic changes in the nature of the Western world. Moreover, following in the wake of Michel Foucault's pioneering *Madness and Civilization* (1967), it has been recognised that the history of madness is a crucial moment in the history of reason: in the history of how people in Western societies have come to think of themselves as – and have been encouraged to turn themselves into – 'rational', 'normal' and 'responsible' human subjects. Thus the story of how 'we' have learned to identify, institutionalise and treat mad people (with the ostensible goal of making them 'not-mad') is at the same time the story of how 'we' have constituted the conceptual edifices of 'rationality', 'normality' and 'responsibility' upon which the whole functioning of modern social life depends. Arguably, then, the sorts of histories being researched here answer questions about the modern world that are at least as significant as those questions tackled by (say) Marxist historians concerned with the emergence of a capitalist socioeconomic order.

Effort has duly been expended on researching the historical dimension to 'mental health subjects', but considerably less has been attempted with respect to the conjoint historical and geographical dimensions to these subjects, with the consequence – so I would argue – that the studies conducted have not managed to do all that they might have done. In the first instance, and this is the weaker claim, historians have often overlooked the very real geographical differences in the way that past societies have identified, institutionalised and treated mad people. This has led them to produce histories that imply past mad-businesses to have been far more coherent in their contexts and contents than they actually were, and also to portray historical changes as if they involved wholesale and instantaneous shifts from one set of ideas and practices to another. The 'truth' was undoubtedly much more heterogeneous and fragmentary than these histories admit, and it is revealing in this connection to repeat Roy Porter's warning about viewing the asylums that appeared in eighteenth- and nineteenth-century England as comprising a coherent 'system':

The asylum eventually became the preferred medicine for the sickness of a civilization. Yet, until the close of the eighteenth century its rise was slow, limited and piecemeal, and it is arguable that the term 'system' which has been occasionally applied to this development may be misleading. After all, as late as early Victorian times, the nation had only a patchy coverage of madhouses, even in heavily populated areas, and despite the passing of the 1808 Act permitting counties to establish rate-supported asylums, a mere twelve had acted up to 1845. The eighteenth-century madhouse map reveals less a co-ordinated system than a highly uneven spattering of heterogeneous establishments – big and small, private enterprise and charity, subscription and proprietary. The term 'system' hints at a misleading uniformity. Diversity remained of the essence (Porter, 1987, p. 156).

In pursuing this argument Porter clearly displays a sensitivity to the uneven geography of the 'madhouse map', and there is a sense in which his alertness to this map fuses with his more general emphasis upon 'the sheer diversity of developments (relating to madness) in the long eighteenth century' (ibid., p. 14: I will return to this point presently).

In the second instance, and this is the stronger claim, historians of madness have rarely appreciated the extent to which space and place – the spatial distributions and associations of phenomena; the moorings of phenomena in particular locations – have made a crucial difference to the very working out of the histories that they write. Indeed, madness itself (or the population of allegedly mad people) has always been a phenomenon with a definite geography: it has always been more prevalent in certain regions and localities than in others, perhaps because certain types of surroundings – and notably the depressing circumstances of burgeoning nineteenth-century towns and cities – have genuinely prompted more psychological unrest in individuals than have other types of surroundings; or perhaps because certain types of surroundings have made people less able to cope with disturbed dependants and more likely to place them at the mercy of 'social control' agencies (including the managers of asylums) than have others. Alternatively, the various institutions that have arisen to deal with madness over the centuries have depended centrally upon a manipulation of space and place, and this is why Foucault devotes some attention to what he calls the 'geography of haunted places' (Foucault, 1967, p. 57). The mere presence of buildings to

which mad people have often been consigned, with their characteristic and forbidding high walls, barred windows and locked doors,
reveals the use of space as a barrier to put distance between a supposedly sane population and its supposedly insane outcasts. This
means that the historical process mentioned above – the creation
and then splintering apart of the two categories, reason and madness – was buttressed by and effected through a conjoint social and
spatial separation, the product of which was to leave at large a
community that Foucault refers to as 'the Same' and to shut away
a community that he refers to as 'the Other' (see Foucault, 1970,
p. xxiv, where he reflects upon his objectives in *Madness and Civilization*). The details of exactly who was incarcerated, along with the
details of how this incarceration was interpreted, justified and organised, obviously varied greatly according to the time and place in
question, but there can be no doubt that the process of sociospatial
separation was integral to the histories under consideration here.

In addition, the principle of sociospatial separation was sometimes extended as authorities sought to remove the institutions themselves from centres of population, with the consequence that the
specialist lunatic asylums opened in many parts of the nineteenth-
century world became spatially marginalised. They were thereby
located 'over the hill' or in places 'out of sight and out of mind',
and the common occurrence was for these places of madness to be
banished – like their medieval predecessors, the leper colonies – to
rural tracts quite distant from cities, towns and major highways.
This 'ruralised' asylum geography obviously did reflect a 'police
intention' (to use a phrase sometimes employed by contemporaries)
designed to evict troublesome people and experiences from the urban
scene, but there was actually more to this ruralisation than just an
exercise in overt social control. The key point here is that nineteenth-
century authorities were striving quite self-consciously to use the
rural landscape, complete with its natural beauty and its peaceful-
ness, to calm and hopefully to cure the disturbed minds of asylum
inmates. The wider strategy being employed was known as 'moral
treatment' or 'moral management', and it called for a humane institutional regime in which care, affection and the detailed manipulation of local environments (both inside and outside of the asylum)
was calculated to rekindle in 'patients' a moral control over their
wayward propensities. This significant departure in the history of
madness – this founding of a 'moral' response to mad people which
still has its echo today in various psychiatric and mental-nursing

procedures – was hence bound up from the start with a manipulation of institutional geographies:

> Hill, valley, wood and garden were all intended to play a part in moral management. Contemplating these rural and idyllic English landscapes, lunatics were being subtly pressed towards a cultural norm. It was considered a very severe psychopathology when women patients at the Fisherton Asylum for the criminally insane ripped up every flower the minute it showed its head above ground (Showalter, 1985, pp. 35–6).

My discussion here considerably over-simplifies matters, of course, since in reality there were numerous different sorts of institutional spaces taking mad people, each of which had particular sorts of locational associations reflecting particular sorts of arguments about madness and its appropriate treatment (Philo, 1992a). But, and as the above quote from Elaine Showalter ably demonstrates, the very functioning of the nineteenth-century mad-business – what this business was designed to achieve, and how it was supposed to achieve it – was both shaped by and shaping of the spaces and places of its component institutions.

The Mad-Doctors and their Geography

In order to be more specific still in this connection I will turn to what might initially appear an unlikely concern for academic inquiry: namely the 'mad-doctors' or physicians who historically organised much of the treatment received by mad people. The medical men (and they were all men) played a crucial role in developing conceptions of madness and in administering the public asylums that emerged during the nineteenth century in England and Wales (and elsewhere in the world), and an important element in the process whereby they became a 'profession', with special claims to tackle mental distress, was their founding in 1841 of a formal body called the Association of Medical Officers of Asylums and Hospitals for the Insane (for details of this organisation see Hack Tuke, 1879; Hervey, 1985, pp. 109–13; Outterson Wood, 1896; Walk, 1978; Walk and Walker, 1961). The Association was a highly intangible phenomenon, consisting as it did in little more than the commitment of its members and a few scraps of paperwork, and it goes without saying that its impact upon the material landscape was negligible. And yet it was also a phenomenon with a definite geography: a geography that was deliberately moulded as the Association sought to make itself a more integrated agency, to spread its influence more widely and to earn favour in the 'right places'. Let us briefly consider this geography.

The first thing to notice is that one of the reasons for the very founding of the Association was to overcome the isolation of asylum medical officers, many of whom were effectively 'trapped' by their residential commitments to institutions set apart from centres of population (see above). In his circular of 19 June 1841, Dr Samuel Hitch of the Gloucestershire County Asylum hence announced that an Association was to be formed, 'it having been long felt desirable that the medical gentlemen connected with lunatic asylums should be better known to each other' (Hitch, 1841, quoted in several papers, including Outterson Wood, 1896, p. 243). Moreover, also in relation to the founding of the Association, one Dr Blake commented upon how much could be achieved by a 'few men of good will' uniting to combat the enemy of mental disease:

> for each one has been working in isolation, [when] the care of the insane was not a problem which could ever be solved by one man. Here, more than with any other problem, there was need for a combination of a number of experiences over a number of years (Crommelinck, 1843, quoted in Walk and Walker, 1961, p. 617).

A meeting was duly held in Gloucester on 27 July 1841, and it was at this meeting – and despite a poor turnout of only six individuals – that the Association was formally instituted and given its first set of rules. Over the next few years the society's existence was rather precarious, with meetings being few, infrequent and sparsely attended, but an early attempt was made to overcome the geographical scatter of members by building up a library of 'books, plans and pamphlets' in the hands of the society's secretary (from whom members could order items provided that they met the expenses of forwarding and returning). One later writer was sufficiently impressed by this practice to urge its revival on the grounds that 'it would give members, especially those living in remote districts, an additional interest in the work of the Association' (Outterson Wood, 1896, pp. 249–50). It was not until the meeting at Oxford in 1852 that decisive moves were made to strengthen the Association, though, and from this time on it underwent 'progressive growth', which entailed it both 'widening its area and deepening its roots' (Kirkman, 1863, p. 312).

The linchpin of the Association's 'rejuvenescence' (Bucknill, 1861, pp. 4–6) during the early 1850s was undoubtedly the production of a 'house journal' through which the isolated members could keep in contact both with one another and with the latest therapeutic, legislative and administrative advances (Anon., 1855, pp. 3–4: for details of the journal see Philo, 1987; Russell, 1988, pp. 299–301; Walk, 1953; Walk, 1978, pp. 532–36). The result was the *Asylum Journal*, which first appeared in November 1853 and soon became the *Asylum Journal of Mental Science* (in 1856) and then simply the *Journal of Mental Science* (in 1859), the changes of name signalling the increasingly 'academic' character of the journal and also the considerable changes then occurring in the conceptualisation of mental distress. The nurturing of this journal could almost be described as a deliberate 'spatial strategy', and it was clearly successful both in integrating the Association's dispersed membership and in promoting a geographical diffusion of the Association's views. As Dr Charles Lockhart Robertson remarked when assuming the editorship in 1862:

the thought and tone of the articles contributed in the period [1853–62] have materially raised the position of the English psychological medicine both at home and abroad. The *Journal* now circulates in our most distant colonies, and it was only this summer that [I] learnt from a distinguished foreign visitor that no less than seven copies circulated in Sweden (Robertson, 1863, p. 462).

It was even claimed by one president of the Association that there was 'not a speech or a language' in the civilized world where the voice of the *Journal* had not been heard (Kirkman, at the Special General Meeting, 1862, pp. 453–4).

The increasing circulation of the journal went hand-in-glove with increasing membership of the Association, and from lists appended to editions of the journal it is possible both to chart this increasing membership (from circa 120 in 1854–5 to circa 240 in 1863–4) and to map the changing geography of membership (see Figure 10.1). In many ways a comparison of the maps for 1853 and for 1863 speaks for itself, in that it illustrates the considerable 'widening' and 'deepening' of the society's 'area' mentioned above. The dots on these maps represent the home addresses of Association members, which in most cases were also the locations of public asylums, and it is interesting that the mad-doctors were conscious of the need to spread their influence not only to other asylums but also to the public realm beyond the asylum gates. That some success was achieved in this direction was indicated by Dr W. P. Kirkman (1863, p. 315) when noting that the functions of 'psychological physicians' were 'becoming every year more intimately woven with social life', and when suggesting that the 'sphere of our labour' was becoming 'less limited by the radius of an asylum'.

As the Association grew to encompass what one physician referred to as 'so scattered a body' (Monro, in 'Report of the Annual Meeting, 1864', p. 449) certain geographical tensions began to appear, however, and in particular members from Scotland, Ireland and England's remoter counties began to suppose 'that the society was becoming a strictly metropolitan one' (Stewart, in 'Report of the Annual Meeting, 1864', p. 451). This fear was far from groundless, given that by the early 1860s powerful interests within the Association were pressing for 'a building of our own' or 'large rooms' in London so as to give their society 'a more solid existence than at present' (Monro, in 'Report of the Annual Meeting, 1864', p. 449). Furthermore, it was declared by Dr Henry Monro – the Association's president in 1864–5 – that the society should *not* appoint presidents who were superintendents of provincial asylums because they 'lived too far off':

> residing as they do, in different parts of the country at a distance from London, I do not think that they are exactly the persons to be elected to fill the office of president of the Association . . . I believe [that the president] ought to be a gentleman resident in London (Monro, in 'Report of the Annual Meeting, 1863', pp. 424–5).

This was all very well for Monro, who was a visiting physician to St Luke's Hospital in London, but it was not a recommendation that uniformly pleased the membership. For instance, Dr Thomas Harrington Tuke replied by stating the 'great advantage' that had been found in electing physicians from different parts of the country (Tuke, in 'Report of the Annual Meeting, 1863', p. 426), whilst Monro's successor as president – Dr William Wood, himself a visiting physician to St Luke's – confessed upon being elected that

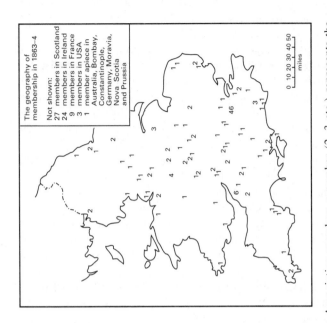

The geography of
membership in 1863–4

Not shown:
27 members in Scotland
24 members in Ireland
9 members in France
3 members in USA
1 member apiece in
  Australia, Bombay,
  Constantinople,
  Germany, Moravia,
  Nova Scotia
  and Prussia

0 10 20 30 40 50
miles

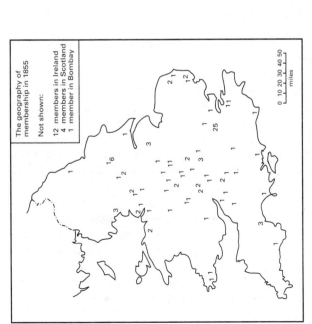

The geography of
membership in 1855

Not shown:
12 members in Ireland
4 members in Scotland
1 member in Bombay

0 10 20 30 40 50
miles

NOTE Each (1) represents the workplace and/or home of one Association member; a number (2, 3 etc.) represents the workplace and/or home of two or more Association members.

FIGURE 10.1 *The Changing Geography of the Association's Membership, 1855–64*

it would have been more appropriate had 'some gentleman connected with the provinces taken the next turn' (Wood, in 'Report
of the Annual Meeting, 1864', p. 454).

An even better index of this tension between metropolitan and
non-metropolitan sympathies was to be found in the bitter disputes
that arose over what Wood described as 'a matter of so much importance to the Association' (ibid., p. 452): namely the choice of
location for the Association's annual meeting. Initially the society
had been happily 'peripatetic' in its choice of venues, since at the
Gloucester meeting in 1841 it had been agreed that meetings should
coincide with 'visits [to] be made annually to some one or more
of the hospitals for the insane in the United Kingdom' (quoted in
several papers, including Outterson Wood, 1896, p. 244; see also
the discussion in Walk, 1978, p. 536). After the 'rebirth' of the
Association in the early 1850s – and despite myriad intrigues and
struggles over this issue – the trend definitely moved towards holding
the annual meeting in London, and at the 1851 gathering it was
resolved that 'the annual meeting . . . be in future held in London,
on the second Saturday in July each year, at the Freemason's Tavern'
(quoted in Outterson Wood, 1896, p. 256). It is true that in 1855
the Association accepted that the meeting could take place outside
London 'in some provincial town or city where there is a public
asylum or where some other object is likely to attract the members'
(Rule XII, agreed upon at the Annual Meeting, 1855, as reported in
Anon., 'Amended Rules', 1855, p. 222), but the expectation remained that most meetings would convene at the Freemason's Tavern
in London. This tendency towards centralising the Association's
activities did not go unchallenged, though, and this was notably
the case in 1860, when it was argued that a meeting in Dublin would
both boost Irish participation in the Association and elevate the
status (and thereby extend the practice) of 'psychological medicine' throughout Ireland (Flynn and Stewart, in 'Report of the Annual
Meeting, 1860', pp. 27–8):

> you would elevate us, you would elevate that branch of your
> society which lives in Ireland, you would do a vast deal of good
> to the poor lunatic by causing us to be recognised as medical
> officers, and you would prevent what has sometimes occurred –
> the Lord-Lieutenant appointing Barony cess-collectors, persons
> having no status whatever (Flynn, in 'Report of the Annual Meeting,
> 1860', p. 29).

Similar arguments were mobilised four years later when speakers agitated for an Edinburgh meeting, but it is evident that the claims being made here about extending the Association's 'sphere of influence' were fighting a losing battle against the claims then being advanced for a regular London rendezvous.

The case *for* London had two basic motivations, and the first of these reflected the reality of London being the most central and accessible city in the realm, and thereby the only place that could guarantee getting a large number of members together at once. Speakers such as Dr C. Mountford Burnett and Mr William Ley turned out to be excellent 'locational analysts' in stressing London's attributes as a 'convenient point', a 'great central point', a 'central position' and even 'the central place where all the great railways meet to a greater extent that at any other point' (Burnett and Ley, in 'Report of the Annual Meeting, 1860', pp. 26–8). Conversely other locations were criticised for their lack of centrality and accessibility, and both Dr Robertson and Dr Edgar Sheppard cited the 'wretched little meeting' held in Liverpool in 1859 as an illustration of 'the extreme difficulty in getting a provincial meeting, whereas everybody comes to London' (Robertson, in 'Report of the Annual Meeting, 1862', p. 326; Sheppard, in 'Report of the Annual Meeting, 1864', p. 452). The second set of reasons for meeting in London reflected a desire to be near the 'levers' of power: a desire to be seen as a large and capable body by the country's most power-ful bureaucrats and politicians, and a desire to use this presence as a tool for influencing both legislative changes and more routine state activities in the lunacy field. In 1858, for example, Dr Henry Stevens asserted that:

> There [is] still a great deal to be done in altering the laws regarding the insane, and [this can] only be done properly in the metropolis where the heads of law [are] collected. It was very pleasant to meet in Edinburgh, and it would be so, no doubt, to meet in Dublin; but these meetings led to comparatively no practical ends (Stevens, in 'Report of the Annual Meeting, 1858', p. 68).

Two years later Burnett pointed out that 'all the great associations meet in the metropolis', and thereby deduced that 'we should do so if we wish to be great' (Burnett, in 'Report of the Annual Meeting, 1860', pp. 27–8), whilst four years later Dr T. Kirkman reminisced about the life-giving role that London had performed for the Association 'when the feebler sporadic efforts in the counties were fortified by electrical connection with the great centre of communication and praise' (Kirkman, 1862, p. 4).

What all of this amounts to, then, is that the Association in question – a phenomenon with obvious importance to the history of madness, but *not* one that would conventionally be studied by geographers – *did* actually possess a geography of some complexity. In fact, and as I hope to have indicated, the seemingly 'simple' geographical matters documented above – the scatter and the isolation of Association members, the circulation of the *Asylum Journal*, the dual 'widening' and 'deepening' of the Association's 'area', the use of places as nodes from which to diffuse influence or in which to cultivate influence – were all inextricably tied up with the society's origins, functioning and endeavours relating to both a specialist branch of *knowledge* (that of 'psychological medicine') and a particular variety of *power* (that of the professional 'pressure group'). We are only talking here about a small chapter in the vast and often tragic history of madness, it must be admitted, but the chapter about the mad-doctors remains a vital one and one that does (after all) merit the attention of the 'geographical historian'.

Michel Foucault and the Spatialising of History

A total description draws all phenomena around a single centre – a principle, a meaning, a spirit, a world-view, an overall shape; a general history, on the contrary, would deploy the space of a dispersion (Foucault, 1972, p. 10).

A number of geographers have begun to trace the implications of Michel Foucault's thought for the reworking of both academic geography itself and social theory more generally (Driver, 1985; Philo, 1986, 1992b; Soja, 1989, especially pp. 16–21), and a key aspect of what Foucault has to offer here involves his practice of what might be described as a 'spatialised' history or even (with a few reservations) as a 'geographical history'. My initial basis for this claim derives from the introduction to *The Archaeology of Knowledge* (1972), where Foucault makes a series of observations about the writing of academic history that (so I would argue) imply a 'feel' for historical inquiry that should prove attractive to geographers. His comments in this respect are perhaps rather polemical and overstated, and it is obvious that some historians (strangely enough, the more source-bound and parochial of them) do not warrant the broadsides being delivered, but it is still instructive to consider the attack that he mounts on what he terms *total history* and also to examine the alternative that he refers to as *general history*.

As far as Foucault is concerned:

> The project of total history is one that seeks to reconstitute the overall form of a civilization, the principle – material or spiritual – of a society, the significance of a period, the law that accounts for their cohesion – what is called metaphorically the 'face' of a period. . . . [And] it is supposed that between all the events of a well-defined spatio-temporal area, between all the phenomena of which traces have been found, it must be possible to establish a system of homogeneous relations (Foucault, 1972, p. 9).

This passage is clearly a difficult one, but its bottom-line message is simple: it is claiming that a great many historical exercises effectively draw a neat line around a particular period and a particular place (the 'well-defined spatio-temporal area'), and then suppose that somehow all of the events and phenomena found within this line are related to one another (through a hypothesised 'system of homogeneous relations') or are in some way bound together by a common 'form', 'principle', 'significance' or 'law'. Take, for example, a crude Marxist account in which it is argued that (say) thirteenth-century Europe was in the grip of a feudal mode of production whose political–economic logic determined everything that went on in that society (from what the peasants ate through to the intricacies of medieval theology); or take a crude 'Whiggish' account in which it is reckoned that (say) Victorian England was energised in every pore by a scientific and humanitarian zeal reaching out to eradicate all backwaters of ignorance and poverty. Foucault's own remarks throw off references to a range of possible historical approaches (Marxist, 'Whiggish', positivist, idealist, structuralist), but in each case he is asserting that the historian proceeds by positing a 'central core' to the period and the place under study – a core which might entail the attainments of a 'great' historical figure, the traditions of a culture, the policies of a state, or whatever – and then by envisaging certain effects and influences rippling out from this core to give order and coherence to all of the things contained within the given period and place.

This project of total history is very much anathema to Foucault, since its ambitions and strategies stand squarely in opposition to his own belief that 'nothing is fundamental: that is what is interesting in the analysis of society' (Foucault, 1982, p. 18). He thereby objects to the way in which historians so often smooth out the chaos and the 'jagged edges' of history by making things appear neatly ordered and coherent, and he objects to how they skate over the minutiae of small-scale and everyday details that may look messy from a distance (from the detached viewpoint of the researcher) but which were the real substance of the practices, struggles, hopes and fears of people in the past. His own alternative is hence to call for a 'new history' – a new mode of thinking to be called 'general history' – that apparently:

> speaks of series, divisions, limits, differences of level, shifts, chronological specificities, particular forms of rehandling, possible types of relation (Foucault, 1972, p. 10).

It is not easy to deduce from these observations precisely how he intends to prevent historians from 'allowing the living, fragile, pulsating "history" to slip through their fingers' (ibid., p. 11), but the point of talking about 'series, divisions, limits, differences' is presumably to insist upon recognising the numerous lines that effectively divide up many of the events and phenomena so often seen by historians as undivided (as undifferentiated elements of a larger and homogeneous whole). And thus a sense of chaos and 'jagged edges', of messiness and diversity, is given prominence.

The image that Foucault mobilises to capture the character of general history revolves around 'deploying the space of a dispersion' (ibid., p. 10), and what he immediately conveys through this spatial image is not a 'central core' radiating effects and influences (the image suggested by total history) but an imaginary plain upon which things (events and phenomena) are dispersed. It is at this moment that Foucault's history becomes 'spatialised', then, since in order to stress the diversity of history he turns to an explicit spatial image in which the unevenness and scatter of a 'dispersion' are quite deliberately 'deployed'. I find this particular tactic of Foucault's highly suggestive, and in like manner I think it revealing that the historian Roy Porter writes of the 'madhouse map' – and in the process flags both the 'patchy coverage' and the 'uneven spattering' of institutions – when insisting that diversity rather than a coherent system was the 'essence' of eighteenth- and nineteenth-century asylum provisions (see above). This mention of Porter's substantive inquiries inevitably raises the question of whether or not Foucault is alert to spatial dispersion (to geographical or areal differentiation) in his own substantive historical studies of deviancy, sickness and madness, and – whilst in one interview he does concede the requirement for 'making the space in question precise' (Foucault, 1980, p. 68) – the answer to this question must remain largely in the negative. Indeed, Porter actually criticises Foucault for the *in*sensitivity displayed in *Madness and Civilization* towards differences in how mad people were treated in different parts of early-modern Europe (Porter, 1987, p. 9).

Having said this, I think that there *is* a dimension to Foucault's 'spatialising' of history that goes some way beyond merely the use of an image, and I would argue that his abstract remarks about 'the space of a dispersion' connect up very directly to a more concrete concern for spatial relationships. In making this claim it is necessary to appreciate that, whilst his account of dispersion is chiefly designed to emphasise the diversity of history, it is also the case that he sees in this dispersion more than just a chaos resistant to all attempts at understanding. Instead what he sees are the spatial relationships that appear in the dispersion – however momentarily – between things (events and phenomena) according to whether or not they occur close to one another in space or whether or not they are somehow joined to one another across space. And this is perhaps why he suggests that we are now living in the 'epoch of space', since in order to understand the social world around us we must think spatially:

> We are in the epoch of simultaneity: we are in the epoch of juxtaposition, the epoch of the near and far, of the side-by-side, of the dispersed. We are at a moment, I believe, when our experience of the world is less that of a long life developing through time [the temporal or historicist understanding of things] than that of a network that connects points (Foucault, 1986, p. 22).

These suggestions could still be read as little more than a metaphor gesturing towards a particular style of 'doing' social research, of course, but the possibility that Foucault's insistence upon the 'epoch of space' amounts to more than a metaphor is indicated in his accompanying thoughts on 'the problem of siting or placement' (the deceptively simple problem of *where* human creations are located in space relative to one another):

> This problem of the human site or living space is not simply that of knowing whether there will be enough space [for humans] in the world – a problem that is certainly quite important – but
> . also that of knowing what relations of propinquity, what type of storage, circulation, marking and classification of human elements should be adopted in a given situation in order to achieve a given end. Our epoch is one in which space takes for us the form of relations among sites (ibid., p. 23).

Thus, from his abstract image of 'the space of a dispersion' through to his more concrete observations about 'relations among sites' in the workings of the social world, Foucault does indeed provide a 'feel' for history that is attractive to geographers.

Moreover, even a casual glance at many of Foucault's substantive historical inquiries into such complex and often intangible phenomena as madness and reason, sickness and medicine, deviancy and discipline reveals that he accords spatial relationships – the distribution and arrangement of people, ideas, activities, institutions and buildings in space – a pivotal role in the historical processes under study. In *Madness and Civilization* he draws various conclusions about what he terms 'the geography of haunted places' (Foucault, 1967, p. 57), as briefly indicated above, and in *The Birth of the Clinic* (1976) he deals with the three different forms of 'spatialisation' involved in nosologies of disease, in the practices of pathological investigation and in the provision of medical facilities or 'cure centres' (and it is intriguing to speculate what a medical geography informed by this text would look like). Meanwhile, in *Discipline and Punish* he explores the notion that 'discipline proceeds from the distribution of individuals in space' (Foucault, 1977, p. 141), and also discusses in detail the physical and psychical control over individual human subjects achieved through the manipulation of spatial relationships in Jeremy Bentham's notorious 'Panopticon' (an ideal-type disciplinary institution of the late-eighteenth century that greatly influenced the design of subsequent prisons, workhouses and asylums). Foucault's masterly dissection of the spatial strategies employed by institutional managers to isolate, maximise the visibility and regiment the lives of inmates has already interested a number of geographers (see Dear, 1981; Driver,

1985, 1993a, 1993b; Philo, 1989), but less attention has been paid as yet to his accounts of (for instance) the spatial strategies employed in transmitting lepers, lunatics and other undesirables to houses beyond the city gates or in 'opening up' bodies to an early-nineteenth-century medical gaze. I can obviously do no more here than hint at the contents of Foucault's texts, but what I should add is that (insofar as Foucault does specify broader 'principles' organising his histories) he reckons the spatial relationships that he uncovers – the countless interactions and movements of people, ideas, activities and so on – to be at root relationships of knowledge and power: to be relationships implicated in the making and then the diffusion of knowledge about particular matters, and at the same time to be relationships constitutive of the power whereby particular social groups exert their will over others or (less manifestly but maybe even more significantly) whereby a general 'vision' of social orderliness is conveyed to and inculcated in members of a population. It is this alertness to the spatial relationships built into both knowledge and power that informed my study above of the mad-doctors, given that my purpose was to show how the mad-doctors shaped their own geography in order to nurture mental science and wield professional influence over a problematic sphere of social reality (mental distress and its disorderly tendencies).

I do not want to conclude by giving the impression that Foucault's work comprises the last word on what a 'spatialised' history might entail, in part because his efforts are in no sense consistent or systematic in their treatment of space and place. In addition, it might be objected that he does not balance his remarks about space with a similar awareness of place, in that – to give an example – he might be sensitive to the 'geometry' inside an asylum (to the configuration of rooms, corridors, stairs and windows), and yet remain insensitive to the 'geography' outside the asylum (to its setting amidst fields or factories; to its location in one particular part of the world rather than in another). But these objections should not detract from the brilliance of Foucault's insights, nor from the various possibilities that he opens up for a 'spatialised' form of historical inquiry cognisant of what spatial relationships (if not so much associations with place) *actually do in history*. If I am correct in my overall assessment that the endeavours of today's historical geographers are closer to the spirit of what was once called 'geographical history' than to the letter of a narrowly conceived historical geography, and if this means that we are now asking questions about the influence of geography in all of its 'richness' (in its myriad guises of space, place, environment, location, region, distribution, dispersal) upon all manner of important but not immediately tangible historical processes, then historical geographers have both something to learn from the historical writings of people like Foucault and something to teach them as well.

Acknowledgements

This has not proved an easy chapter to write, and I must acknowledge the help, encouragement and criticisms of various people: Alan Baker, Sarah Byrt, Felix Driver, Derek Gregory, Ron Martin, Miles Ogborn, Jenny Robinson and Graham Smith. I would also like to thank Maureen Hunwicks and Caron McKee for typing drafts of the chapter and Miles Edwards for preparing the maps.

Bibliography

Anon. (1855) 'Prospectus', *Asylum Journal*, vol. I, pp. 1–7.

Anon. (1855) 'Amended Rules of the Association', *Asylum Journal*, vol. I, p. 222.

Beaujeu-Garnier, J. (1952) 'The Contribution of Geography' (published address, Ibadan, Nigeria: Ibadan University Press).

Bucknill, J. C. (1861) 'President's Address, 1860', *Journal of Mental Science*, vol. VII, pp. 1–23.

Cosgrove, D. (1984) *Social Formation and Symbolic Landscape* (London: Croom Helm).

Daniels, S. (1993) *Fields of Vision: Landscape and National Identity in England and the United States* (Oxford: Polity Press).

Darby, H. C. (1953/1957) 'The Relations of Geography and History', *Transactions of the Institute of British Geographers*, vol. 19 (1953), pp. 1–11; reprinted with alterations in G. Taylor (ed.), *Geography in the Twentieth Century* (London: Methuen, 1957, 3rd edn), pp. 640–52.

Darby, H. C. (1989) 'Address, 1989', *Historical Geography Research Group Newsletter* (spring).

Dear, M. J. (1981) 'Social and Spatial Reproduction of the Mentally Ill', in M. J. Dear and A. J. Scott (eds), *Urbanisation and Urban Planning in Capitalist Society* (London: Methuen), pp. 481–7.

Dennis, R. J. (1984) *English Industrial Cities in the Nineteenth Century: A Social Geography* (Cambridge University Press).

Dodgson, R. A. (1987) *The European Past: Social Evolution and Spatial Order* (London: Macmillan).

Driver, F. (1985) 'Power, Space and the Body: A Critical Assessment of Foucault's *Discipline and Punish*', *Environment and Planning D: Society and Space*, vol. 3, pp. 425–46.

Driver, F. (1988) 'The Historicity of Human Geography', *Progress in Human Geography*, vol. 12, pp. 497–506.

Driver, F. (1993a) *Power and Pauperism: The Workhouse System, 1834–1884* (Cambridge University Press).

Driver, F. (1993b) 'Bodies in Space: Foucault's Account of Disciplinary Power', in C. Jones and R. Porter (eds), *Reassessing Foucault* (London: Routledge), forthcoming.

Dunford, M. and D. Perrons (1983) *The Arena of Capital* (London: Macmillan).

East, G. (1938) *The Geography Behind History* (London: Thomas Nelson).

Febvre, L. (1932) *A Geographical Introduction to History* (London: Kegan Paul Trench Trubner).

Foucault, M. (1967) *Madness and Civilization: A History of Insanity in the Age of Reason* (London: Tavistock).

Foucault, M. (1970) *The Order of Things: An Archaeology of the Human Sciences* (London: Tavistock).

Foucault, M. (1972) *The Archaeology of Knowledge* (London: Tavistock).

Foucault, M. (1976) *The Birth of the Clinic: An Archaeology of Medical Perception* (London: Tavistock).

Foucault, M. (1977) *Discipline and Punish: The Birth of the Prison* (London: Allen Lane).

Foucault, M. (1980) 'Questions on Geography: Interview with the Editors of *Hérodote*', in C. Gordon (ed.), *Power/Knowledge: Selected Interviews and Other Writings, 1972–1977, by Michel Foucault* (Brighton: Harvester), pp. 63–77.

Foucault, M. (1982) 'Interview with Michel Foucault on Space, Knowledge and Power', *Skyline (March)*, pp. 17–20.

Foucault, M. (1986) 'Of Other Spaces', *Diacritics*, spring, pp. 22–7.

Geographical Association/Historical Association (1932) 'What is Historical Geography? (Account of a Joint Meeting, 1932)', *Geography*, vol. 17, pp. 39–45.

George, H. B. (1901) *The Relations of Geography and History* (Oxford: Clarendon Press).

Gregory, D. (1982) *Regional Transformation and Industrial Revolution: A Geography of the Yorkshire Woollen Industry* (London: Macmillan).

Guelke, L. (1982) *Historical Understanding in Geography: An Idealist Approach* (Cambridge University Press).

Hack Tuke, D. (1879) 'Historical Sketch of the Association', in G. F. Blandford (ed.), *General Index to the First Twenty-Four Volumes of the Journal of Mental Science* (London: Churchill), pp. iii–viii.

Hartshorne, R. (1939) *The Nature of Geography: A Critical Survey of Current Thought in the Light of the Past* (Lancaster, Pa: Association of American Geographers).

Harvey, D. (1985) 'Paris, 1850–1870', Ch. 3 in D. Harvey, *Consciousness and the Urban Experience: Studies in the History and Theory of Capitalist Urbanisation*, Vol. 1 (Oxford: Basil Blackwell), pp. 63–220.

Hervey, N. (1985) 'A Slavish Bowing Down: The Lunacy Commission and the Psychiatric Profession, 1845–1860', in W. F. Bynum, R. Porter and M. Shepherd (eds), *The Anatomy of Madness: Essays in the*

History of Psychiatry, Volume II, Institutions and Society (London: Tavistock), pp. 98–131.

Kirkman, T. (1862) 'An Address Delivered at the Royal College of Physicians in London, Before the Association of Medical Officers of the Insane' (published address, Woodridge: Loder).

Kirkman, W. P. (1863) 'President's Address, 1862', *Journal of Mental Science*, vol. VIII, pp. 311–21.

Langton, J. and R. J. Morris (eds) (1986) *Atlas of Industrialising Britain, 1780–1914* (London: Methuen).

Mackenzie, S. (1989) *Visible Histories: Women and Environments in a Post-War British City* (Montreal: McGill-Queen's University Press).

Mitchell, J. B. (1954) *Historical Geography* (London: English Universities Press).

Monkhouse, F. J. (1955) 'The Concept and Content of Modern Geography' (published inaugural lecture: University of Southampton).

Outterson Wood, T. (1896) 'The Early History of the Medico-Psychological Association', *Journal of Mental Science*, vol. XLII, pp. 241–60.

Philo, C. (1986) 'The Same and the Other': On Geographies, Madness and Outsiders', Occasional paper no. 11, Loughborough University of Technology, Department of Geography.

Philo, C. (1987) '"Fit Localities for an Asylum": The Historical Geography of the Nineteenth-Century "Mad-Business" in England as Viewed through the Pages of the *Asylum Journal*', *Journal of Historical Geography*, vol. 13, pp. 398–415.

Philo, C. (1989) '"Enough to Drive One Mad": The Organisation of Space in Nineteenth-Century Lunatic Asylums', in J. Wolch and M. J. Dear (eds), *The Power of Geography: How Territory Shapes Social Life* (Unwin Hyman: London), pp. 258–90.

Philo, C. (1991) 'Brief Thoughts on Older Words and Older Worlds', in C. Philo (comp.), *New Words, New Worlds: Reconceptualising Social and Cultural Geography* (Lampeter: St. David's University College, Social and Cultural Geography Study Group of the Institute of British Geographers), pp. 1–13.

Philo, C. (1992a) *The Space Reserved for Insanity: Studies in the Historical Geography of the Mad-Business in England and Wales* (unpublished PhD thesis, University of Cambridge, Department of Geography).

Philo, C. (1992b) 'Foucault's Geography', *Environment and Planning D: Society and Space*, vol. 10, pp. 137–61.

Porter, R. (1987) *Mind-Forg'd Manacles: A History of Madness from the Restoration to the Regency* (London: Athlone).

'Report of the Annual Meeting, 1856' (1857) *Asylum Journal of Mental Science*, vol. III, pp. 1–14.

'Report of the Annual Meeting, 1857', (1858) *Journal of Mental Science*, vol. IV, pp. 1–42.

'Report of the Annual Meeting, 1858' (1859) *Journal of Mental Science*, vol. V, pp. 56–102.

'Report of the Annual Meeting, 1859' (1860) *Journal of Mental Science*, vol. VI, pp. 1–38.

'Report of the Annual Meeting, 1860' (1862) *Journal of Mental Science*, vol. VII, pp. 23–59.

'Report of the Annual Meeting, 1861' (1862) *Journal of Mental Science*, vol. VII, pp. 309–38.

'Report of the Annual Meeting, 1862' (1863) *Journal of Mental Science*, vol. VIII, pp. 309–54.

'Report of the Annual Meeting, 1863' (1864) *Journal of Mental Science*, vol. IX, pp. 421–42.

'Report of the Annual Meeting, 1864' (1865) *Journal of Mental Science*, vol. X, pp. 448–68.

'Report of the Special General Meeting, 1862' (1863) *Journal of Mental Science*, vol. VIII, pp. 444–58.

Robertson, C. L. (1863) 'Notes', *Journal of Mental Science*, vol. VIII, pp. 461–4.

Rose, G. (1988) 'Locality, Politics and Culture: Popular in the 1920s', *Environment and Planning D: Society and Space*, vol. 6, pp. 151–68.

Russell, R. (1988) 'The Lunacy Commission and its Staff in the Second Half of the Nineteenth Century, With Special Reference to the West Riding Lunatic Asylum', in W. F. Bynum, R. Porter and M. Shepherd (eds), *The Anatomy of Madness: Essays in the History of Psychiatry*, vol. III, *The Asylum and its Psychiatry* (London: Tavistock), pp. 297–315.

Sauer, C. (1941) 'Foreword to Historical Geography', *Annals of the Association of American Geographers*, vol. XXXI, pp. 1–24.

Showalter, E. (1985) *The Female Malady: Women, Madness and English Culture, 1830–1980* (London: Virago).

Smith, C. J. and J. A. Giggs (1988) 'Preface', in C. J. Smith and J. A. Giggs (eds), *Location and Stigma: Contemporary Perspectives on Mental Health Care* (Boston: Unwin Hyman), pp. vii–viii.

Soja, E. J. (1989) *Postmodern Geographies: The Reassertion of Space in Critical Social Theory* (London: Verso).

Walk, A. (1953) 'The Centenary of the *Journal of Mental Science*', *Journal of Mental Science*, vol. 99, pp. 633–7.

Walk, A. (1978) '"Forty Years of Wandering": The Medico-Psychological Association', *British Journal of Psychiatry*, vol. 132, pp. 530–47.

Walk, A. and D. L. Walker (1961) 'Gloucester and the Beginnings of the R.M.P.A.', *Journal of Mental Science*, vol. 107, pp. 603–32.

Williams, D. (1959) 'Chartism in Wales', in A. Briggs (ed.), *Chartist Studies* (London: Macmillan), pp. 220–48.

Williams, M. (1983) '"The Apple of My Eye": Carl Sauer and Historical Ge-ography', *Journal of Historical Geography*, vol. 9, pp. 1–28.

Wreford Watson, J. (1957) 'Sociological Aspects of Geography', in G. Taylor (ed.), *Geography in the Twentieth Century* (London: Methuen, 3rd edn), pp. 463–99.

Index

Notes: this index is in word-by-word alphabetical order; page references in *italics* indicate tables or figures; contributions to this publication are shown in **bold** type.